Word Processing Buyer's Guide

by Arthur Naiman

BYTE/McGraw-Hill, 70 Main St., Peterborough, NH 03458

Because a major purpose of this book is to evaluate hardware and software products, numerous such products are mentioned by their trade names. In most, if not all, cases these designations are claimed as trademarks by the respective companies. It is not our intent to use any of these names generically, and the reader is cautioned to investigate all claimed trademark rights before using any of these names other than to refer to the product described.

Library of Congress Cataloging in Publication Data

Naiman, Arthur.
    Word processing buyer's guide.

    Includes index.
    1. Word processing equipment.   I. Title.
HF5548.115.N343   1982   681'.6   82-17898
ISBN 0-07-045869-3

Edited by Bruce Roberts.
Design and Production Supervision by Ellen Klempner.
Production Editing by Tom McMillan.
Typeset by LeWay Composing Service Inc.
Printed and Bound by Halliday Lithograph Corp.
                Arcata Company
                North Quincy, Massachusetts.

Table of Contents

Dedication

This book is dedicated to everyone
who works on uses for computers that serve people
(like word processing)
and not on uses that oppress them
(like guidance systems for weapons)

Acknowledgements

Tony Pietsch taught me half of what's in this book. Ron Lichty was a great help, as always. He, Tom Crosley, Charley Maher, Meg Holmberg, Susan McCallister, and Roz Kulick read drafts of various chapters and made many helpful comments and suggestions.

My editor at BYTE, Bruce Roberts, must have felt like a man in a hospital waiting room being told by the nurse that he was the father of twins . . . no, triplets . . . wait a minute, quadruplets. I'm grateful for the patience he showed as this book grew longer and longer, and more and more overdue.

Ed Kelly and Tom McMillan were great to work with. Dan Donelly reviewed several programs for me and did a careful, diligent job of it. In a variety of ways, the following people also helped with the book: Albert and Nettie Naiman, Rita Gibian, Steve Goldstein, Sharon Mason, Dennis Foley, Harvey Mayes, Matt Helmerich, Meg Gawler, Linda Spangler, and Lichen Gawler-Brown.

Introduction

I originally thought of calling this book *The Complete Buyer's Guide to Word Processing Programs and Equipment*. That was before I understood the enormity of the task. There are dozens of companies manufacturing dedicated word processors.* They make hundreds of models. There are almost a hundred word-processing programs for microcomputers on the market, and almost as many different machines to run them.

Like Brooklyn — which, according to Thomas Wolfe, is so immense and various that no living person can ever truly know it — word processing, even at this early stage in its development, is beyond the scope of any one book. So I've had to settle for writing the *most* complete buyer's guide to word processing programs and equipment (which doesn't sound quite right as a title).

It's not that I'm presenting less information than I thought I would; in fact, I'm presenting quite a bit more. But I've had to narrow my sights anyway. As a result, I don't discuss electronic typewriters or any word processor without a screen — except incidentally (and I don't call something a "screen" unless it displays at least 12 lines of text). I also don't cover word-processing programs that run on large computers or word-processing systems designed primarily to have many terminals (although almost everything I say is applicable to them).

A **word processor** is just a computer that has been adapted for the typing, editing, and printing out of text. This is done by giving the computer a set of instructions called a **word- processing program** (although the equipment itself can also be modified and sometimes is).

All word processors are computers; **dedicated word processors** are simply computers that can't do anything *but* word processing. (Even that's changing, though. Many dedicated-word-processor manufacturers are adapting their machines to run other sorts of computer programs.)

There isn't really all that much difference between a dedicated word processor and a

---

* Use the glossary at the end of the book if you aren't familiar with some of these terms. After this introduction, you won't have to, because I'll define the terms as I go along.

microcomputer running a word-processing program. I call them both word processors and discuss them both in depth.

The information I present is designed to help you decide what word-processing products to buy, either for yourself or for people who work for you. Chapter 1 tells you what word processors are good for (in case you don't already know). Chapter 2 describes how they work and what they're made up of.

Chapter 3 gives a short history of word processors and describes all the different kinds that are available. Chapter 4 offers some general advice about what to look for, and what to avoid, in a word processor. Then things get specific.

The next three chapters talk about software. Chapter 5 discusses (at great length) how to go about evaluating a word-processing program — what you can expect one to do. Fourteen actual programs (including six that run only on the dedicated word processors they are sold with) are evaluated as examples. At the end, there's a checklist for you to use when evaluating software on your own.

Chapter 6 tells you why those 14 programs got the points they did, details their features and failings, and briefly describes 90 additional word-processing programs and dedicated word processors that aren't evaluated in this book. Chapter 7 describes other kinds of software that work closely with word processing — for example, programs that proofread your text and catch spelling errors or automatically generate indexes and tables of contents.

The last four chapters cover hardware and provide checklists of things to look for when buying it. Chapter 8 is about keyboards and screens, whether separate or as part of a video terminal. Chapter 9 covers printers. Chapter 10 discusses a couple of dozen microcomputers. And Chapter 11 is about dedicated word processors from a hardware point of view (the software having been covered in Chapters 5 and 6).

Since, if this book does its job, you'll want more information about word processing, Appendix A lists many sources for it — magazines, reports, books, fairs, etc. Appendix B gives you conversion tables for several common measures (for example, how many words in a K). This will help you make sense out of ads and brochures.

Appendix C gives you some information about my own personal history with word processing and reveals the biases that have grown out of it. I do this because ''objectivity'' doesn't exist — as anyone who's ever genuinely tried to attain it knows. Values always enter into any judgment. When people say they're being ''objective,'' what they really mean is: ''Rather than admitting to my prejudices, I'm going to hide them behind a facade of phony objectivity.'' (TV news is a perfect example.)

So, instead of pretending to be objective, I've tried instead to be fair; that's difficult, but at least it's possible. My model in this is George Orwell, whose approach was not to conceal his own personal feelings. That way, when he was off the wall, it was immediately obvious to his readers. Like Orwell, I try to be reasonable; but, like Orwell, I also try to make it easy for you to tell when I'm not being reasonable.

Last, and certainly not least, there's a glossary of every significant term and concept in the book. This is one of the most essential tools for learning about word processing, so I've tried to give you a *complete* glossary, not the scrap of a glossary you usually get.

You can skip around in the book if you like, but I've introduced terms and concepts in order. So, for maximum intelligibility, it makes sense to read the book straight through. But if you don't and get lost, the glossary or the index should get you pretty quickly to the information you need.

To make it easy for you to find a term or concept when skimming through the book, I boldface it wherever it's defined or discussed in any detail. In the index, the numbers of the pages where a term is boldfaced are also boldfaced. So, for example, if you saw an entry in the index that read like this:

Computers, irrational fear of — 4, 14, **34,** 42, **59,** 125

you'd know to look for a definitive treatment of the subject on pages 34 and 59. On pages 4, 14, 42, and 125, the irrational fear of computers would merely be referred to and the phrase would not be boldfaced there.

There's a saying around Silicon Valley that by the time a microcomputer product hits the market, it's already out-of-date. Books, including this one, are no exception. On the average, three or four new word-processing programs come out every month. Weekly newspapers have trouble keeping up with them; a book doesn't stand a chance.

I've tried to deal with this problem in a couple of ways. The first is to discuss emerging technologies and products as much as possible. So, for example, one of the programs reviewed in this book wasn't even out when the book was completed, and others had just been introduced.

But I think the second way is even more important. It's based on the idea that if you give people fish, you feed them for one day, but if you teach them to fish, you feed them for the rest of their lives. So this book not only tells you about the word-processing software and hardware that's presently available, but also teaches you how to judge whatever comes along in the future.

I discuss and evaluate a lot of different products in this book. As new products come out and prices drop, this information will undoubtedly become dated. But these specific examples help you see how the principles of evaluation should be applied, and the prices give you an idea of the relative cost of things. (You should be aware that most computer products are available at discounts of at least 20 percent.)

There's no way I can address this book to everyone, so I think of you, gentle reader, as a sort of generalized word-processor user — someone with just about any need that anybody has, but no intense ones. You're probably not like that, but it doesn't matter, because I've made it easy for you to tailor what I say to your own particular requirements.

One audience I definitely don't address is programmers. They have significantly different needs, and there are even word-processing programs (like Wordmaster) designed specifically for them. I don't cover those programs in this book.

Let me emphasize an important distinction: A **programmer** is someone who *writes* programs; a **user** is someone who uses programs written by somebody else. (It's possible to be both, of course, although not at the same instant.)

A lot of people think that to use a computer — even a word processor — you have to be at least a little bit of a programmer. This is completely untrue. I've written two books about computers and I don't know how to program. (I am, however, an experienced user of other people's programs, which makes me a pretty good judge of them.)

As computers get more common, programmers are going to make up a smaller and smaller proportion of the people using them. In the long run, there's no reason to expect that the percentage of computer users who know how to program will be any greater than the percentage of drivers who know how to repair their own cars.

Since it would be tedious for me to always write ''you or your operator,'' I just talk directly to ''you.'' It's not hard for a business owner or manager who's buying machines for employees to make the necessary translations, and, in any case, it's from the standpoint of the actual user that any word-processing product should be evaluated.

OK, now, for ten points — what's Chapter 6 about?

1

Word Processors: What They Do

From the time the first Cro-Magnon used a stick to scratch a map in the dirt so his tribemates would know where he hunted that day, the aim of all writing instruments has been to communicate thoughts as clearly, rapidly, and easily as possible. In the last ten years, the ability to do that has taken a giant leap forward, and the instrument responsible for that leap is called a **word processor.**

Word processors replace typewriters (and are as far beyond them as an electric typewriter is beyond a quill pen). The main difference is that on a word processor, what you write is stored as electronic (or magnetic) impulses instead of as marks on paper. You type just as on a typewriter, but the text appears on a screen — a **cathode ray tube (CRT)** similar to the one on your television set.

Since your text is electronic, pieces of it can be moved around and changed *very* quickly and easily. A copy only shows up on paper when you order a **printout** (also called a **hard copy**). It doesn't matter when, or how often, you make a printout. You can go through dozens of drafts without ever putting one on paper. Or you can make printouts at every stage of your work.

Word processors give you the freedom to make whatever changes are necessary, to revise as many times as you want without having to worry about the retyping that revision normally involves. For example, consider my own case:

I wrote my first book on a word processor. The day of my deadline, after working all night, I began printing out a 220-page draft at six in the morning, making last-minute changes and corrections on the typescript as it emerged from the printer. When the printout was finished, I entered the changes into the text and, at ten that same morning, began printing out a second, letter-perfect, 220-page draft. It was finished, packaged and in the mail by one that afternoon. And I didn't even have to run off to make a copy of the typescript for myself; I just had the word processor print one out for me after the first one was already on its way.

On a smaller scale, the ability to revise without retyping frees you forever from correction fluid and tapes, typing words backwards to lift them off the paper, writing in letters you left out as neatly as you can with a fine-tipped pen, and so on. If you discover a mistake on a printout, you just crumple it up, circular-file it, go back to the screen, correct the mistake, and have the word processor print out a perfect new copy.

Word processors also make it possible for you to change a word (or an entire phrase) everywhere it occurs in a document in a matter of seconds. (By **document,** I simply mean whatever it is you're writing — a letter, a report, an article, or a book.)

Since word processors vary in how powerful they are, not all of them can do everything I describe. But these capabilities are typical of the sort of machine it makes the most sense to buy.

Suppose you've just finished an 800-page epic. Suddenly it hits you — the heroine's name should be Helen, not Trixie. And wouldn't it be better if everywhere you talked about the sea, you called it the "wine-dark sea"?

If these changes were really important to you and you were working on a typewriter, you'd have to seriously consider whether it would make more sense to retype all 800 pages or just to commit suicide. With a good word-processing program, both changes will take only a few minutes — by means of something called **global substitutions** ("global" because they make a change everywhere).

In this case, you give your word processor two commands: everywhere you find the word "Trixie," change it to "Helen;" and everywhere you find the word "sea," change it to "wine-dark sea." (Naturally you don't actually have to type all that out; the commands themselves are a letter or two long.) Then you go off and get yourself a cup of coffee or something while the computer does the job for you.

A third thing a word processor lets you do is move whole sections of text around from one place to another. This is the computerized equivalent of "cut and paste," and in fact is sometimes called **electronic cut and paste** (the more common name is **block moves**). You can also insert (or delete) extra words, lines, or paragraphs anywhere in a document you want.

For example, let's say that as I originally wrote this chapter, this paragraph didn't exist. On rereading, I realize I want to add something at this point. All I have to do is move to the start of the next paragraph (the one that starts "Or consider . . ."), push a key, and start writing. A new paragraph (this one) is inserted here; the next paragraph (and everything that follows it) is pushed down.

Or consider how easy it was for me to remove the paragraph after this one (the one that isn't there now — the digression about growing healthier broccoli). All I had to do was move to the start of it and hit a key for each line I wanted to kill. The text below moved up to fill the gap. (I could also have deleted the whole paragraph in one fell swoop with a different command.)

With a word processor, you never have to type the same piece of text twice. You can store blocks of text you use repeatedly, and print them out in various combinations. This is the key to many powerful applications.

Let's say you want to send the same (or a similar) letter to a lot of different people. On a word processor, you type the basic letter once and then change just the name on subsequent letters. And by using a **merge-print program** (also called a **form-letter program**), you can tell the word processor to pull each name off a mailing list, write a letter personally addressed to that person, and then go on to the next name. You can even have the word processor vary other parts of each letter.

In any case, the finished product — called a **customized** or **personalized form letter** — is indistinguishable from an individually typed letter (and, in fact, it *has* been typed individually — but by the word processor, not by you).

Perhaps what you write is composed almost entirely of **boilerplate** — standard blocks of text that you use over and over again. Different pieces of boilerplate go in each document, in different orders, interspersed with new material, and surrounded by different introductory and transitional material. (Contracts, wills, and legal letters are one example of this sort of document. Grant proposals are another.) On a typewriter you'd have to retype the individual sections of text many times; on a word processor, you just type them once.

Word processors also shine when you need to create more than one version of a given piece of writing (one example is an academic paper you want to turn into a popular article). You just copy the original version electronically (which takes a few seconds) and rework the copy into your new version. If you're not happy with what you've done, you can just dump that copy and make a new one to work on. Or you can keep several different versions around until you decide which one is best.

A related application is preparing two or more resumes. In one, you emphasize your teaching experience; in another, your writing experience (using block moves to put different sections of the resume first). The basic layout (which you may have slaved over for hours) stays the same, as does all (or most) of the actual text.

Printouts from word processors look just as good as what the best electric typewriter produces — if that's all you need. But word processors also let you do things you can't do (or can do only with great difficulty) on a typewriter. In addition to printing in boldface, they can automatically:

- center lines.
- number pages in sequence, starting with any number you specify (you can also change the page number within the text as often as you want).
- decide when a page of text is full and move the printout on to the next page.
- indent blocks of text.

- put headers and footers on each page.
- justify text to both margins.
- put the justifying spaces between letters, rather than words, or even space proportionally (giving m's more room than i's, etc.). When you justify to both margins with proportional spacing, the result looks like typesetting.

Some word processors can even automatically suppress **widows** (the last line of a paragraph alone at the top of a page) and **orphans** (the first line of a paragraph alone at the bottom of a page).

Another advantage of word processors is that they're faster to type on. One reason for this is that most word processors will automatically move words that don't fit at the end of a line down to the start of the next, so you only have to hit a carriage return at the end of a paragraph or a title. You just keep typing and let the word processor worry about what line to put things on.

Word processors also tend to have a very fast and light key action, because nothing mechanical has to happen when you hit a key. An electrical impulse is sent out and that's all.

But fast as a word processor is when you're typing on it, it's even faster when you're not. Good typists do from 80 to 120 (standard, five-letter) words per minute on a good office electric. The slowest letter-quality computer printer does 204 wpm, the fastest turns out 960.

You don't have to be even near the machine, much less slaving over the keyboard, when it's printing out. Nor do you have to feed each sheet of paper manually; most printers have ways to do that automatically.

It is true that if you're going to do just one draft of a document, never revise it, never use any part of it again, and make no mistakes typing it, a typewriter will be faster than a word processor (because fewer steps are involved in using it). But that describes maybe five percent of all business and personal typing jobs.

In typical office use, word processors are so efficient that they pay back their purchase price in less than a year. One person on a word processor can do the work of three on electric typewriters and do it better.

And even that may be understating it. *Time* magazine reports that when the Atlantic Richfield company installed Xerox word processors in their Los Angeles office, they were able to reduce the ratio of secretaries down to one for every nineteen other employees. In other Atlantic Richfield offices, the ratio is one to five.

I'm not trying to put secretaries out of work, by the way. I just think they should have what every secretary I've ever known wants — more meaningful, challenging work and a higher-paying job. In the long run, inefficiency makes for fewer, not more, jobs.

That same *Time* article points out that the average blue-collar worker today is backed up by $25,000 in machinery, while the average white-collar worker uses only $2,000 worth. This is despite the fact that white-collar workers now account for more than a quarter of the gross national product while basic manufacturing accounts for less than a quarter.

The benefits to personal word-processor users are harder to put a precise value on. Most writers say that the ability to enter text rapidly and then revise it endlessly greatly improves the quality (as well as the quantity) of their work.

That certainly has been my experience. In a period of 16 months, I've written four books (and several shorter pieces) on my word processor. In more than 20 years of trying to be a writer before that, working on a series of typewriters, each one more sophisticated and expensive than the last, I managed to write no books (and not much else either).

Obviously I can't give a machine all the credit for the change. On the other hand, what always stopped me before was a feeling of despair when I thought of what it was going to be like to revise and polish something the size of a book. (I'm one of those people who puts a phone message through three drafts.)

Before I got a word processor of my own, I used to leave my Correcting Selectric and the comfort of my home — carpeted, pleasant, with a refrigerator full of food and a stereo, TV, books, and a phone — and travel to a nearby university whose computer I had wangled the right to use.

There I would sit — in a huge room filled with terminals, harshly lit with fluorescent lights, always too hot or too cold and stuffy in either case, usually filled with computer twerps who treated the place like a clubhouse and shouted their puerile conversations across the room — and work on a system which was so crowded with other users it sometimes took minutes (instead of fractions of a second) for a command to execute, which used a word-processing program that was clumsy even when it was running right, and which cost me a couple of dollars an hour.

Why? Because being able to revise as much as I wanted, without ever having to retype, made it worth it. At that point I would have sold my soul to get a word processor of my own. (It turned out I didn't have to go to that extreme — which is fortunate, considering what I was offered for my soul when I had it priced.)

I'm not the only writer sold on word processors; so is every other writer I know who has ever used one — without exception.

Well, that's enough raving about what word processors can do; let's go on to how they work.

2

Word Processors: How They Work

This chapter tells you what word processors are made up of and what goes on inside them. It explains the meaning of the technical terms you're most likely to run across in ads, brochures, and articles about them.

If some of the jargon intimidates you, skip over it, and use the index or glossary later on when you come across a term you don't know. But you should at least skim the chapter so you have an overall idea of how a word processor works.

Let me stress again that word processors *are* computers; there's no way to understand what a word processor is without knowing something about what a computer is. Although most books about computers are pretty incomprehensible, there's really nothing about the subject itself that's particularly hard to understand, if it's explained clearly (as I've tried to do).

Don't worry if you don't get everything in this chapter on your first reading. What's important is to get a general sense of what word processors are all about and to learn enough of the necessary language so you feel comfortable reading about them.

There are many different sizes of computers, from programmable calculators on up to giant IBM and Amdahl **mainframes** whose number-crunching abilities stagger the imagination. The size that's best suited to individual word processing is called a **microcomputer,** or simply a **micro.**

Sometimes micros are called **personal computers** or **home computers** and, of course, those that are sold exclusively for word processing are called word processors. But microcomputers is what they all are.

If several people are going to do word processing on the same computer, a **minicomputer** may be what's used — although some micros can also handle this kind of **multi-user multi-tasking** (several people doing different jobs at the same time).

Don't be fooled by the word *mini*computer, by the way. Minis are incredibly powerful machines, way beyond the needs of any one user. It's only in comparison to the monster mainframes that they can be thought of as mini-anything. (For more about

A typical microcomputer—the IBM Personal Computer.

different kinds of computers and word processors, see Chapter 3.)

The equipment, the actual nuts-and-bolts machinery that makes up a word processor (or any computer) is called the **hardware.** (Sometimes a computer is simply called a **machine** or, with all the equipment it's connected to, a **system**.)

Unlike most machinery, computer hardware can't just be turned on and expected to work. It's much too complex — and flexible — for that. You have to tell it what to do. The instructions which tell computers how to do things are called **software,** or **programs.** So, in addition to the hardware described below, another essential ingredient of any word processor is a word-processing program.

(By the way, ''software'' is a noun like ''butter.'' It makes no more sense to say ''a software'' than it does to say ''a butter.'' I mention this because I once saw the following (illiterate) sentence in an ad: ''One product, WordStar, is the top-selling CP/M business software in the world.'' ''One product'' cannot be ''the software.'' You say ''*a* program'' or ''*a piece* of software,'' ''many programs'' or ''lots of software.'')

I'll discuss word-processing programs later on in this chapter. First, let's consider the hardware.

There are lots of different sorts of machines that are sometimes called word processors. But in order to focus the book, I consider only the most useful models, those that have the components shown in Figure 2.2.

You can buy all these pieces in one neatly-tied-up package. Or you can get them separately. If the company that puts them together doesn't actually manufacture any of the items, it's called an **OEM** — which, ironically enough, stands for "original equipment manufacturer." (**System integrators** is a better name for such companies.)

Any or all of the components can be combined in the same box. For example, sometimes the computer is part of the keyboard. (For word-processing applications, however, the printer is almost always separate.)

In any case, each kind of component has the same functions from one computer to the next, regardless of what's packaged with what.

Frequently the screen and the keyboard are combined, to make a **video display terminal (VDT)** — sometimes called a **VDU** (for "video display unit") or just a **terminal.** (There are also terminals that combine the keyboard with a printer; in fact,

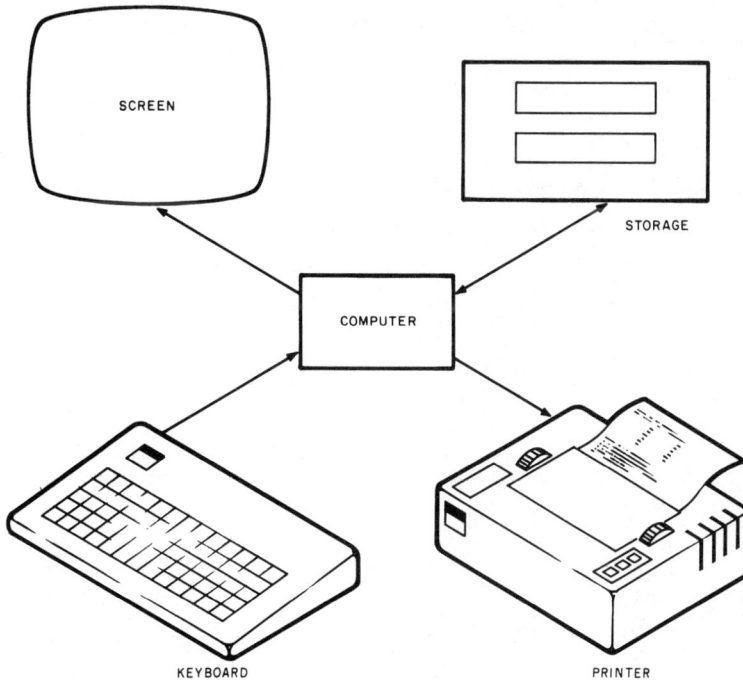

The basic components of a word processor.

originally all terminals were **printer terminals.** So, basically, ''terminal'' means a keyboard plus some means of displaying information. When I use the word, however, I mean a VDT.)

Every component but the computer itself is called a **peripheral** (or **peripheral device**). A peripheral can be **dumb,** which means it has no computational power of its own and just does what the computer explicitly tells it to do, or a peripheral can be **smart** — which means, of course, that it does have computational ability of its own and can modify and transform what the computer tells it. (*Really* smart peripherals are called **intelligent**.) For example, a smart terminal or printer might be able to accept raw text from the computer and justify the lines or proportionally space them.

A smart peripheral isn't necessarily better than a dumb one; sometimes you'd rather do the fancy stuff in software, so you can change it whenever you want and so you don't have to adapt to the peripheral manufacturer's idea of how things should be done.

The arrows in the diagram show the *direction of information flow* between the various peripherals and the computer. So, for example, information only travels from the keyboard to the computer, never from the computer to the keyboard. And information goes only to the screen, never from it (unless you have a light pen or touch-sensitive screen, neither of which are very useful on a word processor).

I'm going to cover each of the components of a word processor in turn, starting with the screen.

THE SCREEN

As I've said, when you enter text on a word processor, it appears on the screen. The characters on the screen are made up of little dots called **pixels.** There's a box, or grid, of pixels — so many across and so many down — for each character. This is called a **dot matrix.** The more pixels in the dot matrix, the easier-to-read each character will be.

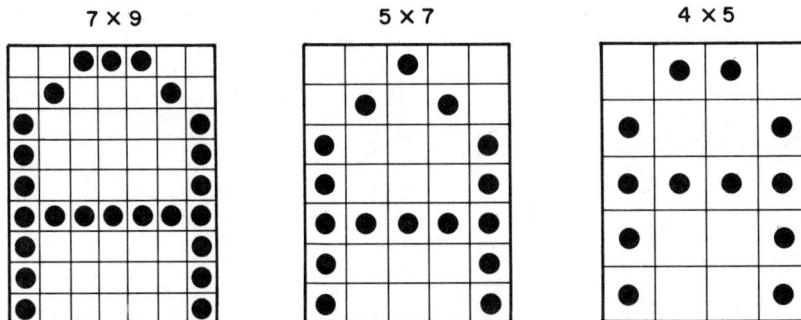

7 X 9   5 X 7   4 X 5

The letter *A* in various dot matrixes.

On a typewriter, you know where you are by the position of the ribbon slot (the place where the hammers or the ball hit the paper). But on a word processor, the ribbon slot is on the printer, and the text (while you're editing it) is on the screen. So you need some sort of marker to tell you where you are in it (where the next letter you type will appear, for example).

This marker consists of a rectangular block of light the size of one character (assuming that your screen, like most, shows light letters on a dark background. If it shows dark letters on a light background, the marker will be a rectangular block of darkness). On some machines, the marker is an underline mark, or a small, up-pointing triangle. Whatever its shape, it's called the **cursor** — which is a Latin word meaning "runner."

If you're unlucky, the cursor will flash on and off at a rate designed to trigger an epileptic seizure — or at least cause permanent brain damage.

As you type, the cursor moves along. Each new letter appears in the space where the cursor was and the cursor moves to the next space to the right. Since the cursor also indicates the place where text is going to be deleted or changed, you want to be able to

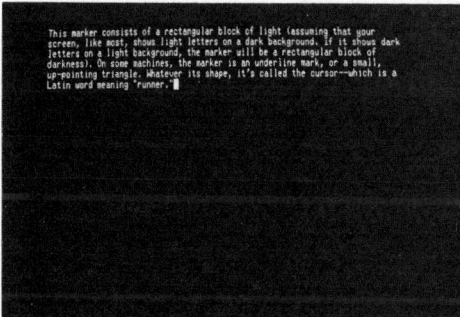

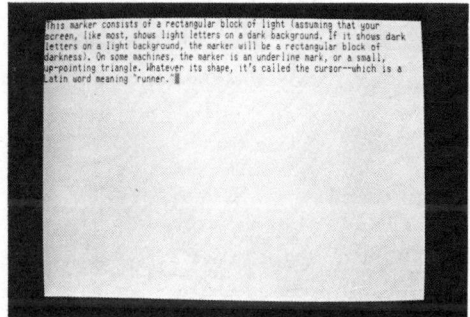

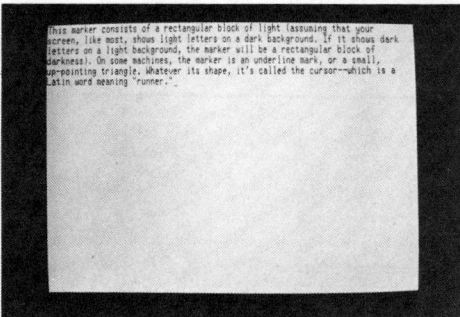

Cursors can have different shapes.

move it in some other way than just by slowly entering text. (After all, to live up to its name it has to run and not just walk.)

If you can move the cursor anywhere you want on the screen, you say it's **controllable** (or **addressable**). Some old-fashioned word-processing programs and equipment don't have controllable cursors. All the lines of text in a document are numbered, and you have to type the number of the line you want to be on rather than just moving the cursor to it. Programs that work this way are called **line** (or **line-oriented**) **editors** — as opposed to **screen editors.** With a few rare exceptions, this book is concerned exclusively with screen editors running on hardware that has a controllable cursor.

The screen provides a ''window'' into your text. If you have a long document, lots of it will be above the portion displayed on the screen (which is called a **screenful**) and lots below it. The word processor can move you up and down in the document, and this is called **scrolling** (since you move through a scroll in just the same way).

Sometimes your text will also be wider than the screen can show, and some machines will let you move sideways to see it. This is called **horizontal scrolling.** (Screens are covered in detail in Chapter 8.)

THE KEYBOARD

The most common way to tell the cursor where to move involves a key that doesn't exist on typewriter keyboards — the **control key.** On many dedicated word processors it's called the **code key;** it goes by other names as well.

Close-up of a keyboard showing the control key (CTRL).

The control key is similar to the shift key in one respect: they both change the effect of other keys. For example, if you hit the ''a'' key while holding the shift key down, you get an ''A'' instead of an ''a.'' Everything the shift key produces shows up on the screen, and subsequently on paper.

But the control key is different. When you hold it down while hitting another key, you get a **control character.** Control characters generally don't appear on the screen or on paper. Instead, they *do* things. So control-S, for example, might move the cursor one space to the right (over already existing text); control-W might move it up one line; control-B to the beginning of your text; and so on. (It takes up a lot of space to always write ''control-'' when referring to a control character, so I follow a standard convention in this book — the ˆ symbol in front of a letter (or other character) means ''hold down the control key while hitting that character.'' Thus control-A is written as ˆA.)

Control characters are written as caps to make them easier to pick out of the text, but in most word-processing programs, it doesn't matter whether you hold down the shift key, as well as the control key, while hitting the letter; that is, ˆX and ˆx have the same effect. In other programs, however, **control shift commands** are used, and capitals do count. In PIE Writer, for example, control-shift-N and control-N do completely different things.

On some word processors, certain operations are assigned to special **function keys.** This has at least one advantage over using control characters: you only have to hit one key instead of the control key plus another. And it has at least one disadvantage: if you're a touch typist, you have to move your fingers from the home position to hit the function keys.

On a completely integrated system (like a dedicated word processor), each function key is marked with the command it invokes, so you don't have to remember which control character goes with which command. These are called **dedicated keys.**

More often, however, function keys are labelled f1, f2, etc. (or in some similar way); the software assigns various jobs to them. These are called **soft keys** or **programmable function keys.**

It's no easier to remember what function a particular soft key performs than it is to remember what various control characters do. On the other hand, several different pieces of software can assign different functions to the same key, or one piece of software — like a word-processing program — can give it several different functions at different times. For that reason, fewer soft keys are needed than dedicated keys.

Dedicated keys.

A row—at the top—of programmable function keys (also called soft keys).

Both soft keys and the regular keys that get used for control characters can be labelled with little stickers that come with many word-processing programs. You put them on the front of each key to remind you of its function (sort of do-it-yourself dedicated keys).

Soft keys are usually on separate rows from the other keys, and this makes possible another kind of recall aid — a strip that can be laid alongside the keys.

Cursor arrows are a special kind of dedicated function key. With them, you don't have to remember anything — you just hit the arrow that points in the direction you want to go. Cursor arrows are most effective when arranged in a diamond, like the points of a compass. (Keyboards are covered in detail in Chapter 8.)

Stickers can be used to remind you of a key's functions.

Reference cards can also help you remember commands.

A typical cursor movement diamond.

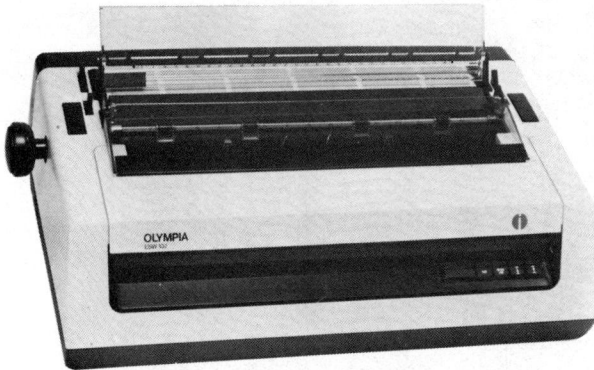

An RO (receive-only) printer. (*Courtesy of Olympia USA, Inc.*)

A KSR (keyboard-send/receive) printer. (*Courtesy of Olympia USA, Inc.*)

THE PRINTER

Printers make hard copies (on paper) of what you write so that you have something to send to other people or to leaf through yourself.

Because (on almost all systems) the keyboard is separate from the printer, most computer printers have no keyboard of their own; that is, they're "receive only" (**RO** or **R/O**). The other alternative is **KSR** ("keyboard send/receive" — because you can transmit data from this kind of printer as well as send text to it for printout).

Computer printers have several different ways of putting characters on paper, all of which are discussed in detail in Chapter 9. And, for the purposes of this general introduction, that's all you need to know about printers.

THE COMPUTER ITSELF

There's no consensus on what to call this main component. You can simply refer to it as "the computer," but that can also mean the whole system with all its peripherals. The **computer box,** if not exactly an elegant phrase, is an unambiguous one, and for that reason it's favored by many computer professionals. The word **mainframe** is also used, although it also means a very large computer (larger than a mini). In this book, I use either "the computer" or "the box" depending on the context.

When you type text on a word processor, it doesn't go to the screen directly. First it gets sent into the computer's **memory,** which is on a **card** or **board** (the names are interchangeable) in the computer box.

The memory card is just one of several boards in the computer box, each made up of **chips** mounted on fiberglass or pressboard. The chips on a board are connected together either by wires or, more usually, by **printed circuits** — metallic ink etched into the board in intricate patterns (from which comes the name **printed-circuit board** or **PC board**).

Chips are the heart of a word processor. About the size and thickness of a baby's fingernail, composed mostly of sand (silicon), a chip contains the equivalent of thousands of transistors (transistors, like tubes, are basically electronic on-off switches). Chips are also called **integrated circuits** or **ICs,** because they're made up of a bunch of very complicated circuits that have been put together (integrated) and shrunk down to a tiny size — a process known as **microminiaturization**.

Chips work *fast*; for example, a new "super-chip" developed by Hewlett-Packard was promoted as being faster than a speeding bullet because it can perform 500 operations in the time it takes for a bullet to travel across the entire one-quarter inch of it.

A memory card for a microcomputer.

Close-up of a printed circuit board.

Magnification of an integrated circuit. (*Courtesy of Intel Corporation.*)

So that they can connect up with the rest of the circuitry on the board, chips get mounted into a caterpillar-like affair called a **dual in-line package (DIP).**

This is as good a place as any to tell you that the two great enemies of computer chips and boards are cigarette smoke and heat. Smoke coats the boards with tar, obscuring connections, and heat makes layers with separate circuits on them melt into each other.

A DIP.

A computer's memory usually takes up all of one board, and sometimes more than one. The actual computing capability — the part of the computer that manipulates information, is called the **central processing unit (CPU) board,** the **microprocessor board,** or the **microprocessor unit (MPU).**

The CPU board is built around the **CPU chip** or **microprocessor.** It's typically the most complex chip in the computer (which isn't surprising, since in a certain sense, the microprocessor *is* the whole computer). I'll have more to say about the various kinds of CPU chips later on, when I discuss operating systems.

Often there are a couple of other boards as well — one to control the disk drives and another to control the display of text on the screen. However, it is possible to put all the functions on just one board (as in the Osborne 1).

Some computers are **expandable** — that is, they have empty **slots** where you can put new cards so that they'll do things like communicate over phone lines or operate different peripherals. There's a wonderful name for what you put boards into, by the way — it's called the **motherboard.**

Boards are connected together by a **bus.** A common one for microcomputers is the **S-100 bus.** Machines with the same bus can generally use the same cards, which means that you can take a card out of one S-100 machine and put it in another and it will work, even if the machines were made by different manufacturers.

In some computers, some of the memory is set up so you can't change it and is called **read-only memory (ROM).** ROM is used for basic instructions to the computer or for programs that are used all the time. ROM is supplied on a chip that is plugged into your computer.

A motherboard in a computer box.

A motherboard with three boards in it.

ROM (read-only memory) chips.

Your text goes in the portion of memory that can be changed (of course). This is called **read/write memory, R/W memory, user memory,** or **random-access memory (RAM).** Since ROM is also "accessed randomly" (don't worry about what that means), the first three terms are more accurate. But RAM is much more common (probably because it's so much easier to say), and I use it throughout this book.

BITS, BYTES, AND WORDS

The amount of RAM a word processor has is measured in characters. A **character** is any letter, number, punctuation mark, or other symbol. Blank spaces are characters, as are the symbols which tell the printer to go on to the next line or the next page.

Another word for a character is a **byte.** Technically, a byte is the amount of information required to specify a particular character (eight bits), but for the purposes of this book, just think of it as a character. You won't need to know much about bits to understand word processors, but in the interest of general computer literacy, let me give you the basics.

Computers are basically large switching devices (in fact, the first ones used actual mechanical switches, rather than vacuum tubes, transistors, or integrated circuits). All the information stored in any computer boils down to a series of switches being on or off. **Binary numbers** — that is, numbers in base two where everything reduces to either a one (on) or a zero (off) — are what a computer understands, because they tell it which switches to throw.

For a computer to be able to understand text, it has to be converted into binary numbers, typically by using the **American Standard Code for Information Interchange (ASCII).** In ASCII, 01000001 (off, on, off, off, off, off, off, on) equals capital A; 01100001 equals lowercase a; and so on. There are ASCII codes for 128 letters, numbers, and symbols.

Each of those ones and zeros is called a **bit** (short for "*bi*nary dig*it*"). Everything a computer produces is ultimately made up of bits. But in talking about word processors, bytes are talked about much more frequently than bits, since each byte equals one character.

Because the number of bytes in a system's RAM is quite large, it's usually given in **K (Kbytes** or **kilobytes**). A K is 1024 bytes. (Why not an even thousand? Because bits have two values, and $2 \times 2 = 4$; $4 \times 2 = 8$; and so on — 16, 32, 64, 128, 256, 512, 1024.) Just as you can think of a liter as a quart and a little bit more, so you can think of a K as a thousand and a little bit (about 2½ percent) more. (By the way, the plural of K is K, not Ks; you wouldn't say "64K*s*" any more than you'd say "64 thousand*s*.")

Unfortunately, K is used to refer not only to Kbytes, but also to Kbits (kilobits). Since there are eight bits in a byte, a Kbit is one-eighth the size of a Kbyte. To add to the confusion, some ads mean Kbits when they refer to K, while others mean Kbytes.

Thus, to add 16K of RAM to your system, you need *eight* 16K memory boards, because the first K means Kbytes and the second Kbits. When K refers to the total number of RAM in a system, however, it always means Kbytes. Sometimes you see the abbreviation **KB** instead of K. KB always means kilobytes, never kilobits.

A **megabyte** (abbreviated **MB**) is a K's worth of kilobytes — that is, 1024×1024 bytes, or 1,048,576 bytes. You can think of it as a million bytes, but it's actually about 5 percent more.

A minimum amount of memory for word-processing applications is 32K (32,768 bytes). 48K or 56K is better, and 64K (65,536 bytes) is adequate for most purposes. (A word processor with 64K of RAM has more than half a million little electronic switches inside it — just to give you an idea of how complicated these machines are.)

But how many words are there in a K? Answering that involves a short digression into how long the average **word** is.

Officially (that is, in typing classes, ads for typewriters and printers, etc.), the average word is five characters — i.e., four letters and a space. There's only one problem with this — the average word happens to be longer than that.

Until recently, counting the number of letters in all the words in a piece of text was about as tedious a job as you could imagine. But word processors make it easy (of course). Mine gives me the length of what I'm working on in both words and K. All I have to do is divide.

In a sample of more than a hundred thousand of my own words, I've found that they average almost exactly six characters each (five letters and a space). Since I tend to use short words, I can only conclude that the people who first defined a word as five characters were the victims of their benighted, pre-computer times.

In this book, when I use the word *word* without qualification, I usually mean six characters, not five. Sometimes I'll call these six-character words **real words** and the five-character words **official words.** Appendix B tells you how to convert official wpm figures in ads to real words per minute, how to estimate the number of words on a page, and how to convert from K to words to pages.

(By the way, there's a technical, computer-science meaning for ''word'' and also for ''page.'' These have no necessary relation to actual words and pages of text; I just mention them so you won't be confused if you come across them.)

So — 32K is about 5500 words, 48K about eight thousand words, and 64K about eleven thousand words. Unfortunately, you don't get all this RAM to use for your text.

Various programs (including the word-processing program you're using) also have to fit in there. More about this later.

While eleven thousand words might be more text than you need to work on at any one time, you obviously will accumulate more words than that over a period of time. Not only that, but a computer's RAM (unlike its ROM) goes blank when you turn it off. For both these reasons, you need a way to store your text, in volume and permanently. Read on.

STORAGE DEVICES

Storage — which implies a certain amount of permanence — is distinguished from **memory** — which, in computers, unlike elephants, doesn't last. (Storage is also called **permanent, bulk,** or **auxiliary storage,** or **auxiliary** or **secondary memory,** but these names seem confusing and/or redundant to me.)

Storage devices put information on and take information off **magnetic media.** At the present time, virtually all storage media used on word processors share the same basic technology — and share it, in fact, with tape recorders. Magnetic impulses are put onto an oxide coating and stay there permanently (unless the medium comes near a strong magnetic field). Media differ only in terms of what the oxide coating is on.

The simplest storage device is a **cassette recorder. Cassette tapes** and recorders are cheap, but they are awfully slow for any serious word-processing applications. You can spend a long time just locating information on a cassette, for the same reason it takes more time to find a song on a cassette than on a record — you have to go past all the other stuff to get to it.

At the other extreme from cassette tapes are **hard disks** (sometimes also called **rigid disks** or **fixed disks**) — flat platters that spin at very high speed inside an enclosure. The information on a hard disk comes around on each rotation, and thus can be put on and pulled off the disk much, much faster than it can on a cassette. You can get between a hundred and a thousand characters off a cassette in one second but more than a million per second off a hard disk.

Most hard disks sold today are called **Winchesters.** They keep the disk in a dust-free enclosure from which you can't remove it.

There are many other forms of storage media — streaming tape, stringy floppies, bubble memory. But almost all word processors use **floppy disks** (also called **floppies, diskettes, flexible disks** or **flexible diskettes**) as their storage device.

Floppies get their name from the fact that, unlike hard disks, they are bendable (although if you *do* bend one, you ruin it). A floppy disk is made up of mylar coated with magnetic oxide (essentially the same material recording tape is made out of). It's in the

A hard disk drive. (*Courtesy of Tandon Corporation.*)

An 8-inch and a 5¼-inch floppy disk.

shape of a circle and is enclosed in a square cardboard jacket.

Floppies are about 1/16 inch thick and either 8 or 5 1/4 inches square (although even smaller, 3 1/2-inch floppies have been introduced). The 5 1/4-inch disks are called **mini-floppies** or **mini-diskettes.** Either kind costs about five to eight dollars each.

Storage media have information **written** onto them and **read** off of them by devices called **disk drives.** (Writing is the equivalent of recording on a tape recorder, and reading is the equivalent of playback.) Both are done by a **read/write head,** which is mounted at the end of a short arm that moves back and forth over the disks while they spin around at high speed (it's sort of like the tone arm of a turntable with the read and write heads of a tape recorder on the end of it).

Because floppies are so widely used as the storage device for word processors, I refer to them simply as **disks** throughout the book. So when you see the word *disk* by itself, remember that I'm talking about a floppy and not a hard disk.

Floppies are intermediate in speed between cassette tape and hard disks. Information can be pulled off them at one thousand to ten thousand characters per second.

The exact capacity of different floppies varies greatly, depending not only on their size but also on whether information is stored on both sides (**double-sided**) or just one (**single-sided**) and on how much the information is compacted (**single-density** or **double-density**). How the disk is **formatted** (where and how it stores information) also makes a difference. Roughly speaking, the range is from about 70K to 1.2 MB — that is, from about 12,000 to 200,000 words.

Storage media like floppies are the word processor's equivalent of filing cabinet drawers. So it makes sense that the groupings of information on them are called **files.**

A file is any piece of text you give one name to. It can be thousands of words long or just one word long. You can split long files in two and combine short files into one. *You* decide what makes up a file by giving a hunk of text a distinct name.

Each system has a maximum length for a file name. Some let you add an **extension** after the name to identify what type of file it is (in fact, this extension is sometimes called a **type**). You might use "TXT" as a type, to indicate a text file, "LET" to indicate a letter, or "LST" to indicate a list. File names are usually written all in caps:

CHAPTER1.TXT
DEARJOHN.LET
LAUNDRY.LST

(These are CP/M file names; they would have different formats on different kinds of systems.)

Each floppy has two limits on the amount of information that can be written onto it — the total number of characters and the total number of distinct file names. Floppies accommodate up to 256 files (depending on size, density, and the software they're running under). Usually the total number of characters, rather than the number of files, is the effective limit to how much you can squeeze onto a disk, unless you have a lot of short files, like business letters.

```
A>xdir

DISK:A    FILES:22     ENTRIES:28  (36  LEFT)   SPACE USED:181K  (60K    LEFT)

CHAPTER1 TXT  10K | EDIT     COM  13K | MAINDICT CMP  50K | UPDICT   CMP   1K
CHAPTER2 TXT  18K | ERRWORDS TXT   1K | MARK     COM   2K | WC       COM   1K
CHAPTER3 TXT  13K | FIND     COM   1K | MBASIC   COM  18K | WORDFREQ COM   2K
CHAPTER4 TXT  16K | LAUNDRY  LST   1K | PRINT    COM  18K | XDIR     COM   1K
DEARJOHN LET   2K | LIST     COM   4K | REVIEW   COM   2K |
DICTSORT COM   2K | LOOKUP   COM   2K | SPELL    COM   3K |

A>
```

A directory of files on a disk.

PROGRAMS AND TEXT FILES

There are two basic kinds of files: data files and programs. In the case of word processing, the data in a **data file** is text, and thus word-processing data files — the files you fill with your own writing — are called **text files.**

Programs are made up of instructions rather than text. They tell computers how to do things. (Creating new programs is called **programming** and the people who do it are called **programmers**.) A mistake or problem in a program is called a **bug.** Programs are also called **software,** and they come to you on disks.

In the Introduction, I pointed out something that's worth repeating here: as the user of a word processing program written by someone else, you never need to do any programming of your own. And that's not just because you're a beginner. It's possible to be a very knowledgeable user of computers without ever writing a program. There will soon be millions of computer users who have no need or desire to write programs.

Taking a file from the disk and making a copy of it in memory — i.e., making it into the work file — is called **loading** (or **getting**) the file. (The original remains on the disk, unchanged.) The file you are editing at any given moment — the one that's loaded into memory — is called the **work file.**

Taking a file from memory and making a copy of it on the disk is called **saving** (and on some dedicated word processors, **archiving**) the file. (The original remains in memory, unchanged.)

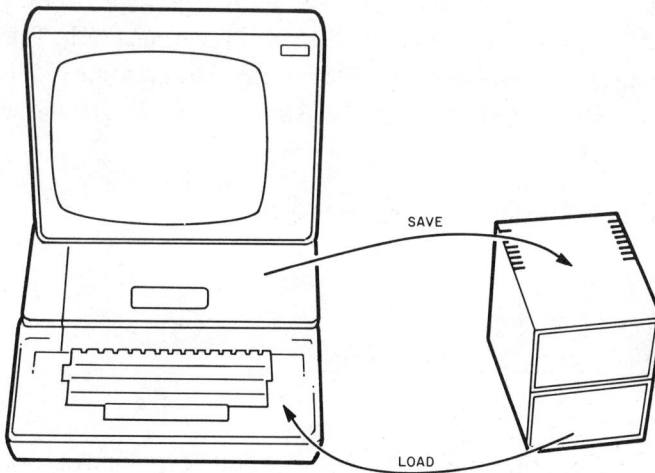

Saving (to the disk) and loading (from the disk) text files with a computer and its disk drives.

Since both programs and data files are stored on disks, both can be loaded or saved. The difference is that programs do things when they're in memory, and text files have things done to them. As a user, you won't ever need to save a program, because you don't change programs when they're in memory. But you will load programs and both load and save text files.

Removing an old file you no longer need from a disk is called **killing** or **deleting** it. Abandoning a work file without saving it is called **dumping** it.

On a system with two or more disk drives, the one that files are loaded from and saved to is sometimes called the **logged** drive (usually drive A). The disk in that drive is called the logged disk. Most systems let you change the logged drive, and all systems let you specify a different drive for each individual load or save.

The disk a program comes on from the publisher or computer store is called a **distribution disk** or **master disk.** You should immediately make a copy of it and put it in a fire-proof, moisture-proof, radiation-proof vault under a mountain somewhere. If possible, post a 24-hour armed guard around it. Then make two copies of the copy. (Having to get a replacement copy of a distribution disk is a needless hassle.)

A word-processing program is called an **applications program,** because it's used for a specific application. There are other kinds of applications programs to help you do just about anything — from generating form letters, taking care of a mailing list, making financial predictions, and using a spreadsheet to creating graphics, checking a document for spelling errors, sorting lists of information, and playing games.

Applications software is written in **programming languages.** Some programming languages available on microcomputers are BASIC, Pascal and Forth. These are called **high-level languages,** because they resemble natural languages like English. High-level languages can typically be used on different machines, regardless of what chip each machine uses for its CPU.

A high-level language looks something like this:

```
10 INPUT F$
20 OPEN ''O'',1,F$
30 PRINT ''NUMBER OF EMPLOYEES''
```

Assembly (or **assembler**) **languages** are specific to each kind of CPU chip. They can only be used on machines which use that particular chip. Assembly language translates directly into **machine language,** which is what the machine itself understands. If you could see it written out, it would look like this:

0010110101011010110001010000100100101110110101 0

Assembly language is harder to program in than a high-level language, but it **executes** much faster — that is, it does its work much more quickly. In general, a word-processing program written in assembly language will be more efficient than a word-processing program written in a high-level language. The advantages of the latter are that it's easier for you to modify yourself and it's likely to be usable on a wider variety of machines.

WORD-PROCESSING PROGRAMS

A **word-processing program** is a set of instructions that tells your computer how to do word processing; it adapts your computer so you can create, edit, and print out text on it.

Sometimes the phrase ''word processor'' is used to refer to a word-processing program itself rather than the whole computer system on which this program runs. (This is particularly common among people who have been around computers a long time. The logic of it is that a word-processing program is what makes a computer a word processor, so it makes sense to refer to the program, rather than a machine, as a word processor.) When I use the term, the context always makes it clear whether I'm referring to a machine or a program.

Word-processing programs are made up of two parts — the **editor** (also called the **text editor**), which lets you insert, delete, and change text, and the **formatter,** which lets you control how that text appears on paper (and sometimes also on the screen). Editors and formatters are occasionally sold separately, so what looks like a whole word-processing program in an ad may actually only be half of one.

Formatters tend to give you a lot of choices about how you want your printouts to look; margin width, character spacing, line spacing, and page numbering are just a few of them. So that you don't have to go to the bother of setting all of them each time you want to make a printout (and so you don't have to deal with them at all when you're just learning), most word-processing programs have default values for these choices.

A **default** value is what something is set at until you change it. So, if double-spacing is the default, your printouts will be double-spaced until and unless you ask for different line spacing. Usually anything that can be changed — not just a formatting feature — has a default value; for example, drive A might be the default for which drive is logged.

The editor and formatter are loaded into memory together in most word-processing programs, but some require you to exit one and load the other. Other programs use **overlays** for certain functions — additional program files that sit on the disk until the main program needs them. A program can go to an overlay and get just the little bit of information it requires, rather than having to load the whole overlay into memory. Overlays slow down the operation of a program tremendously, but they save space in RAM for your text files.

Many word-processing programs list commands that are available to you on the screen. Since you can pick from this list the way you do from a menu in a restaurant, a **menu** is what it's called. (Programs that use menus are described as being **menu-driven**).

There are a few concepts that have to do with formatting that you'll need to know. One is the idea of a **line break.** Most word processors have **word wrap,** which means that words that don't fit at the end of a line get moved down automatically to the start of the next, without your having to hit a carriage return. So the only time you need to ask for a line break is when you want one regardless of whether or not the line is filled — as you would at the end of a paragraph or after a title, subtitle, or some other line you want to stand alone.

The situation with **page breaks** is similar: when a page of printout fills up, the word processor automatically moves on to the next. But there are situations — like the end of a section or a chapter — when you want to force a page break, and there will typically be a command to let you do that.

Some word processors show on the screen where all the line breaks and page breaks will appear in the printout. The ones that don't have special symbols to show where you have inserted your own line breaks and page breaks.

There are two basic ways you can give a word processor formatting instructions: you can tell it what you want each time you print out, or you can **embed** commands in the text file, so that when the word processor comes across them, it will read and obey them. The second method is generally more convenient because it saves your having to retype a series of commands each time you want to print out a file.

In order to embed commands, you need some way to distinguish them from normal text. (Otherwise the word processor will just print it out, rather than doing what it says.) The trick is to use something that never could appear in normal text:

- a peculiar symbol, like a backslash (\ ) — on systems that have that character.
- an unusual sequence of characters, like %%.
- some strange format, like a line that begins with a period. (This last is very common; so, for example, the command .ce, sitting on a line by itself, means ''center the next line'' in a dozen different word-processing programs.)

I'll have much more to say about word-processing programs in Chapters 5 and 6 (as well as elsewhere), but that will do for an introduction.

OPERATING SYSTEMS, CHIPS, AND BRANDS OF MACHINES

In order for a word processor to be able to load any program or text file, you first have to **boot** it — that is, you have to load a very basic program that tells the computer how to load other programs. (The word *boot* comes from the idea that this basic program pulls the computer up by its own bootstraps.) Each system has a different procedure for booting; some do it automatically.

This basic program you boot a word processor with is called an **operating system** (sometimes abbreviated **OS**). Since it controls the disk drives, it's also often called a **disk operating system** (or **DOS**, pronounced dawss or dahss). Every computer system has an operating system; if it didn't, you couldn't use it. But on dedicated word processors, it's an integral part of the word-processing program and you don't even know that it's there.

The operating system takes up some RAM (memory) of its own, on top of which you have your word-processing program. Conceivably, if the word-processing program was written in a high-level language, you might even need to load a language in too. What's left over after all these programs are loaded is the **workspace** (or **buffer**) in which you create your text. See Figure 2.24.

TOTAL *RAM*: 64 K

OPERATING SYSTEM: 6K

WORD-PROCESSING PROGRAM: 31K

WORKSPACE: 27K

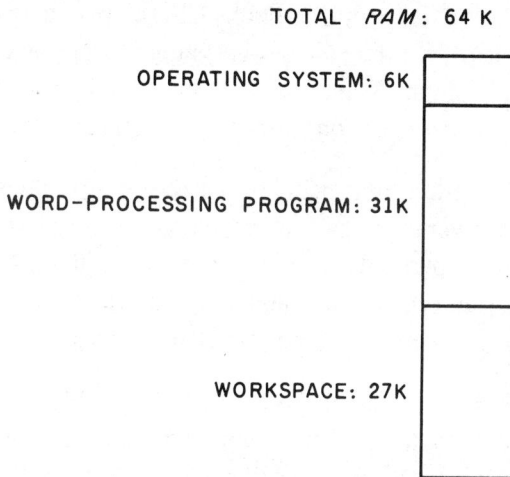

An example of how RAM might be allocated.

Any disk with a copy of the operating system on it is called a **system disk.** Disks with your text files on them are called **work disks.** Ideally, you'll be able to put your operating system, word-processing program, and text files all on the same disk, making every work disk a system disk as well.

When an operating system works on a particular microcomputer, you say that machine **runs** it ("Does the Apple III run CP/M?"). You can also say that it **supports** it ("UNIX is supported on a wide range of machines"). You also speak of machines running and supporting word-processing programs and other applications programs ("I don't care what else it can do, as long as it will run WordStar").

Applications programs are said to **run under** an operating system, and all kinds of programs **run on** machines ("I know Scripsit runs under TRSDOS. What I want to know is if TRSDOS runs on the Color Computer").

Some operating systems run on a wide variety of machines from different manufacturers; CP/M, Oasis, Flex, and UNIX are examples. But many microcomputer manufacturers (Apple, Radio Shack, Commodore, etc.) and most dedicated-word-processor makers use **proprietary** operating systems that only run on their own machines (TRSDOS, Apple DOS, SOS, etc.). Sometimes other companies will adapt independent operating systems to run on those systems (Digital Research's CP/M-86 for the IBM Displaywriter, for example).

It's the operating system that really gives a computer its individual flavor. A Wangwriter running CP/M is more like a Cromemco running CP/M than it is like a Wangwriter running Wang's own operating system.

Operating systems tend to be tied to one particular CPU chip, or at least to a chip family (a **chip family** is a series of chips, made by one company, that have evolved from each other). But even this is changing. As the competition gets stiffer, many publishers are adapting their operating systems to run on the widest possible variety of machines.

Most word-processing programs run under just one operating system. And those that have been adapted to run under more than one operating system are still usually limited to machines based on one particular chip family. Some aren't, but they're pretty rare. This is because each chip and chip family has a different way of doing things and a different group of commands it understands (called an **instruction set**).

Thus, for a word-processing program to work on a different chip, it has to completely change its way of doing things. Exceptions to this are word-processing programs that are written in high-level languages like BASIC, because BASIC "interpreters" and "compilers" have been written for many different chips. (Of word-processing programs I know about, PIE Writer is the one that has been adapted to work with the most different CPU chips.) See Figure 2.25.

So the first decision you have to make is which operating system and chip combination is going to provide you with the software you want. This is important for giving you a wide choice not only of word-processing programs, but also of other applications programs you're going to need in the future (whether or not you anticipate needing them now).

There's no way to avoid this decision, although if you buy a dedicated word processor or some other system that's all put together for you, you can let someone else make it for you.

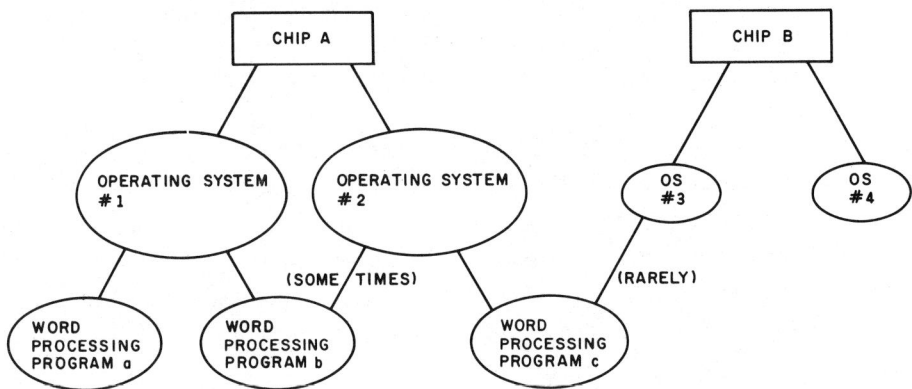

A chart of chip, operating system, and word-processing program organization.

There are two basic kinds of microprocessors (CPU chips) used in microcomputers — **eight-bit chips** and **sixteen-bit chips.** The difference has to do with how much data a chip bites off when it does its computing. Eight-bit chips — the most common in micros — grab data eight bits at a time (which is handy for word-processing applications, since each character is eight bits).

Sixteen-bit chips take data in sixteen-bit chunks (naturally). They're faster and more powerful, but there's less good, inexpensive software available for them. Personally, I think that building a single-user word processor around a sixteen-bit chip is a little like swatting a fly with a hammer. For more than one user at a time, however, they're ideal.

There are also several ''half-breed chips'' that combine eight-bit and sixteen-bit features; like most half-breeds, they end up with the best qualities of both parents. The **8088** (the chip used in the IBM Personal Computer) and the **6809** are two examples.

Most of the chips I discuss in this book are eight-bit chips; when I mention one that isn't I try to indicate that.

CP/M is the most popular operating system for microcomputers (the name stands for ''control program for microprocessors''). It's become a virtual industry standard for computers based on the widely used **8080/Z-80** chip families. Some machines that run CP/M are the Zenith-Heath Z-89, Xerox 820, Wangwriter, Vector Graphics, TRS-80, SuperBrain, Sol, Osborne 1, NorthStar, Imsai, HP 125, Cromemco, Apple II, Altos, and Altair.

The Apple II isn't actually a Z80-based computer; it's built around the 6502 chip. But MicroSoft came out with a separate board you put in the Apple II (called the **SoftCard**). The SoftCard is basically a Z80 CPU board which slaves the whole rest of the Apple (including its own 6502 CPU chip) to it. (**Slaving** means just what it sounds like — putting one computer or device under the control of another.) With a SoftCard, the Apple II runs CP/M (although somewhat more awkwardly than on a machine it was designed for).

TRS-80s are Z80 machines (except for the Color Computer); the name itself stands for **T**andy **R**adio **S**hack **Z80**. But you have to substitute CP/M from another vendor for the operating system that comes with the machine, Radio Shack's TRSDOS.

Many dedicated word processors are 8080- or Z80-based, but only a few run CP/M. The Wangwriter and Lanier have only recently been adapted to support CP/M; CPT has run it for years. CP/M gives dedicated word processors access to literally thousands of pieces of applications software. That's also why HP and Xerox built machines that run CP/M.

CP/M software is the strongest in the area of business programs. All the best-selling word-processing programs (Electric Pencil, Magic Wand, WordStar) have been CP/M programs.

Now — everything I've just said refers to the original CP/M, which was written for 8080/Z80 machines. There's also at least one later version of CP/M; it's called **CP/M-86** and is designed to run on machines based on either the 8086 or 8088 chip. (Sometimes the original CP/M is called **CP/M-80** to distinguish it from CP/M-86, but most of the time both are just called CP/M.)

The reason that it's important to make this distinction is that all that wonderful software *only runs under the original CP/M (CP/M-80)*. *None* of it will run under CP/M-86 without being adapted to do so, and that adaption is not an easy job. So while IBM says in its ads that the Personal Computer will support CP/M, what they don't say is that they're referring to CP/M-86, for which much less software has been written so far.

I've never heard anyone claim that CP/M is the best operating system around; in my own experience, I've found it to be awkward, confusing, wretchedly documented, and hard to learn. Aside from the fact that (unlike some of its competitors) CP/M actually does work, almost the only good thing you can say about it is that it doesn't take up much RAM. But there's so much good software written for CP/M (CP/M-80, that is) that most people don't care what CP/M itself is like.

Another popular chip is the **6502.** In addition to the Apples II and III, 6502-based computers include the Ohio Scientific Challenger, Commodore Pet/CBM, and Atari. There is no industry-standard operating system for 6502 computers the way there is for 8080/Z80 computers. Each manufacturer tends to have its own operating system, which limits the total amount of software usable on their machines (although people who publish software for 6502s sometimes adapt it to run on each machine's operating system).

6502 software is strongest in the area of graphics and light-hearted applications-like games, but there is also a whole lot of 6502 business software.

The 8080/Z80 family of chips was the first, which is why so much software has been written for it. But here again, no one argues that it's the best. That honor is usually awarded to the **6800 family,** and particularly its most recent eight-bit member, the **6809.** Some makers of 6809 computers are the Radio Shack (TRS-80 Color Computer), Commodore (Micro Mainframe), SWTPC, Smoke Signal, Hazelwood, Helix, Gimix, and Canon. You can also get a plug-in board for the Apple II that makes it into a 6809 machine.

The **Flex** operating system has been the clear choice of 6800 users, but on 6809 machines it's running neck and neck with a new multitasking operating system called **OS-9.**

There are also several **proprietary chips** that only appear in the computers of the company that manufactures them. Most HP computers use proprietary chips, as does the Texas Instrument 99/4.

Some popular sixteen-bit chips are the **Z8000** (used in Onyx computers, among others), the **8086,** the classic **LSI-11** (from DEC), and the **68000.**

The dominant position that CP/M occupies in the world of eight-bit chips, an operating system called **UNIX** occupies in the world of sixteen-bit chips. UNIX, developed by the phone company's Bell Labs in New Jersey, runs on PDP-11 machines. It is much admired for its power, flexibility, and the ease with which it interacts with the user. However, CP/M-86 seems intent on giving it a run for its money.

COMMUNICATION BETWEEN COMPONENTS

Word processors vary in the way they transmit text from the computer to the screen. Some use a system called **memory-mapping** or **direct memory access (DMA).** On a memory-mapped system, a separate **video board** reads information directly off circuits in the computer and puts it on the screen. This has the advantage of being very fast.

The other way to transmit text to the screen is called **terminal mode** and requires that the screen be part of a terminal which has some memory of its own. Information goes from the computer's memory into the terminal's memory and *then* onto the screen. This lets the terminal alter how information is displayed. The smarter a terminal is, the more fancy things it can do with the text. (The differences between DMA and terminal mode are discussed in more detail in Chapters 5 and 8.)

When a system is running in terminal mode, the speed at which a screen is **updated** (shows changes made in the text) depends on the rate at which characters are transmitted to it. This is measured in bits per second (**bps**), also called the **baud rate.**

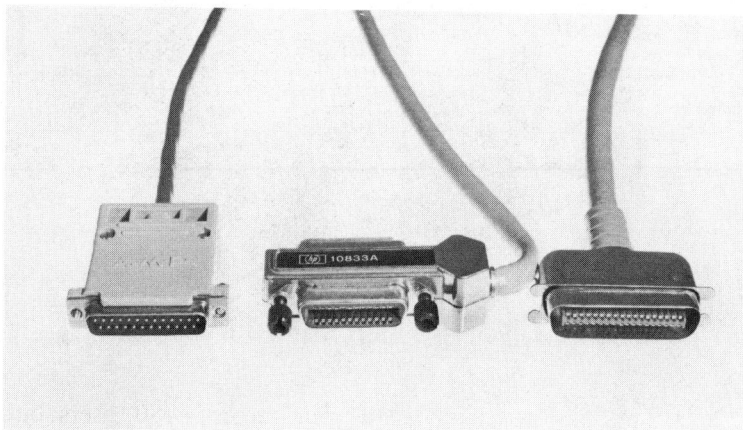

RS-232, IEE-488, and Centronics-type connectors.

The baud rate is important in figuring how quickly a terminal's screen will respond. Three hundred baud is agonizingly slow, 1200 baud is tolerable, 9600 is very good, and 19,200 is almost indistinguishable from memory-mapped video.

Transmission speed also depends on the code used. Sometimes eleven bits are required to send each character, so you have to divide the baud rate by eleven, and other times ten bits are required. (The extra two or three bits are required to tell the terminal, ''OK, here comes another character.'')

To connect components together, you need cables, jacks, and plugs, To not go crazy doing it, you need standard cables, jacks, and plugs. Fortunately, they exist and are in common use.

The whole shebang — a standard plug with so many pins in a certain pattern, a matching jack, a certain type of cable, and an agreement about what kinds of stuff goes over what wire — is called an **interface.** (''Interface'' can also refer to the software, as well as the hardware, necessary to connect devices.) A jack is usually called a **port** — which is a general term for the place where anything comes into or goes out of a computer.

RS-232 is the name of industry-standard **serial interface.** ''Serial'' means information travels over each wire in the cable one bit after the other. **IEEE-488** is the name of a very common **parallel interface.** ''Parallel'' means several bits (usually eight) travel over separate wires simultaneously, next to each other. **Centronics** is the name of another common parallel interface.

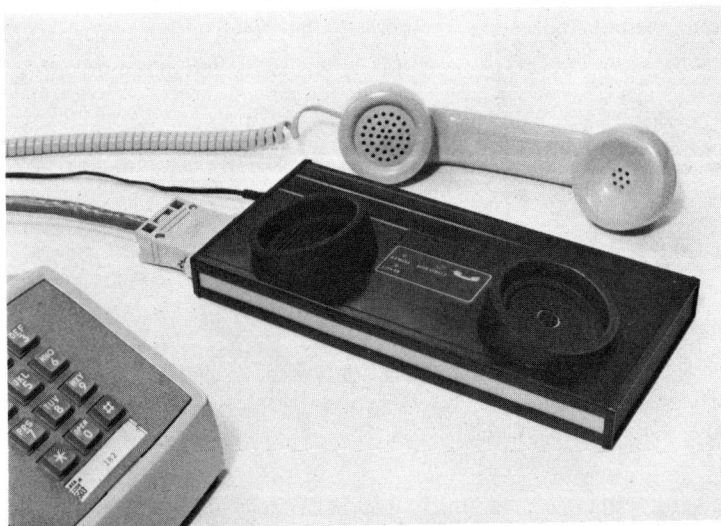

A modem.

COMMUNICATIONS BETWEEN MACHINES

So far I've just been talking about communications inside of one computer system. But it's also possible for one whole system to talk to another. Usually this is done over phone lines with a device called a **modem** (pronounced ''MOE-dum'', it stands for *mo*dulator/*dem*odulator).

Modems usually work at one of two transmission rates — 300 baud or 1200 baud. 1200 baud modems are more expensive and require a 1200 baud port on the computer you're calling (300 baud ports are much more common). It also costs more per hour to connect up with a 1200 baud port.

Modems can connect directly to a phone line with a modular plug like the one that comes on telephones or use an **acoustic coupler** into which you put the handpiece of the telephone (sometimes the acoustic coupler and modem are integrated into one unit). Obviously the direct connection is more accurate and dependable.

On some systems, modems are built into the computer rather than being a separate unit. A **modem board** can be inserted into computers with empty slots for additional boards.

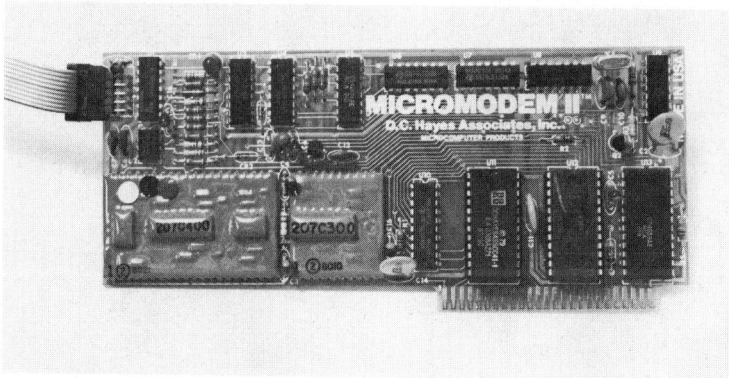

A modem board for the Apple II computer.

POWER SUPPLIES

Word processors, like all computers, are very sensitive to variations in the electrical power that's fed to them. If it isn't perfectly steady, it can cause big problems.

Many sorts of malfunctions in your system may indicate that your power line needs to be cleaned up, but two common symptoms of **dirty power** are **hash** (visual static on the screen) and **dropouts** (characters missing from your text). Drpouts look lik ths. Usualy ther arn't so mny. If u cn rd ths, u cn gt a gd jb. . . .

Since your electrical utility is already providing you with the cleanest power it can (or intends to), it's up to you to solve the problem at your end by modifying your **power supply.**

This term is quite misleading, since power supplies don't actually supply power. Rather they convert the 110 or 220 volts AC from your wall into DC current of the correct voltages for a computer, printer, terminal, etc. Various sorts of electrical filtering are included in some computers' power supplies. Whether they are or not, you may have to add some protection of your own.

If you have a problem with **spikes** (sudden surges of power coming over your electrical lines, caused by a heavy machine like an air conditioner shutting off or by lightning), you'll want to protect your system with a **surge suppressor.**

If you have a problem with **noise** or other kinds of **electromagnetic interference (EMI)** — which can be caused by CB radios, fluorescent lighting, radar, television sets, car ignitions, photocopiers, elevators, home appliances, or most electrical motors, you need a **line filter** (also called a **line isolator**).

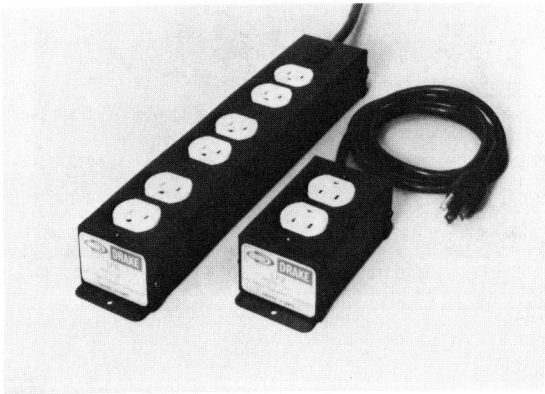

A combination line filter and surge suppressor. (*Courtesy of R. L. Drake Company.*)

If you have a problem with brownouts (long-term drops in line voltage caused deliberately by your power company or as a side effect of a machine like a vacuum cleaner operating in your building), you need a **constant voltage transformer (CVT).**

(Sometimes brownouts are caused by a coffee maker or the like on the same line as your computer. The solution for this is much simpler — give your word-processing system a line of its own.)

All three kinds of devices (surge suppressor, line filter, and CVT) can be combined into a single unit, usually called a **line conditioner** or **line stabilizer.**

A line conditioner. It gives protection against power line noise, brownouts, and voltage sags and surges. (*Courtesy of Topaz, Inc.*)

Remember — dirty power isn't just annoying; it can destroy electronic circuits. Make sure the power coming into your computer is clean.

Well — that's more than you probably ever wanted to know about word processors. But the more information you have, the easier it will be for you to figure out what programs and equipment best fits your needs. The first decision you need to make is which basic kind of machine to buy. That's what the next chapter is about.

3

Different Kinds of Word Processors

Word processors were sired by computers out of typewriters, and perhaps the best way to begin describing the children of that union is to give a short history of each of the parents.

The first patent ever recorded for a typewriter was granted to the Englishman Henry Mill in 1714. The first commercially practical machine was developed by the Americans Christopher Latham Sholes, Carlos Glidden, and Samuel Soulé in 1867, and manufactured — beginning in 1874 — by Philo Remington, son of Eliphalet Remington (I love those nineteenth century names).

Typewriters were clumsy machines at first; in fact, Sholes et al. rearranged the keys to cut down the speed with which they could be hit to prevent them from jamming (he originally had them in alphabetical order). Over the years typewriter design has become more efficient, but the original, designed-to-be-slow keyboard is still with us. (More on this in Chapter 8.)

The first electric typewriter came out around 1935, and the first IBM Selectric — the most advanced of the non-electronic typewriters — in 1961. To follow what happens to typewriters after this, we need to turn to computers.

An early typewriter.

An IBM Selectric typewriter.

It's hard to know where to begin the history of the computer; certainly the abacus, which is thousands of years old, is a predecessor. The first programmable machine of any kind was the automatic loom invented around 1800 by the Frenchman Joseph-Marie Jacquard. His **Jacquard loom** was programmed by large, stiff punched cards that told it what pattern to weave.

This idea was taken over by the Englishman Charles Babbage. In 1833, Babbage designed what he called an **analytical engine,** to be powered by a steam engine and programmed by punched cards. It would make complex mathematical computations and store the results in its memory.

Although the technical expertise of the time wasn't capable of actually constructing Babbage's machine, it would have worked if it had been built. The analytical engine was the first design for a machine to process large amounts of information in basically the same way a computer does.

A collaborator of Babbage was Ada, Countess of Lovelace, the gifted daughter of the Romantic poet Lord Byron. A talented musician, Ada's abilities as a mathematician were even more extraordinary. While still a child, she became fascinated with one of Babbage's earlier inventions and impressed him with her understanding of it. She ended up spending the rest of her life working with him.

Lovelace planned problems for the analytical engine, suggested that information be stored in binary (rather than decimal) notation and discovered several errors in Babbage's work. In short, Ada Lovelace was the world's first computer programmer.

But she was also a victim of the age she lived in. As a woman, only her initials could appear on the translation she made of a French description of the analytical engine. Although she was one of the few people who understood the workings of the machine and could clearly explain them, her identity remained a secret. Her career as a mathematician was stunted by the lack of educational opportunities.

Lovelace and Babbage took to betting on horse races to finance development of the analytical engine and lost heavily; she had to pawn her family jewels to pay her debts. She died of cancer in 1851, at 36 (the same age as her father). A new computer program developed for the government — Ada — is named after her.

Little direct work was done on computers for the next hundred years, but much progress was made in related devices. The **cathode ray tube** was developed in the late nineteenth century, and the **vacuum tube** around 1905. In 1939, IBM began work on the **Mark I,** which was completed at Harvard University in 1944. The Mark I was based on mechanical relays and thus was very slow.

A faster machine, based on vacuum tubes, was **ENIAC,** developed by Presper Eckert, John Mauchly, and Herman Goldstine in 1943 (based in part on ideas of John von

Neumann). The first computer sold commercially was Remington Rand's **Univac,** which began being delivered to customers in 1950.

When I was a kid, I remember reading somewhere that if a computer was built as smart as a human being (they didn't say which human being), it would have to be as large as the Empire State Building and you'd have to divert the Hudson River to cool it. This referred to **first generation** computers like the Univac, which were based on vacuum tubes. Vacuum tubes are big and they put out a lot of heat.

The **transistor** (invented in 1947 by William Shockley, Walter Brattain, and John Bardeen) paved the way for the **second generation** of computers. Transistors allowed computers (and everything else made with vacuum tubes) to become much smaller and lighter — not only because transistors are physically smaller than tubes, but also because they generate much less heat and thus require much less space between them for cooling.

In the early '60s, the **third generation** of computers arrived. They were based on the **integrated circuit** (IC), the product of the work of several people, notably Jack Kilby and Robert Noyce. IC's take up even less room than transistors and generate even less heat. (All three devices — vacuum tubes, transistors, and IC's — function basically as electronic switches and are thus very useful in computers, which are essentially just assemblies of switches.)

Transistors, integrated circuits, and computers spawned a huge industry; it grew up around major universities and concentrated in two areas — along Route 128 (which circles the greater Boston area) and in the Santa Clara valley (near Stanford University, south of San Francisco). Once famous for its beautiful fruit orchards, this tranquil, idyllic valley was rapidly overrun by computer companies. Today it goes by the name of **Silicon Valley** (because silicon is used in transistors) and produces about two-thirds of all of this country's computer products.

The first actual **microprocessor** (or **CPU chip**) was the **4004,** announced by Intel on November 15, 1971. It contained the equivalent of 2300 transistors. (Today there are chips that contain the equivalent of one-half million.) The 4004 — the size and weight of a fingernail — was as powerful as the tons of computer equipment that filled whole rooms in 1951.

Microprocessors like the 4004 form the heart of all word processors today. If you took any one of them and transported it 25 years backwards in time, it would be the most powerful computer in the world. Likewise, in 25 years, we can look forward to buying a micro (or probably something much smaller) as advanced as any computer in the world today, and we'll pay a few thousand dollars for it.

Other CPU chips followed fast and furious on the heels of the 4004 (which itself grew into the 8080 and beyond). And soon whole stand-alone microcomputers based on these chips were being built. The first was the MITS Altair 8800, sold as a kit beginning in January, 1975. This was rapidly followed by the IMSAI 8080. (Despite their claims, Apple did *not* invent the personal computer. All this had happened before the chip on which Apples are based, the 6502, was even invented.)

Soon many other companies jumped into the fray. By the end of 1975, about 20,000 microcomputers had been sold. Today the number is in the millions.

Meanwhile, the makers of typewriters and office equipment were not standing still. IBM took the lead in merging the new electronic technology with word-processing functions. In 1964, IBM introduced the first machine to be called a word processor, the **MT/ST** (for magnetic tape Selectric typewriter). As its name implied, this machine used a tape cartridge to store text and a Selectric typewriter to print it out. In 1969, the tape cartridges were replaced by magnetic cards on the **MC/ST.**

The first word processors with video displays were introduced in 1972 by Lexitron and 3M/Linolex. In 1973, Vydec incorporated floppy-disk drives.

Today there's a broad range of word-processing equipment. At the low end of the spectrum are the **electronic typewriters.**

These have a small memory for stock phrases or short files, which generally goes blank when you turn the machine off. They also have features like automatic centering of lines of text and automatic underlining. Electronic typewriters are one step up from electric typewriters and are suited for short documents you don't revise extensively and don't want to use over again.

Next come the **no-screen word processors.** These differ from electronic typewriters by having some way to store data permanently, like a magnetic card, cassette tape, tape cartridge, or floppy disk. No-screen word processors have been in use since the mid-'60s (the MT/ST and MC/ST fall in this category), and there are lots of them around. But they no longer represent the best value for your money.

The next step up is word processor with a **thin-window display** which runs across the top of the keyboard and shows you one line — or part of a line — of text as you type it in.

As I mentioned earlier, this book doesn't cover word processors that display less than 12 lines of text. Given the state of the art, I believe it will be worth your money (for any application I can think of) to get a word processor with a full screen display, especially since you can get one (a microcomputer with word-processing capabilities) for less than you'll pay for a dedicated word processor without a screen (and maybe even for less than an electronic typewriter).

Word processors with full CRT displays come in two flavors: **microcomputers** and **dedicated word processors.** I'll discuss several examples of the former in Chapter 10 and several examples of the latter in Chapter 11. Here I'll talk in general about the difference between the two categories.

SUITABILITY TO THE TASK

Since dedicated word processors are designed from scratch to do word processing (and other jobs only secondarily), much thought has gone into — or should have gone into — every aspect of their design. They should make sitting in front of them and typing for eight hours as painless as possible. (Some ways to do that are discussed in Chapter 8.) And they should have all kinds of special features not found on microcomputers.

On the other hand:

1) Most word processor components — and features — are standard and are found on some microcomputer systems as well.

2) Because dedicated word processors are designed to be used primarily by secretaries, some of their features may not be very well suited to the needs of creative writers, editors, owners of small businesses, or others.

3) Secretaries don't get listened to, or cared about, as much as they should. There's no question that the human engineering of dedicated word processors would be better if they were used primarily by top executives.

In my experience, dedicated word processors are *in general* easier and more comfortable systems to use — if money is not an object. However, I wrote this book (and several others) on a microcomputer, using a program specially designed for creative writers (WRITE). A dedicated word processor would have given me somewhat better hardware than I had, and its software would have been better in certain ways but worse in others. I'm not convinced I would have preferred it overall, and in any case, I couldn't have afforded it.

BUNDLED VS. UNBUNDLED

Dedicated word processors have traditionally come **bundled** — which means you buy everything in one package from one manufacturer. The advantage of this is that everything works well together, or should; and if it doesn't, you know who to go to to get it fixed. The disadvantage of a bundled system is that you can only choose components from a very limited selection (if you have any choice at all).

Stereo equipment is somewhat analogous. You can buy a system that's put together by the manufacturer. If the manufacturer cares about its reputation, none of the components will be terrible and they'll be matched to work well together.

On the other hand, if you know something about audio components, you can mix ones from different manufacturers and end up with a system that's better (and/or less expensive) than one that's put together for you. Where this analogy breaks down, of course, is that you need to know a whole lot more about computer components than audio components to make them work together.

Of course you don't have to do the assembling yourself. Most computer stores function as OEM's — that is, they'll put together microcomputer components from different manufacturers to make up a system that's designed to do word processing. If their customers don't like a given component, it's easy for the store to change it.

Some dedicated word processors manufacturers are also moving in the direction of unbundling their systems. The new Wangwriter, for example, features an unbundled printer (that is, they'll sell you the system without the printer).

COMPATIBILITY

A problem that's related to bundling is compatibility with machines made by other manufacturers or with software published by other companies. I need to rant a little before I discuss it.

There are two different (and opposing) philosophies of how to make your company bigger than the competition. One approach is to milk your current customers for everything you can. A good way to do that is to make them buy all their supplies and parts from you. Thus if you own a Plymouth, you can't put a Chevy or Ford wheel on it because the bolts are in different places. If you own a Sanyo portable tape player like the one I have, you can't buy a cord to plug it into your car's cigarette lighter from anyone but Sanyo, because only Sanyo's (non-standard) plug will fit.

This once-you-got-'em-squeeze-'em approach is widespread, and it's been the traditional approach for large computer manufacturers. But so far, the world of microcomputers has been a refreshing exception to it. Microcomputer software tends to run on lots of different kinds of machines, and microcomputer hardware tends to be industry-standard. If you have single-density eight-inch floppy disks on your computer, there's a standard format that will let you interchange your disks with dozens of other brands of machines.

This philosophy of widespread compatibility has produced a vital, growing, and extremely responsive industry which serves the needs of its customers well.

Unfortunately, dedicated word processors are not part of it. A Micom's disks will not run on a Lanier. Lexitron software will not run on an NBI. And so on. Once you buy a dedicated word processor, you're locked into the company that sold it to you — which, of course, is just what they want.

CHOICE OF SOFTWARE

Incompatibility presents the greatest problem in the area of software. Because huge numbers of microcomputers have been able to share software, an incredible library of programs has grown up. There are many systems you can buy which have more than a thousand different programs available to them — like most Apples, TRS-80s, and systems that run CP/M(-80).

Since most dedicated word processors have not been able to share software, however, each brand has much less of it. Of course if the software a dedicated word processor does have is just what you want and you plan never to grow beyond your present needs (dream on), this won't present a problem.

More realistically, if you use a machine solely as a word processor — eight hours a day in an office setting, for example — it might make more sense to buy a separate computer to run the other software. But, as a general rule, remember that computers (including ones used as word processors) are potentially very useful and adaptable. It's silly not to exploit their potential.

As I mentioned before, several dedicated-word-processor manufacturers have seen the error of their ways and have decided to offer systems that will run microcomputer software.

PRICE

Dedicated word processors tend to cost more than microcomputers (although the overlap is extensive). And their software tends to cost more. So even if a dedicated word processor has the programs you want, you're likely to pay a lot more for them. For example, The Word — a CP/M program that checks text for spelling errors — cost $75 (or $150 for a new version with many new features). The program that Xerox sells to do the same job on the Star costs $1500.

SERVICE

Service for microcomputers tends to be less expensive, but also less convenient, than service for dedicated word processors. Dedicated word processor manufacturers normally offer service contracts. The typical amount is either ten percent of the system's total cost per year or one percent of the total cost per month (i.e., twelve percent per year). This comes to a lot of money, but you get great service for it. If something goes wrong with a machine, someone is usually there to repair it within a few hours.

It seems to me that a word processor shouldn't need repairs with the frequency that justifies spending hundreds of dollars a month on a service contract. But then I can spare the time to take a microcomputer somewhere to be fixed, and I can also afford to wait a few days to get it back. In an office, where time is money, things are different.

With these thoughts in mind, sit down and work at a good dedicated word processor and a good microcomputer for a while. You'll be able to judge for yourself which machine best meets your needs.

SHARED-RESOURCE SYSTEMS

Up until now, I've been talking exclusively about **stand-alone** systems. This means they are complete unto themselves, and only one person can use them at a time. However, if you're going to need more than one word processor, it probably doesn't make sense for you to buy several complete, stand-alone systems. For example, the printer is used only a small fraction of the time. The same is true of the disk drives. So you don't need one for each terminal.

It's possible to buy interconnected systems that share these peripherals. They're called **shared-resource systems,** and linking machines together in this way is called **clustering.** Most dedicated word processors are set up to cluster, but most microcomputers must be modified to do it.

To share the computer itself, however, is a much trickier proposition. Even with dedicated word processors, you need a system specifically designed to do just that. Systems where the computer itself is shared by many users, each of whom has just a terminal to work at, is called a **shared-logic system.**

(Multi-user dedicated word processors are discussed in Chapter 11 and the software for one shared-logic system — the A.B. Dick Magna SL — is evaluated in Chapter 5 and described in Chapter 6.)

If you already have a large computer system in place at your office, it may make sense to use it for word processing. But in certain situations, it may also work out better to set up independent word processors. In any case, word processing on large computer systems is beyond the scope of this book.

There's one further possibility: you can sign onto a **timesharing** service that offers word processing. You connect with it via a phone line and pay hourly charges. This might be the route to take if you have little capital and/or if your need for word processing is infrequent.

4

What To Look For (And Avoid) In A Word Processor

In other chapters I discuss specific features that are desirable — software in Chapter 5, keyboard and screen features in Chapter 8, printer features in Chapter 9, etc. But there are general principles more important than any individual feature, and these are discussed in this chapter.

SUPPORT, SUPPORT, AND SUPPORT

Computers are *very* complex machines. The average *micro*computer contains the equivalent of more than half a million transistors and over 100,000 separate connections. Since you almost certainly don't want to spend the time required to understand how a computer actually works (a much larger project than learning to understand a simple machine like an electric typewriter or a car), you need someone to go to with your questions and problems.

This is particularly important since many things that seem insurmountable to a beginning user are just the result of confusion and can be cleared up in a couple of minutes on the phone. This willingness to answer questions and fix problems is called **support.**

Computer software requires support just as much as hardware does. Word-processing programs are so complex that it's virtually impossible to write one without several **bugs** (mistakes) in it. There are just too many different possibilities to check them all out. Programmers debug their software as best they can and then have friends or associates test it (by using it) for several months to catch the other errors. (This is called **beta testing.**)

Here's another indication of how complex word processors are: in the next chapter, it takes me over 15,000 words just to come up with a vague, imprecise way of evaluating word-processing programs. I ask 160 questions and still end up with nothing more than a rough sketch that doesn't begin to capture all the nuances.

You should expect a certain amount of support from a program's publisher. This consists mostly of fixing bugs and adding features and also occasionally answering questions about the program. But most of your support should come from the **vendor,** the dealer that actually sells you the product.

The best guarantee of good vendor support is a friend who's patronized them for several years and likes them. The next best alternative is to ask the vendor for two or three satisfied customers you can call. Ask these people if they know anyone else who's used the same vendor and call them up as well. Try to talk to an owner of the same product you're thinking of buying.

Unfortunately, businesses change, and so does the level of support they offer. Even mail-order companies who've built their whole reputation on giving great support have been known to suddenly cut back on it. Still, a good record of providing support in the past is the best indication — although not an infallible one — that a vendor will continue to provide it in the future.

It's a good sign when a vendor emphasizes support in advertising, like a computer store I know whose ad promises ''service *after* you buy your computer.'' And how you feel when talking to the salespeople is a very good indication of how you'll like dealing with them after the sale. (Keep in mind that the salespeople who work for a vendor may vary widely in both their helpfulness and knowledge. If you have trouble with one, try another.)

Some vendors (usually those selling products at top dollar) offer ongoing training seminars. These can be helpful, but ultimately what you need is a knowledgeable person you can call with a question.

Top-of-the-line vendors — like dedicated-word-processor makers and other manufacturers who sell their hardware directly to the public — often use **support contracts** as the way to pay for the level of support users actually need. But unless your product is going to be used in an office for eight hours every day, you'll probably be paying for more support than you're likely to need. If you're an individual user, look for support you don't have to pay for. If the vendor is decent, that should be adequate.

Sometimes dedicated-word-processor manufacturers will give you free support regardless of whether you have a support contract (or a service contract), but for only a limited number of hours. What you want is *unlimited* free support.

In the case of software, you need support when you're learning to use it; it can't malfunction later on. (Good manuals could substitute for most of the support, but they're rare.)

Several companies have come up with an interesting way to market programs — stores that sell nothing but software and therefore have a wide range of it. Since the sales staff doesn't have to learn about hardware too, they'll tend to know more about the programs they sell than if they worked in a regular computer store. Software stores will also let you spend as long as you want trying various programs out (regular computer stores usually do this too, but they have a much smaller selection). But the question still remains: what level of support will software stores provide after you've bought a product from them?

Frequently you'll see in computer publications mail-order ads for products at very low prices. They may be real bargains, but there's a good chance you'll lose more in support than you save in money. If the vendor is in another city, find out what the long distance phone charges are. And make sure they have a staff to answer questions.

Don't tell yourself that you won't need support on the products you buy; it's likely that you will. If you do need support and your vendor can't (or won't) provide it, you'll end up having to consult with someone else. Computer consultants make $50/hour . . . and up.

It's a good idea to buy both your hardware and software from the same vendor if you can. This avoids the dread **pointing-finger syndrome,** in which the people who sold you the hardware say, ''There's no problem with it, there must be something wrong with the software,'' and the people who sold you the software say, ''There's nothing wrong with it, it must be some kind of hardware failure.''

Obviously *you* have no way of figuring out who's right. It's perfectly possible that both vendors sincerely believe the problem lies with the other vendor's product. In any case, you're caught in the middle and stuck with a system that doesn't work.

I'm impressed by the approach of Taranto and Associates of San Rafael, California, who call themselves ''the total system store.'' They offer completely integrated business software systems (general ledger, accounts payable, accounts receivable, etc.) and the TRS-80s to run them on. Then they support both, which eliminates the pointing-finger syndrome.

Taranto's ads feature their founder talking to you in the first person. Under a headline that reads, ''Most people just sell disks. I sell you a complete system, and then I help you make it work,'' he promises that ''when you buy one of my systems, you buy me. . . . And you buy my telephone number.'' He offers you ''hand-holding'' and characterizes his approach as ''a far cry from that collection of program disks they're selling down the street.''

Now, I've never had any dealings with Taranto and Associates and I have no idea whether they do what they promise (although I bet they do). I've quoted from their ad simply because this is *exactly* what you want a computer vendor to be saying to you.

I may have been making the same point over and over again, but, to paraphrase the famous real estate adage (which says that the three most important things to look for in a property are location, location, and location), the three most important considerations in deciding which computer product to buy — and who to buy it from — are support, support, and support.

SOFTWARE, THEN HARDWARE

"You don't buy a computer, you buy a use," the saying goes. And software is what adapts computers to particular uses. It's what actually does whatever it is you want done. So first find the word-processing software that most efficiently handles the kind of work you anticipate doing, then find hardware that accommodates that software.

And be sure to look for software that meets your particular needs. If you do a lot of work with columns, give the ability to handle them easily all the weight it deserves. Don't shortchange yourself. No one program is ideal for everybody, and no one feature is what everybody needs. (Of course in the case of dedicated word processors, software and hardware come together in one bundle. But you should still generally consider the software's capabilities first.)

THE ADVANTAGES OF SHARING

As I say many times throughout this book, word processors (like all computers), can be *very* versatile machines. It's a waste not to use them that way. So, if you can find more than one word-processing program that fits your needs, go with the one that runs the machine that has the most other kinds of software.

The three with the most software (in the range of a thousand programs each) are the Apple II, the TRS-80 Model II, and machines that run CP/M (CP/M-80 that is). So — if you can find a word-processing program that runs on one of those machines and does everything you want it to do — you'll be better off buying one of them rather than a less common machine (with a less popular operating system) because you'll have access to a lot more programs.

Software for Apples and TRS-80s tends to be less expensive than CP/M software — although there is considerable overlap. There's one other factor to consider when you're deciding which operating system to use — how well does it work? I've never heard anything good about Apple DOS or TRSDOS, and very little good about CP/M. The advantage of all three is the tons of applications software that's been written to run under them.

Operating systems I *have* heard good things about are NEW DOS (which substitutes for TRSDOS), FLEX (which runs on 6800/6809 machines), and the integrated operating systems of some dedicated word processors. Some of the things to look for in an operating system are a wide range of capabilities, ease of use, understandable manuals, and specific features like how long it allows file names to be.

SAFETY FIRST

There's nothing more maddening than working for hours (or, God forbid, days) on a project, only to lose everything because the person who wrote your software or designed your hardware didn't consider all the possibilities carefully enough. Nowhere does Murphy's Law apply with greater regularity or with more devastating effect than with computers.

Your time is *always* worth more than the difference in price between a product that's been meticulously thought through and one that's just been slapped together.

GOOD DOCUMENTATION — THE IMPOSSIBLE DREAM

Documentation is the name for all the materials that teach you how to use a computer product and serve as references to it. Manuals are the most common kind of documentation, but the term also covers training programs on cassette tapes or actually on the screen, key tops and similar stickers for the keyboard, reference cards, wall charts, and so on.

It's unlikely that you'll ever buy a more complicated product than a word-processing program or a dedicated word processor. Unfortunately, it's also unlikely that you'll ever buy a product with worse documentation. There must be some secret course they teach in engineering school — Gibberish 101 or Seminar in Advanced Gobbledygook.

I could just let you discover bad documentation yourself, but it's hard to pass up this opportunity to complain about it.

1. One of the things that annoys me the most is the practice of numbering every sentence.

2. I mean, we all know that the text goes from the top of the page to the bottom.

3. What information do the numbers add?

In addition to being hard to understand, bad documentation puts you in a self-doubting frame of mind. In a sea of disorganized bureaucratese, common sense does you no good, and you begin to feel like there's no way you'll ever understand anything. The other reaction I have is rage: "What right does anyone have to subject me to this torture? And to make me *pay* for the privilege . . . !"

Remember that it's meaningless to talk about what a piece of software can do if you can't figure out how to make it do it. So look for well-organized, complete, readable documentation. It *does* exist.

USER-FRIENDLY — WHAT ELSE?

Computer professionals talk about making their products **user-friendly** (or sometimes just **friendly**). What user-friendly means in practice is that there's some faint hope that people without doctorate degrees in computer science will be able to figure out how to use the product.

It's hard to argue with this goal. But the fact that something so obvious even needs to be stated shows how wretchedly user-*un*friendly most computer products are. It's as if you overheard two hot dog manufacturers talking and one of them said, ''Yeah, we've *really* improved the product — now you can actually *eat* it!'' (By the way, dedicated word processors are *much* better than microcomputers and microcomputer programs in this regard.)

THE TIME/MONEY TRADE-OFF

As a rule, you have a choice of spending more time or more money when you decide on a word processor. At the high-money, low-time end, you buy a top-of-the-line dedicated word processor from a large, established manufacturer and have it covered by a service contract. This will cost you twelve to twenty thousand dollars, plus an additional one to two hundred a month.

At the low-money, high-time end, you get an inexpensive microcomputer (or possibly build a kit or buy one used), a slow printer (also possibly used), and a word-processing program for $100 or $150. Together they might cost you as little as $2500, plus *many* hours running around looking for good deals, figuring out what will run with what, and getting various questions answered.

Of course it's also possible to minimize the amount of time per dollar or the amount of money per hour (that's what this book is all about). You should decide what your time is worth — put an actual dollar value on it. This will help you avoid two kinds of mistakes: spending days researching various alternatives so you can save $100, or plunking down a bunch of money when a simple inquiry could have saved you most of it. (This is the voice of experience speaking here.)

THE ONLY REALITY IS HERE AND NOW

This general truth, brought to us by Eastern philosophy, applies with special force to computers. Whatever it is the manufacturer or programmer is working on will probably never get completed. No matter how sincerely a new feature is promised, a million things can prevent it from ever being perfected and marketed. As that early computer buff T. S. Eliot put it: ''Between the conception and the creation . . . falls the Shadow.''

BE FUSSY

Any word processor, even an electronic typewriter, is so much better than a regular typewriter that it's hard not to be impressed by it. I know people who are absolutely ga-ga over inferior products (inferior to other word processors, that is, but much superior to typewriters). But the capabilities of the finest systems are even more amazing. So don't jump at the first wonderful system you try; you may find something even more wonderful for even less money.

That's it for general principles. On to the specifics.

5

How To Evaluate A Word-Processing Program (With Ratings Of 14 Actual Programs)

What you have below is a set of very detailed questions to ask about any word-processing program you come across. After I explain each group of questions, I apply them to fourteen actual word-processing programs (including six that only run on the dedicated word processors they're sold with). At the end of the chapter there's a blank checklist with the same questions on it. If I've failed to review a program you're interested in — one that came out after this book did, for example, or a later version of a program I did review — just use the checklist to rate it yourself.

(Let me pause here to say a word about language. I'll go batty if every time I say ''word-processing program'' I have to add the phrase ''or dedicated word processor.'' And it's really unnecessary, since everything I talk about in this chapter is a word-processing program, regardless of whether it's designed to run on several different brands of microcomputers or just one brand of dedicated word processor. So understand that when I use the term ''word-processing program,'' I'm talking about both types. Likewise, when I write ''software publisher,'' I mean to include ''dedicated word-processor manufacturer.'')

Although you can learn to use a powerful word-processing program in a matter of hours (if it has good documentation and you don't try anything fancy), it takes much longer — usually several weeks — to go beyond this basic level and really get a feeling for the program's capabilities and limitations.

Yet it's in terms of advanced, and sometimes infrequently used, functions that word-processing programs really differ. For example, a powerful global editor or the ability to link files can save you an enormous amount of time. On the negative side, a **fatal error** (one that crashes the program and destroys your text) doesn't have to happen very often to be significant.

By the end of 1981, there were already more than a hundred word-processing programs for microcomputers on the market, and there were dozens of dedicated word processors. There is no way anyone could have possibly obtained a hands-on, in-depth working knowledge of all of them.

So I was left with two choices: I could limit the range of the programs I evaluated, or I could evaluate them in some way other than actually learning to use them all.

Limiting the range to the "major" programs is the strategy adopted by most books of this kind. But it has a serious drawback — the programs that are the most popular today aren't necessarily the ones that will best meet your needs (nor, for that matter, are they necessarily the programs that will be the most popular tomorrow). Interestingly enough, of the fourteen programs and dedicated word processors I looked at in detail, the "major" ones ended up ranking seventh, ninth, tenth, twelfth, thirteenth, and fourteenth.

You'll hear people say things like, "There are lots of programs out there, but you really don't need to concern yourself with any but these three." Usually they'll tell you that in order to sell you one of those three. Since I'm not trying to sell you anything, I didn't want to dismiss any programs out of hand just because I hadn't heard much about them. So here's what I did:

First, I wrote to the publishers of every word-processing program I could find the name of and to all the major dedicated-word-processor manufacturers, requesting detailed information. (The letter I sent is in Appendix C.) Unfortunately, most of them blew their chance for some free publicity.

I wrote 54 publishers of microcomputer word-processing programs; of these, only seven (Mince & Scribble, NewScript, PIE Writer, Word Juggler and WP Daisy) sent me the information I asked for within a month of getting my letter (information from three others — Writemaster, SuperScribe II, and VEDIT — arrived within six weeks). The dedicated-word-processor manufacturers had a better record, although still not a good one — five out of sixteen responded (A.B. Dick, CPT, Dictaphone, Lanier, and Micom). So a lot of my selecting was done for me.

This is a sad commentary on how unprofessional the computer industry still is, and all the more reason to pick a system carefully. After all, if a company can't answer a business letter, do you want to depend on them for support?

The dedicated-word-processor makers I wrote are listed in Appendix C. Ninety-four microcomputer-program publishers and ten dedicated-word-processor manufacturers are listed in Chapter 6. If I wrote a company and they didn't respond, I indicate that in their listing. If I list a publisher and don't indicate that I wrote them, it's because I heard about their program too late to send a letter.

I wanted to review all the programs that sent me information, but my rating scale got so detailed that this wasn't possible. I had to pick and choose, and I'm sure that a certain amount of pure, random chance was involved in my choices. If I'd had more time, I would have liked to review The Benchmark, and also SuperScribe II, Lanier, and

Writemaster. (As it was, this book was three times larger than I thought it would be — and three months late.)

If a publisher *didn't* answer my letter, I dropped that program from consideration, except in the case of some popular products — WordStar, Magic Wand, Scripsit, Easywriter, and Wang — that I felt I had to review (they got one or more follow-up phone calls).

Then I evaluated the programs on the basis of what their documentation said they could do and/or their publishers' responses to questions about that. I supplemented this with information about the publishers' reputations and, in the case of dedicated word processors, with demonstrations.

To structure my evaluation, I came up with six main areas — safety and error handling, documentation, ease of use and human engineering, editing power, formatting power, and the publisher's responsiveness and support. (I'll explain what all these are as we go along.) Not everything fell neatly into one category or another, of course, but they were still helpful. I gave from 4 to 25 points to each area and broke them down into a series of questions, each of which also had a number of points assigned to it. When I was done, I had a detailed, weighted, 100-point evaluation scale. (Actually, the scale goes up to 105 points, but the extra 5 points involve hardware.) Here's an outline of it:

```
Total possible score for program . . . . . . . . . . . . . . .100  (105)
    Safety . . . . . . . . . . . . . . . . . . . . . . . . . . . . . . . . . . . . . . .18
    Documentation . . . . . . . . . . . . . . . . . . . . . . . . . . . .18
    Ease of Use . . . . . . . . . . . . . . . . . . . . . . . . . . . . . . .18
    Editing Power . . . . . . . . . . . . . . . . . . . . . . . . . . . .25
    Formatting Power . . . . . . . . . . . . . . . . . . . . . . . . .25   (30)
    Responsiveness . . . . . . . . . . . . . . . . . . . . . . . . . . . 4
```

Some items under these categories can give negative points as well. For example, the first item under safety can award four points or take away as many as 75 (although that would be quite unusual).

One hundred points was nowhere near enough, however, as all the half-point and quarter-point items illustrate. Although this scale is far and away the most detailed one available for evaluating word-processing software, it doesn't come close to describing all the subtle nuances of these programs.

I based how many points each item got on my idea of general use of a word processor — a little of every kind of work. So if there's some particular job you do all the time, you'll want to give related items more points than I do and downgrade others. Some people will say I give documentation too much weight. *I* say most software publishers give it too little.

In any case, it's unlikely that my weightings will exactly match your own. But this chapter will teach you what kind of things to look for and what level of thoroughness makes sense in evaluating these programs.

The time is not far off when there will be specialized word-processing programs for a whole variety of different applications. For example, there's already a special version of PIE Writer for playwrights.

When I had rated all fourteen programs on my 100-point scale and ranked them, I requested a demonstration of the only one of the top seven programs I hadn't already tried (PIE Writer) to make sure it did what they said it could do.

This isn't an infallible approach, of course, but it's yielded useful information about a relatively large number of programs. Since my judgement isn't perfect, since the weightings I give each area are subjective, and since there are undoubtedly questions I forgot to ask, a variation in scores between programs of less than ten percent of the total score — in any given area, or overall — may be insignificant.

In presenting the 100-point scale, I'll first discuss an area, say some general things about it, and talk about each question and the number of points I've given to it. Then I'll list the programs in a chart in the order of their score *in this particular area*. The chart also includes each program's score on each question.

I do that because people have different needs. If you're a beginner who's a little intimidated by computers, you'll want to pay special attention to how various programs rank in the areas of documentation, ease of use, and error handling. If you're an experienced and sophisticated user of word processors, you may be willing to sacrifice good documentation or publisher support to get particular advanced features.

Giving separate rankings for the programs in each area helps you to customize your approach to finding a word-processing program that's right for your needs. (In any case, there's too much detail in each area to put all the information together in one chart.)

After each area has been covered individually, there's a master chart which lists all the programs in the order of their overall scores, along with their scores in each area and their prices. Following that is the blank checklist for your own use.

Chapter 6 lists all the programs in alphabetical order, with general comments about each one and explanations of why it received the various scores it did. So, for example, the Safety and Error Handling chart in this chapter will tell you that WordStar got two points on "how easy is it to lose text?"; the WordStar listing in Chapter 6 will tell you why.

Also listed in Chapter 6 are the programs of the companies which failed to respond (in the same alphabetical list with the others). If I know anything about them, I mention it. Addresses and phone numbers of the programs' publishers are given in these listings.

Below is a list of the fourteen programs evaluated in this chapter, the version number of the software that I reviewed, and, if applicable, what particular machine the version I reviewed was designed to run on:

- A. B. Dick Magna SL (dedicated word processor), software version 7
- CPT 8100 (dedicated word processor), software version G-2
- Dictaphone Dual Display (dedicated word processor), software version D
- Easywriter, version 1.0 for the IBM Personal Computer
- Magic Wand, version 1.11
- Micom 2001 (dedicated word processor), software version 5.1R
- Mince, version 2.6, and Scribble, version 1.3
- NewScript, version 7.0
- PIE Writer (for the Apple II), version 2.1 (pre-release), with PRO/FORMAT, version 2.2 (pre-release)
- Scripsit (for the TRS-80 Model II), version 2.0
- Wang System 5, Model 3 (dedicated word processor), software version 3.2
- Wangwriter 5503A (dedicated word processor), software version 3.1
- WordStar, version 3.0
- WRITE, version 1.4 (pre-release).

SAFETY AND ERROR HANDLING — 10 POINTS

It doesn't really matter in what order I cover the various areas, but I've put this one first for a reason — it seems to me that if a program can do nothing else, it can at least refrain from losing material you spent hours typing in. Actually, it should never amount to hours, because you should save your file *at least* every half hour and make a backup of it when you're finished editing it (if this doesn't happen automatically each time you save). But even to lose 15 minutes' work is a maddeningly frustrating experience. In fact, if safety were easier to measure, I'd give it more than ten points.

(Many safety problems are a function of hardware, of course, and these are discussed in Chapters 8 and 10. But software can be more dangerous than you might at first realize.)

The first question for evaluation is: How easy is it to lose text? For example, what happens if you run out of RAM or disk space? Do you get a simple, clear message like NO MORE ROOM, after which the program returns you to the text with nothing changed, or do you get something like:

ERROR 0273B BUFFER PARAMETER CONFABULATION

which, when you finally find it in the manual, turns out to mean that you've crashed the program and sent your text off in the general direction of Alpha Centauri?

I give four points to a program that makes it as hard as (humanly?) possible to lose text. It should ask you, after *every* command that results in the deletion of more than a line of text, ARE YOU SURE YOU WANT TO DO THAT? (or words to that effect), to which you must answer with one specific keystroke (usually ''y'' for ''yes''). Another way to handle that is to require that three keys be held down simultaneously to execute the command.

Such precautions protect you not only from mistakenly giving the wrong command, but also from accidentally hitting the wrong key. There's no feeling in the world quite like realizing you just did in several pages of text because your finger slipped.

To get three points, a program must do an almost perfect job of protecting your text against loss. And the conditions under which the loss can occur should be covered clearly and fully, early on in the training manual.

Clearly, a program that loses a significant amount of text half the time doesn't deserve a two, or, for that matter, a zero. If it loses your text even one time out of a hundred, a zero isn't adequate. This is a catastrophic malfunction and requires a catastrophic penalty.

So if a program has (one or more) fatal errors that result in a loss of text about one percent of the time, I subtract 25 points from its score. If the loss occurs an average of two percent of the time, minus 50 points. Three percent, minus 75.

Obviously a program with any such problem is going to have its score reduced so much that it will be removed from consideration. And that's the idea.

One way of preventing the loss of text is ''protecting'' files or disks — either internally in the program or with **write-protect slots** on the disk itself (little notches you have to cover over before you can alter a disk). I think this method is ineffective because you always unprotect whatever file or disk you're working on *before* you make your mistake. The right way to protect a disk is by making lots of copies of it (all of which are alterable); the right way to protect a file is with programs that make automatic backups, verify saves, and don't crash.

The next two questions are: How well does the documentation steer you clear of possible errors — all kinds, not just the fatal ones (two points)? And how clear and informative are the **error messages** — the words that appear on your screen when something goes wrong (one point)?

If there are codes which refer you to clear explanations in a manual, I give a half point. If there is no clear explanation on the screen *or* in the manual, no points. One point is reserved for messages which are clear in themselves and which are backed up, if necessary, by further clear explanations in the manual.

It's essential to save your text to disk and to back up that disk copy as often as you can. So I give the last three points to features which make doing that easier and more certain.

Sometimes your computer will make a bad copy (this can be due to several different kinds of hardware or disk failures). The only way to make sure a copy is exact is to verify it. Verification means that after the file has been copied, the program goes back and compares the copy with the original, letter for letter, and tells you if there's any discrepancy. (Under CP/M, you get this feature by adding [v] to the end of your PIP command.)

Any word-processing program should not just allow you to verify saves and/or copies, but should do it automatically, by default (some operating systems, like FLEX, also verify by default). It's hard to imagine a circumstance in which you wouldn't want to be sure that a copy you made was accurate. It takes twice as long to do this, of course, but the time spent is trivial when compared with the time it takes to restore lost or jumbled text. So I give one point to programs that automatically verify all saves and/or copies.

When you save a file, the previous version on the disk should be automatically made into a **backup file** and labelled as such. This gives you three versions of the file at any given time — the most recent, which is in the workspace; the version at the time of the last save, which is on the disk; and the version at the time of the save before that, which is also on the disk and labelled as a backup file (in most CP/M programs, it will have the type .BAK, as opposed to .TXT, .DOC, or whatever).

Without automatic backups, you either have to rename the file each time you save or overwrite the previous version, neither of which makes much sense. Automatic backups earn one point.

It's also useful to be able to make a backup of a file on a disk other than the one you're working on without exiting the word-processing program and going back out to the operating system. Having to exit discourages you from making extra backups as often as you should. For example, you should definitely make one or two backups on separate disks whenever you finish editing a file and are about to go on to another. But you'll tend to skip it if it requires dumping and reloading the word-processing program.

There are two ways to get a backup copy on another disk — you can switch to the other drive (if you have two) or you can remove the disk you've been working on and put a new one in. If a program has an internal way to do either of those things, it gets one point.

Those are the ten points given for safety and error handling. Here's how the various word-processing programs did in that area:

SAFETY	Total score	How hard to lose text?	How well errors documented?	How clear error messages?	Saves automatically verified?	Automatic backups?	Switch or save to either disk?
WRITE	10	4	2	1	1	1	1
PIE WRITER	9½	4	1½	1	1	1	1
CPT 8100	9	4	2	1	1	0	1
NEW SCRIPT	8½	4	1¾	¾	1	0	1
WANGWRITER	8	4	2	1	0	0	1
A. B. DICK MAGNA SL	8	4	2	1	0	0	1
MICOM 2001	7¾	4	2	¾	0	0	1
WORD STAR	7½	2	1½	1	1	1	1
MINCE & SCRIBBLE	7	3½	1½	1	0	0	1
DICTAPHONE DUAL DISP.	7	3½	1½	1	0	0	1
WANG SYSTEM 5	6	4	½	½	0	0	1
MAGIC WAND	3¼	0	½	¾	0	1	1
SCRIPSIT	2	0	0	1	0	0	1
EASYWRITER	−24	−25	0	0	0	0	1

I may be conservative on this issue, but I personally wouldn't want to use any program that scored less than seven points for error handling.

There doesn't seem to be any clear difference between dedicated word processors and microcomputer programs in this area, except that most dedicated word processors can recover lost text.

Note that even if Easywriter corrects that fatal bug that caused it to lose 25 points, it would still have the lowest score in this area — one point.

DOCUMENTATION — 18 POINTS

Without software to tell it what to do, a computer is just a big hunk of metal. It makes a hell of a door stop, but it's not much use for anything else. Similarly, without documentation that tells you how to use it, a program is just a bunch of gibberish. It won't do you any good at all. Despite this obvious fact, most computer documentation is about as helpful and informative as your local postmaster.

To be minimally adequate, a word-processing program should have two manuals — a **training manual** (sometimes called a **tutorial**) to teach you how to use it, and a **reference manual** you can look things up in after you know how to use it. (It's possible to combine these, but it's hard for both of them to be adequate if you do.) There should be an index (at least to the reference manual, ideally to both) so when you want some information, it won't take you all day to find it. And the manuals shouldn't be actually painful to look at.

Here's how I give points for documentation.

Training manual (seven points):

- Is it well organized (three points)? If the information is presented in just the order you need to know it, I give all three points. If section headings are relatively clear and descriptive but aren't arranged in the best order, I give two points. If you pretty much have to read the whole manual before proceeding to work with the system, one point. And no points if it's a morass.
- Is it readable (three points)? If the training manual is actually a pleasure to read, enjoyable as learning should be, I give it three points. If the style is clear but somewhat stuffy, two points. If it's difficult to wade through, one point. And no points for a manual which is harder to understand than the program itself (that is, you'd be better off just floundering through the program on your own).
- Is it complete (one point)? Just one point because a training manual is only supposed to get you off to a good start, not necessarily cover every facet of the program (although one that does certainly deserves an extra point.)

Reference manual (seven points):

- Is it complete (three points)? This is the one that needs to cover absolutely everything. If some details are missing, I give two points. If many details are missing, I give one point. If what's missing is crucial, no points.
- Is it well-organized (two points)? The purpose of a reference manual is to be referred to. But you can't refer to it if you don't know where the information you're looking for is. If it's unclear where to find things or if material is repeated unnecessarily in several places, I give one point. And no points if the reference manual is a labyrinth.
- Is it understandable (two points)? A reference manual just has to be clear, not well written. There's really no reason why it shouldn't be well written, but, as a practical matter, I've given up on this one. Programmers are going to want to write the reference manual themselves, and in general, they write about as well as I program. So I give two points if the writing is clear, one point if it's obscure and/or stilted, and no points for gobbledygook.

In addition to those fourteen points, I give one more point if there's a good index (and some fraction of that for indexes that are less than good). If the manual(s) are typeset, which makes them much easier to read, another point. (If they're not typeset but are proportionally spaced, half a point.) If the design and layout are such that you can bear to look at them before breakfast, another point (or a fraction thereof for a design which doesn't meet that high standard, but still isn't completely horrendous).

Although I find that where information appears is a lot less important than how it's presented, I reserve one final point for special kinds of documentation other than manuals. Scripsit, for example, gives you a training program on cassette tapes. Select has an on-screen tutorial that walks you through the learning process. WordStar has a series of on-screen explanations on various topics. Many programs have reference cards, key tops, wall charts, or the like. These vary in how useful they are, but they can be a big help.

Here's how the programs' documentation stacked up:

DOCUMENTATION	Total Score	Training manual Subtotal	Well-organized	Readable?	Complete?	Reference manual Subtotal	Complete?	Well-organized	Understandable?	Index?	Typeset (or prop. space)?	Design quality?	Special kinds of documentation
DICTAPHONE DUAL DISP.	16¾	6½	3	2½	1	6½	3	1½	2	¾	1	1	1
CPT 8100	16¾	6	3	2	1	7	3	2	2	¾	1	1	1
A. B. DICK MAGNA SL	16½	6½	3	2½	1	6½	2½	2	2	¾	1	¾	1
WANGWRITER	16	6¾	3	2¾	1	5¾	3	1	1¾	¾	1	1	¾
MICOM 2001	15¾	6½	3	2½	1	6	2¼	2	1¾	¾	1	1	½
NEW SCRIPT	15½	6	2	3	1	6½	3	2	1½	¾	½	¾	1
WRITE	15½	7	3	3	1	7	3	2	2	¾	0	¾	0
PIE WRITER	15	6¼	2¾	2½	1	5½	2½	1	2	¾	1	½	1
WANG SYSTEM 5	14¾	6	3	2	1	5½	3	1	1½	¼	1	1	1
EASYWRITER	14½	5¾	2½	2½	¾	5	1½	1½	2	¾	1	1	1
SCRIPSIT	14¼	6	2¾	2½	¾	4½	2	1	1½	¾	1	1	1
MAGIC WAND	12¾	6	2½	2½	1	4¼	1¾	½	2	¼	1	½	¾
MINCE & SCRIBBLE	12¼	6¼	2¾	3	½	4	2	0	2	0	½	½	1
WORD STAR	11¾	5½	2½	2	1	4½	2½	1	1	¼	0	½	1

Here's an area where dedicated word processors really do excel, although there's no reason why microcomputer programs *have* to have inferior documentation. Perhaps the most startling thing about this chart is that not one of the fourteen programs rated had a good index. This has to be because indexes are not considered important and because it takes time to do one well. But it seems to me that a good index is vital and well worth the time spent on it.

EASE OF USE AND HUMAN ENGINEERING — 18 POINTS

Many of the things that make word processors easy to use are functions of the hardware — a comfortable keyboard, an easy-to-read screen, no flashing cursor, etc. But there are also important ways in which the software contributes to ease of use. One major one is how many keystrokes it takes to execute given commands.

Some programs have quick ways to do one thing and lengthy ways to do another (Easywriter, for example, requires seven keystrokes to order a page break and eleven to center a line). So I set up a sequence of 23 commands to run each program through. It covers all the major areas of editing, formatting, and printing out and therefore gives a good indication of how much effort on your part a program will require to do its job. (This is my equivalent to *Consumer Report's* 195-mile test drive for cars; both measure energy efficiency.)

In figuring keystrokes for this sequence, control characters count for one and a half strokes, as do shifted characters. Shifted control characters (or any other commands that require you to hold down three keys at once) count for two keystrokes.

Sometimes cursor arrows are the fastest way to execute a command. I count a minimum of three strokes (because it takes a while for the auto-repeat to kick in) and a maximum of ten strokes (because once you're moving, it doesn't take long to get to where you're going, even if it's on the other side of the line, or the other end of the screen).

Since some microcomputer keyboards have special function keys like those on dedicated word processors, and since certain word-processing programs have been designed to work with them, the number of keystrokes such a program will need to finish this sequence depends on what system it's being used on.

To equalize things, I evaluated all programs as if they were running on a system without special function keys and therefore needed to use control characters — except for the dedicated word processors, which of course only run on systems with function keys, and Easywriter, because the version I had was configured to run on the IBM Personal Computer.

Several programs would have gotten higher scores if I'd rated versions of them that were integrated with a keyboard's function keys. WRITE, for example, can be adapted to work with a 103-key keyboard so that there's a dedicated key for every major function.

Although the 23-command sequence is designed to be as general as possible, not all programs are able to follow it precisely. For example, some have you type out the name of the file when you're saving it, instead of when you open it. Variations from the strict sequence are not important, as long as all the commands are included. If a program can't execute a command at all (can't boldface, for example), it's penalized five keystrokes.

Since this 23-command sequence involves many separate measurements, I give it five points (maximum). I count how many keystrokes (aside from those required to actually enter text) it takes to:

1) open a new text file (don't count the characters in the file name itself; they're free this first time. But if you have to type the file name more than once in this sequence, it counts as a standard eight keystrokes each time);

2–4) center, boldface, and underline a title;

5) skip a line;

6) indent the next line of text five spaces;

7) indicate the end of that paragraph;

8) skip a line;

9) indent the next paragraph five spaces;

10) put a page break at the bottom of that paragraph;

11–14) reset the top, bottom, left, and right margins (just count the commands, not the numerical values);

15) order the file to be double-spaced (if single-spaced is the default), or vice versa (again, not counting the numerical values);

16) save the file;

17) print it out (some dedicated word processors have what I call **virtual representation** — that is, they can show on the screen exactly how the text will look on the page, right down to boldfacing and proportional spacing. On such systems, it's just as likely that a mistake will get caught on the screen as on the page, so they're exempted from this step and the next two);

18) stop in the middle of printing out;

19) return to the text;

20) delete a word (five characters and a space);

21) delete a line (of 60 characters);

22) save this new version of the file, keeping the old version for a backup; and

23) begin printing out again at the top of the page.

I give five points for programs that finish the sequence in fewer than 55 strokes; four and a half points if it takes between 56 and 60 strokes; four if it's between 61 and 65; three and a half for 66–70; three for 71–75; two and a half for 76–80; two for 81–85; one and a half for 86–90; one for 91–95; half a point for 91–100; and no points if the sequence takes a program more than 100 strokes.

I also make another, subjective judgement about keystrokes — is there a clear, logical **command structure,** or are there twelve ways to do everything and a confusing array of complex commands? Obviously, the more keystrokes there are, the harder it is to remember them (not to mention the feeling of being lost in a jungle).

Mnemonics (assigning a command to a letter or letters that remind you of the function, like S for ''save'' or P for ''print'') also aid recall, although it's been my experience that you just end up memorizing the commands more or less by brute force, regardless of how mnemonic they are.

Having the basic cursor movement commands arranged in a diamond — with the key for "up" at the top, the key for "right" on the right, etc. — makes the cursor commands much easier to learn and use.

It's also possible for other commands to be logically placed on the keyboard. For example, if ˆD means move right one character and ˆS move left one character, it makes sense for ˆF to move you right one word, and ˆA left one word, since the F key is just to the right of the D key and the A key is just to the left of the S key. Or similar commands might be grouped together — delete a character, delete a word, and delete a line on adjacent keys, for example.

Even if there aren't a lot of commands, it's a big help to have them listed on menus, reference cards, key tops, or the like (and the more commands, the more help these aids are). Some programs, like PIE Writer, even let you reconfigure the keyboard any way you want, so you can choose each command yourself. And, of course, some systems have dedicated keys which make commands unforgettable.

Since a logical command structure, mnemonics, a cursor movement diamond, menus, reference cards, key tops, reconfigurable commands, and dedicated keys are all intertwined, since the adequacy or inadequacy of one changes how necessary each of the others is, and since at times they are in fact opposed to each other (mnemonic cursor movement commands as opposed to a cursor diamond, for example), I lump them all together and evaluate them all together as command recall aids.

Command recall aids earn three points maximum. A program doesn't have to be missing every feature mentioned above to get no points at all for command recall aids; it just needs a combination of features that make remembering commands extremely difficult.

If the main editing menu is always on the screen, it cuts down the number of lines of your own text you can see. And after you've learned the commands, you don't need it up there most of the time. So I give half a point to programs that let you suppress it or that keep it off the screen until you call it up.

It's useful to know what page your text would be on (if what's on the screen were printed out). Some programs give you this information on a **status line;** I give them half a point for doing that. It's also nice to know how far through the file you are — that is, what percentage of it is in front of and what percentage behind the present cursor location. Programs that tell you that get an additional quarter point.

And it's helpful to know the total size of the file you're editing without having to exit the word-processing program. Programs that make it possible for you to find that out without too much trouble earn another half point. If they let you get that information and return to the same place in the text in less than three keystrokes (or two control characters), I give them an additional quarter point.

It's essential to be able to make copies of a program, so that if a disk is damaged all is not lost. Most publishers allow you to do this, but some do not. They send you a couple of copies of the program, and that's all you get. This is *not* the way to protect against software theft (there *are* other ways; they just take more effort). I give two points if the program is copyable and no points if it isn't.

Another virtue of copyable programs is that you can put them on the disks you actually work with. Otherwise you have to put a program disk in the drive, load the program into memory, and then either replace the program disk with a work disk or put the work disk into the other drive and get no use out of the first drive. But it doesn't make any sense to put the word-processing program on every disk if it's too large. The disk space you lose negates the convenience of having the program right there.

Another problem with the program's being large is that it takes up a lot of memory space that you could otherwise use for something else, like your own text. Some programs, usually the larger ones, get around this by holding most of the workfile on disk and only bringing into memory the small portion that's being worked on at any given time. On the other hand, since disk operations are much, much slower than memory is, this strategy dramatically slows down the speed with which you can move through the text.

Swapping (sometimes called **spooling**) the workfile on and off of disk allows it to be as large as the disk allows, instead of just as large as RAM. On the third hand (just think of Shiva, rather than your ordinary mortal), such large files are *very* slow to work with and not even recommended by the publishers of such programs. They also take longer to save, thereby discouraging you from saving as often as you should.

If a word-processing program is small enough, there will be plenty of room left over in RAM for the workfile. The system I use keeps all its text in RAM and yet I can have files as big as 37K, which is larger than I ever need them to be (since I can link them during printout anyway).

Another advantage of keeping the workfile in RAM is that you can work most of the time with your disks out (that is, sitting in the drives with the doors open) and just pop them in to save and copy. Since the disk drive heads will probably be the first things on your computer to wear out, and since most of that wear comes from just having disks brush past them when they're in but not being used, you should try to minimize the amount of time that disks are in.

Keeping disks out while you work also prevents them from being damaged by the heads in case you lose power for some reason. A better solution to the problem is having the drives turn off between uses, which many do (particularly minifloppy drives). But if your system doesn't have that feature, it's nice to be able at least to get the disks out of them when you're not actually saving or loading.

Shiva has run out of hands, and the question of workfile-on-and-off-of-disk vs. workfile-all-in-memory is still undecided. Some people appreciate the flexibility of the former; others (like me) want the speed and security of the latter. I think that linking files during printout (with continuous page numbering and no page breaks required between files) completely solves the problem of file size.

Another advantage of a long file is that you can make global substitutions over a larger amount of text, but there's a better way to do that too: global substitutions that travel from one linked file to another.

In view of all the ways to get around the problems of workfile size, it seems to me that files need to be only long enough not to break your train of thought — 25–30K maximum. But the exception to that is if you have a hard disk. Then you can make a whole book one file, if your software will let you, and still get to each part of it quickly enough. With a hard disk, swapping text on and off disk makes a lot more sense.

There are obviously a lot of arguments on both sides of this issue and I don't want to impose my personal tastes on this evaluation process (except when absolutely necessary, as in the case of flashing cursors, where the sanity of millions of people is at stake). So on the chart below, I merely indicate whether a program swaps the workfile onto and off of disk or whether it keeps it completely in RAM; I don't give points for either approach. Decide for yourself which you prefer.

But everything else being equal, the smaller a program is, the better; it will run on systems with less RAM, leave more room on the disk, etc. So I give one point to programs smaller than 25K, including all necessary overlays and messages. If a program is between 25K and 35K, it gets half a point.

The crucial thing, of course, is not how large the program is, but how much room is left for a workspace. There's no way to know this without knowing the total amount of RAM in your system; that's why I rate program size instead. But on a dedicated word processor, you do know the exact amount of RAM (and you probably don't know the program size). So on those systems, I measure the workspace instead, and give one point if it's larger than 30K and half a point if it's larger than 20K.

Some programs conserve the amount of RAM they take up by loading the editor and the formatter separately. This is not a good way to go, because it means that if you're in the middle of printing out and you discover a mistake, to correct it you have to stop the printout, exit the formatter, reload the editor, reload the file you're printing out, make your correction, save the file, exit the editor, reload the formatter, reload the file, and start printing out again. Only to find *another* error.

I find that my documents inevitably have at least one mistake in them, so I always print out the first draft with a faint ribbon, correcting as I go along. Then I print out the copy I'm going to send out with a darker ribbon, and sometimes I have to do that more than once because there are still things I want to change. I can't even imagine how I could work with a program that required me to reload programs and files every time I wanted to make a correction.

So I give one point to programs that load their editors and formatters together and no points to programs that require you to go through the rigmarole described above. I give half a point to programs that load the editor and formatter separately but let you move from one to the other fairly easily — without having to save and reload the file you're working on, for example.

Another thing that slows the program down is the use of **overlays.** As I explained in Chapter 2, these are program files that sit on the disk until the main program needs a piece of them and accesses it. Although overlays conserve RAM and take a lot less time than loading a whole new file, they still drastically reduce a program's responsiveness. So I give one point to programs that don't use overlays at all (in the main program); half a point to programs that use overlays only occasionally for special jobs; and no points if overlays are an essential part of the program.

It's convenient to be able to manipulate files and file names on the disk while you're editing without having to exit to the operating system. Many programs have integrated some of these functions into themselves, and I give points for them as follows:

If you can rename the file you're editing without having to abandon the edit, a quarter point.

If you can rename a file other than the workfile without leaving the word-processing program, a quarter point.

If you can delete a file other than the workfile without leaving the program, a quarter point.

You'll discover that — quite frequently when you're editing — you'll want to know what files are on the disk and how big they are. Such a listing is called a **directory** (or a **catalog**) and no word-processing program worth its salt should make you go out to the operating system to get one. If a program doesn't give you a directory in response to a couple of keystrokes, it loses a point.

It's nice if the directory also tells you the size of each file (usually in K). This is a much less frequent feature, but very useful, so a program that gives it to you, also in two or three keystrokes, gets half a point.

It's also nice to be able to ask for just part of the directory, particularly when you're working with a hard disk or with double-density, double-sided floppies, where there can be hundreds, or thousands, of files in a directory. The ability to display just a given category of files, rather than all of them, earns a quarter point.

Word-processing programs can lose keystrokes if you type them in while they're doing something else. The solution to this is called a **type-ahead buffer** (or **keystroke storage**). It stores the keystrokes you type when the system is unable to digest them and feeds them in when the system is finished with whatever was distracting it. This is a very useful feature; a famous science fiction writer once switched word-processing programs solely to get it.

A type-ahead buffer can be implemented in hardware as well as software; I think the program should always have one, in case the machine doesn't. It's worth one point.

As I discussed in Chapter 2, there are two basic ways information can be brought to your screen — terminal mode and memory-mapped mode. (**DMA,** for direct memory access, is a common kind of memory mapping.)

Terminal mode requires a regular terminal, usually with an integrated keyboard. Information is sent from the computer and stored in the terminal's memory, then displayed on the screen. If you turn your computer off but leave the terminal on, the information will still be there, because it's in the terminal's memory. Many of the larger microcomputers and most multiuser systems run in terminal mode.

The rate at which terminal mode can put information on the screen depends on the transmission rate from the computer — which, if you're lucky, is 9600 or 19,200 baud (bits per second). This is plenty fast, but it still produces a noticeable **rewrite flicker** when it makes changes on the screen.

Memory-mapping doesn't require a terminal, just a monitor (plus a **video board** that goes inside the computer). Instead of information being sent to the screen, the screen (the video board, actually) looks directly into the computer's memory; in fact, memory-mapping is often called "a window into RAM." If you turn the computer off, the screen immediately goes blank, even if it's plugged in separately. Many computers, including the Apple and the TRS-80, are designed to run memory-mapped.

In memory-mapped mode, the screen is **updated** (rewritten) at the speed at which your computer thinks, which, if you're lucky, is four MHz (megahertz) or more. (Computers time everything they do by an internal clock. If it's a four MHz clock, it puts out four *million* timing pulses every *second*.) Actually, in this case, the limiting factor is the CRT's scanning speed, but that's still much faster than 19,200 baud.

Some people say they aren't bothered by rewrite flicker. Others are driven batty by it. Personally I suspect that, like flashing cursors, it's one of the causes of eye strain in people who work with VDTs. Since rewrite flicker may be a problem, and since, in any case, memory-mapping has no disadvantages, I give programs that can run memory-mapped half a point.

That makes eighteen points. Here's how the programs stacked up in terms of ease of use:

EASE OF USE	Total Score	Workfile memory or disk?	# of keystrokes	Score	Command recall aids	Suppress main menu?	Page you're on?	How far thru file?	Total size of file?	Less than 3 keystrokes?	Program copyable?	Small program &/or large workspace?	Editor & formatter together?	Lots of overlays?	Rename work file?	Rename other files?	Delete file?	Directory with file sizes?	Partial directory?	Type-ahead buffer?	Run memory-mapped?
WRITE	16¾	M	51	5	2½	½	0	0	½	¼	2	1	1	1	¼	¼	¼	½	¼	1	½
CPT 8100	14¾	M	56½	4½	3	½	½	¼	½	0	1	0	1	1	¼	¼	¼	½	¼	1	0
WANGWRITER	13½	D	75	3	2½	½	½	¼	½	¼	2	0	1	1	0	¼	¼	½	0	1	0
PIE WRITER	13	M	75½	2¾	2½	½	0	0	½	0	2	1	½	½	¼	¼	¼	½	0	1	½
WORD STAR	13	D	64½	4	2	½	½	0	½	0	2	½	1	0	0	¼	¼	0	0	1	½
NEW SCRIPT	12¾	M	68	3½	3	½	½	0	½	¼	2	0	0	½	¼	0	¼	0	0	1	½
DICTAPHONE DUAL DISPLAY	12	D	75	3	3	½	½	¼	¼	0	½	0	1	1	0	¼	¼	½	0	1	0
EASYWRITER	11¼	M	77½	2½	3	½	0	¼	½	¼	¼	0	1	1	¼	0	¼	0	0	1	½
WANG SYSTEM 5	10¾	D	73	3	3	½	½	0	½	0	1½	0	0	0	0	¼	¼	0	¼	1	0
MICOM 2001	10¾	M	88	1½	3	½	½	¼	½	0	¼	0	1	1	¼	¼	¼	½	0	1	0
A. B. DICK MAGNA SL	9¾	D	93½	1	3	½	½	0	½	¼	½	0	1	½	0	¼	¼	½	0	1	0
MINCE & SCRIBBLE	8	D	172½	0	3	½	0	¼	½	¼	2	0	0	1	¼	0	0	-1	0	1	¼
MAGIC WAND	8	M	108	0	3	½	0	0	½	¼	2	0	0	0	0	0	¼	0	0	1	½
SCRIPSIT	7¾	D	123½	0	2½	½	½	0	½	0	2	0	0	0	0	0	¼	½	0	½	½

WRITE takes a clear first place here, although that may have something to do with the fact that it's the program I know best and thus probably influenced the questions I ask about ease of use. Still, notice how closely the total points for the category correlate with number of keystrokes on the 23-command sequence; if programs were ranked in order of the latter, rather than the former, there wouldn't be all that much difference in the ratings. Since the number of keystrokes is an objective measure — given that the 23-command sequence doesn't have any weird operations in it — this seems to indicate that my ratings for ease of use are not totally subjective.

Surprisingly, dedicated word processors seem to have no particular edge over microcomputer programs in this area.

EDITING POWER — 25 POINTS

By editing power, I mean how many different kinds of ways can you change the text — as opposed to formatting power, which is how many different ways you can change the printout (or output to the screen).

The grossest measure of editing power is the **total number of commands** the program offers; I count as a command any possible option (and I include formatting, editing, disk operations — the *total* number of commands in the program). If a program has more than 170 commands, understood in this broad sense, it gets the full four points. If it has between 150 and 170, I give it three and a half points; 130 to 149, three points; 110 to 129, two and a half; 90–109, two; 70–89, one and a half; 50–69, one point; 30–49, half a point; and no points if there are fewer than 30 editing commands.

Obviously, though, not all commands are equally useful, and the other 21 points are devoted to evaluating editing power in terms of specific tasks. All the programs evaluated in this chapter use visual editors — that is, you can move the cursor around the screen anywhere there's text (and on some, even where there isn't).

As I mentioned earlier, I don't consider systems where the cursor can only move down and to the right, say, or where you have to reference each command to a numbered line, as real word processors — at least not at this stage in the game. Originally, of course, the machines IBM called word processors didn't even have screens.

Visual editors can vary tremendously in how powerful and easy to use they are. I include certain kinds of ease of use in this section because there's always *some* way to do everything, if you go to enough trouble. For example, consider a program that only lets you move the cursor to the right and down, but has a **home** command (which moves the cursor to the upper left corner of the screen). It's still possible to move the cursor up; all you have to do is hit home and then move it down. But it's stretching the point to call the difference between that procedure and a real, up-cursor command merely a matter of convenience, rather than a difference in capability.

Or take a more extreme example — a computer that doesn't have any keyboard at all. You type in letters in ASCII code by flipping a switch for each bit. Capital A in ASCII is 01000001. So all you have to do is flick the switch down, up, down, down, down, down, down, up. That types in A. Now you go on to the next letter. Is it more accurate to say that such an arrangement is merely difficult, or that such a machine can't really be used as a word processor at all?

In other words, in the final analysis, ease *is* power.

One of the features that makes editing the easiest is **word wrap.** This means you never have to tell the word processor when to end a line of text. When it runs out of room, it automatically takes the last word on the line and moves it in one piece to the start of the next line. (You just keep typing when this happens.) The only time you indicate the end of a line yourself is when you want a line break regardless of whether the line is full, as at the end of a paragraph, after a title or subtitle, etc.

If a program doesn't have word wrap (but does have **wraparound**), the words will be broken in half at the end of the line, which makes the text hard to read. Also, you'll have to insert line breaks periodically yourself. Word wrap makes text entry much faster and easier, once you get out of the habit of hitting the RETURN key all the time. It's worth one point.

I give six points for basic operations — moving the cursor around, inserting, and deleting. Programs differ widely in the ways they do this. For example, the Dictaphone word processor is set up to be in *search* mode by default — that is, if you just start to type, it assumes you're entering the piece of text you want to search for. If you want to either insert *or* write over, you have to tell it.

Since searches are so easy on this system, and since a few letters are usually sufficient to indicate the word you're looking for, doing a search is just about as convenient as the more usual ''move to end of line'' or ''move to end of page'' (although Dictaphone has that command too).

Or, to choose another example, any system with cursor arrow keys and auto-repeat has much less need of commands like ''next word'' and ''last word.'' So, although I have a neat little scale which I describe in the next few paragraphs, it's parochial and unfair to use it to evaluate certain systems. In such cases, I make a subjective judgement about power and ease of use for the basic commands.

Here's the approach I use with conventional programs:

First I look for single keystroke commands (because most programs can perform these basic commands some way or another, if you don't care how much time, or effort, it takes you). I consider one control character to be one keystroke as well, and for the rest of this section, whenever I write ''one-stroke,'' I mean to include ''one control character.''

The basic minimum requirements for one-stroke commands are ones to move the cursor right and left one character, and up and down one line. If a program is missing any of these, it loses one point for each. Then I give additional half points for one-stroke commands that do the following things: move the cursor forward one word, backward one word, to the end of the line, to the start of the line, to the top of the screen, to the bottom of the screen, to the beginning of the file, and to the end of the file. (If a program has two-keystroke, or two-control-character, commands for any of the above, it gets a quarter point for each of them.)

Next I want to know if there are one-stroke commands to delete a whole word (half a point) and to delete a whole line (half a point). (Here again, quarter points for two strokes.)

When you add text anywhere but at the end of a file, a question inevitably arises: do you want this new text to replace the existing text, or do you want it stuck into the existing text, which will then be pushed forward, intact, to make room for it? The first option is called **writeover mode** and the second **insert mode.** Any decent word-processing program gives you a choice between them. If it doesn't, it loses two points. And if it lets you switch between them in one stroke, it gets a point.

By the way, some word-processing programs operate in writeover mode by default, and some in insert mode. As long as you can switch between them easily, I can't see that it makes much difference.

Continuous forward scrolling gets half a point, as does continuous and unlimited backward scrolling (some programs can't go back more than a screenful or so). If you can change the speed at which the scrolling progresses, that's worth half a point too.

Some systems (dedicated word processors mostly) move you around by page numbers rather than by scrolling. If you don't know what page you want, you just guess, and then guess again if you're wrong. (If you're looking at a printout, of course, you'll know.) Being able to call up a specific page is at least as convenient as scrolling, and is worth the same one and a quarter points.

Most programs only let you move the cursor where there is text. To move it out into an area of the screen where there is no text you have to insert blank spaces or something like that. But some programs let you put the cursor anywhere at all on the screen, regardless of what is (or isn't) there. This capability is worth half a point.

The next area to cover is **block moves** (also known as **electronic cut and paste**). The most basic of these is copying a block. This means you mark off the block you want to move and put the cursor where you want it moved to. When you copy it, it appears in the new place and remains in the old one too.

It's also possible to simply move a block. This works just like copying, except the block doesn't remain at the old location. The third basic option is to delete a block.

Now — if you have the ability to copy and delete you can quite easily simulate moving by simply copying the block to a new location and then immediately deleting it from its old location. With just the ability to move a block, however, you could never have it in two places at once (without retyping it). So copying, rather than moving, is the more important command. But moving does have its uses.

For example, if you want to move a big block of text within a large file, there might not be room (in RAM or on the disk) for it to exist at both locations. If you can simply move it, rather than copy it, the problem can be avoided. So I give three quarters of a point for copying, one quarter for moving, and a full point for deleting.

There are a couple of other things it's nice to be able to do. One is to make a new file of a block of text you've marked off (without having to stop editing the file you're on) so you can use it later somewhere else. Another is to get a separate file from the disk and merge it into the one you're working on (again, without having to stop editing). These complementary processes get half a point each.

In Chapter 1, I talked about lots of things you can do faster and more easily with a word processor than with a typewriter, but I also talked about one thing you can do *only* with a word processor — **global substitutions** (also known as **global search and replace**). To refresh your memory, this means that the word processor goes through an entire file at very high speed, finds every occurrence of a given word (say), and, if you want, replaces it with another. The part of a word-processing program where global substitutions are performed is called the **global editor.**

You can look for just about anything — a single word or a long phrase, a symbol or a number. You could even find every question mark or every comma. Since there isn't any common English word that covers all these possibilities, what you search for is called a **string** (or a **character string**). This is computerese for "any group of characters."

Global search-and-replace functions get five and a half points, as follows: if the program can find a string (a word or phrase) anywhere in a file, it gets one point. If it can automatically substitute another string for that first one, it gets another point. It gets a third point if it can do **mass substitutions** — that is, make many changes without stopping to ask you to approve each one. (Some programs, like WRITE, let you see them as they happen, which is nice.) If a program lets you do *only* bulk substitutions, and doesn't allow you to approve each one, it loses two points.

Search and replace, with and without approval, are the basic global capabilities. I also give credit for some fancier ones. The first of these is very simple: if the program will let you search backwards through the file from the cursor position, as well as forward, it gets an additional quarter point.

The next two have to do with the fact that computers are very literal. If you search for every occurrence of the word *the,* you'll miss all the *The's,* because capital letters and lowercase letters aren't the same. Some word-processing programs will ignore whether letters are caps or lowercase when you tell them to, and those that do get an extra half point for it.

Similarly, if you search for *the,* you'll not only get the word *the,* but you'll pick up those three letters in the middle of other words, like *other,* for example, or *fathead.* One way around this is to search for *the* (with a space on either side of it). But this misses whole words at the beginnings and ends of sentences and whole words with punctuation — like parentheses and quotation marks — around them. Some programs let you search only for whole words (i.e., the string you're looking for surrounded by either spaces and/or punctuation marks, but not by other letters). This is a convenience and gets half a point.

If you tend to work with long documents, you often find yourself wanting to change a word or phrase in many different files (for example, all the chapters of a book). It's nice not to have to load each file, make the global substitutions, and save the corrected file.

Some programs that let you link files during printout also let you link them for the purposes of global substitutions. You give the command in one file and it goes through all the linked files and makes the change in them too (loading and saving the files automatically as it does it). Linking files for globals is a very advanced feature, although you can certainly live without it. It gets half a point.

No matter what kind of writing you do, there are bound to be **stock phrases** you use over and over again. There are two ways a word processor can help you with that.

Any word-processing program that has a global editor will let you insert codes into your text and then go back and substitute the stock phrases for them. For example, you might use @@ to stand for ''imperialist running dogs and their lackeys.'' When you finish your diatribe, a simple global will substitute the six-word phrase for the two-character symbol everywhere it occurs.

The only problem with this technique is that you have to remember to do the globals at the end or you end up with text that looks like this:

Join in solidarity with // against the @@!

A better system is to insert the stock phrase right when you want it. You set up the codes beforehand — ˆS1 equals ''this antique debt,'' ˆS2 equals ''what you laughingly refer to as your 'credit',''and so on. Then whenever you want the phrase ''this antique debt,'' you just type ˆS1 and it appears.

This is different from merging other files into the one you're working on. The stock phrases are in memory, not on the disk, and they appear instantly.

The ability to generate stock phrases from memory is one of the few features that most electronic typewriters have and most word processors don't. It's worth half a point.

Many other kinds of global capabilities are possible. For example, some programs let you use **wildcards** — symbols which, like wildcards in poker, can stand for anything (or any letter, any number, anything that isn't either a letter or a number, etc.).

Some programs let you insert a whole bunch of characters or words, without having to retype them. This is called **bulk insertion.** For example, let's say you want a dotted line across the page. You could type in 60 dashes (assuming your margins are 60 characters apart). But with bulk insertion all you'd have to do is put the cursor at the left margin, go to the global editor, and type something like ''i (for ''insert'') 60-.''

Any additional global capability earns a program an extra quarter point.

Both block moves and global substitutions can move the cursor far from its previous position. (Certain other commands do this as well.) It's useful to have a command that will put it back where it was, so I give a quarter point for such a cursor-return command.

It's very nice to be able to compare two pieces of text on the screen — an earlier and a later version, say, or two different treatments of the same subject. Some word processing programs let you do this by means of a **split screen.** This useful, advanced feature is worth one point.

Another convenient feature of some programs is the ability to edit one file while printing out another. This isn't totally essential, because usually you want a break after editing anyway. It's also a little hard to think with the printer going. And with most programs, the editor works much more slowly than normal when you're doing a printout. Still, if you have many long printouts, editing while printing is an advantage, and I give one point for it.

The last point and a half are reserved for other special editing features not specified above. One example is keeping the cursor in place during a save. Another is the ability to move a single column of text without disturbing the columns on either side of it (normally, you have to move whole lines).

A third example is the only feature I miss from the minicomputer word-processing program I used to use — the ''undo'' command. When you make a disastrous mistake, it undoes your last command. Most of the dedicated word processors I evaluated, and even some of the microcomputer programs, have some sort of command to restore text, often in a limited way (up to a screenful or a page, for example).

Here's the chart for editing power:

EDITING POWER	Total Score	Total No. Of Commands	Score for that	Word wrap?	Basic commands	Scrolling?	Move to specified page?	Cursor where no text?	Block copy & move?	Block delete?	Make block new file?	Insert file into workfile?	Global find & replace?	Backwards?	All at once?	Ignore u & lc?	Whole words only?	Thru linked files?	Insert stock phrases?	Other spec. global abilities?	Cursor to previous position?	Split screen?	Edit while printing out?	Other special powers?
CPT 8100	24	200+	4	1	5½		1¼	½	1	1	½	½	2	0	1	½	½	½	½	¼	0	1	1	1½
WORD STAR	22	200+	4	1	4½	1¼		0	1	1	½	½	2	¼	1	½	½	0	0	¼	¼	0	1	1½
PIE WRITER	20½	208	4	1	5½	1		½	1	1	½	½	2	¼	1	0	0	0	0	¼	¼	0	0	¼	1½
MICOM 2001	20½	200+	4	1	4¾		1¼	½	1	1	0	½	2	¼	0	½	½	0	½	¼	0	0	1	1½
A. B. DICK MAGNA SL	19¾	200+	4	1	4½		1¼	½	1	1	0	½	2	0	1	¼	0	0	0	¼	0	0	1	1½
WRITE	19	139	3	1	5½	1¼		0	¾	1	½	½	2	¼	1	½	0	½	0	¼	0	0	0	1
NEW SCRIPT	18¾	200+	4	1	4¼		¾	½	1	1	½	½	2	¼	1	0	0	0	¼	¼	0	0	0	1½
WANGWRITER	18¾	200+	4	1	3¾		1¼	½	1	1	0	½	2	0	1	0	0	0	½	¼	0	0	1	1½
DICTAPHONE DUAL DISP.	18¾	115	2½	1	5		1¼	0	1	1	¼	¼	1½	0	1	½	0	0	½	¼	¼	0	1	1½
MINCE & SCRIBBLE	18¼	200+	4	1	2¾	0		½	1	1	½	½	2	¼	1	¼	0	½	0	¼	¼	1	0	1½
SCRIPSIT	18¼	200+	4	1	3½		1¼	¼	½	1	0	0	2	0	1	½	0	0	½	¼	0	0	1	1½
WANG SYSTEM 5	18	200+	4	1	3¾		1¼	0	1	1	¼	¼	2	0	1	0	0	0	½	0	0	0	½	1½
MAGIC WAND	17¼	175	4	1	3¾	0		½	1	1	½	½	2	0	1	0	0	0	0	¼	0	0	¾	1
EASYWRITER	12½	88	1½	1	4½	0		0	½	½	¼	¼	2	¼	1	0	0	½	0	¼	0	0	0	1

CPT is the clear winner here, with WordStar making a surprisingly strong showing for a microcomputer program and taking second place (editing power is WordStar's forte). As usual, Easywriter trails far behind the pack.

FORMATTING POWER — 25 POINTS

Unfortunately (for my sanity), formatting allows for an even greater variety of features than editing does. So I'd better get to them without further ado. Unless otherwise specified, all the questions below apply to controlling printout, not how things look on the screen.

I assume that the size of the side margins can be varied. If it can't, I subtract one point from a program's score. I also assume that the size of the top and bottom margins can be varied. If it can't, I subtract another point.

On the positive side, I ask the following questions:

Can the spacing of characters (horizontal) be varied as much as printers with microspacing will allow — typically, to 1/120 inch? — (one point). This lets you use different sizes of type (pica, elite, micron, etc.) and either spread text out or condense it. If a program gives you some choices, but they're limited (pica and elite and that's all, for example), it gets half a point.

Can the spacing of lines (vertical) be varied as much as printers with microspacing will allow — typically, to 1/48 inch? — (one point). This lets you double space, triple space, space and a half, or do more sophisticated things like compress lines of text or lead them out, the way a typesetter does. If you get some choices but not all (just single spacing, double spacing, or triple spacing, for example), I give half a point.

If you can set all the tabs equal to five, or eight, or any number of spaces you want, I give half a point. Most programs also let you vary the location of each tab stop individually. This gets another half point.

If you do any work with columns of numbers, you'll want all the decimal points to line up. Some word-processing programs do this automatically with a feature called **decimal tabs.** This is worth half a point on this generalized scale (and either much more or much less than that to you).

Is there a feature that lets you indent several lines automatically, as you might want to do for a long quotation? If so, I award half a point. An ability to **outdent** — as you might want to do with the names of characters in a play, notations like HEADLINE: and COPY:, or the first line of a paragraph, in the left margin, keeping all subsequent lines at the old margins — earns a quarter point.

Is there automatic page numbering (one point)? And can you choose where the page number goes — upper left corner, centered at the bottom, alternating sides of the page, etc. (one point), or what text — if any — accompanies it (a quarter point)?

Are there automatic **headers** and **footers** — lines of text that appear at the top or bottom of every page (one point)?

Are there features like **horizontal scrolling** to make special formats like tables and text with extra-wide margins easier to lay out (half a point)?

As I mentioned in Chapter 2, printers with microspacing can produce **boldface** text by printing it once, going back to the start, moving right slightly, and printing it again. A program that can tell them to do that earns three-quarters of a point.

It's also possible to go back and **overstrike** without moving right. This produces a fainter boldface, a nice contrast to regular boldfacing (usually called **doublestriking**). But overstriking has more uses than that. If you ever type foreign language text with tildes (señorita) or umlauts (küssen) or accents graves (très) or aigus (aimé) in it, you need to be able to tell the printer to go back and put those marks over letters that have already been typed. So, for example, if ($^\wedge$H) means go back and print the next character over the last one, re($^\wedge$H)$^\wedge$ve will print out as "rêve".

Overstriking also lets you produce symbols like ¢ (c + /), and it has an application in legal documents as well — overstriking whole sections of text with slashes or hyphens to show that it's been deleted.

Overstriking is important not only because of all the things it can do, but because there's no way to substitute for it if you don't have it. No number of keystrokes will get around the lack. You have to go in there with a fine-tipped pen. So overstriking gets one full point.

Subscripts (H_2O) earn a quarter point, as do superscripts ($e = mc^2$).

I assume that a program has the ability to underline (if it doesn't, I subtract a point). Some programs can underline, but they skip spaces, so only the words are underlined. That looks like this: <u>What Could Be Uglier?</u> Some even skip punctuation (e.g. dont). I don't know who dreamed this up, or why (nor do I care), but it produces truly graceless and unprofessional text. So if a program can underline continuously (even if only as an option), it earns half a point.

If lines can be centered automatically, I award three quarters of a point. If there's a way to produce two columns automatically (without having to run each sheet of paper through twice), half a point.

Can you choose either single-page or continuous output (one point)? Single-page output is for loose sheets of paper. The printout stops at the end of the page and waits for you to put in a new sheet and then tell it to go on. Continuous output is for fan-folded computer paper that's perforated between each sheet.

Can the program link separate files during printout, without requiring a page break between them and with continuous page numbering? As I mentioned under Ease of Use above, this is the solution to the problem of maximum file length. If you never print out long documents, of course, it makes no difference.

There are two ways to link files: by embedding a link command line at the end of each file, specifying the next file to be printed (e.g., ./GO TO CHAPTER2); or by specifying all the file names when you give the print command (e.g., PRINT CHAPTER1, CHAPTER2, CHAPTER3).

If a program lets you link files both ways, I give it a point and a half. If it lets you link files either of these ways, one point. And if you can order multiple copies of the same file printed out with a single command, another half point.

Sometimes you want the printer to stop at some place other than at the end of each page — so you can change your print wheel or thimble, for example. To do this you need an **embedded stop and wait** command. You just type a command line (.wa for "wait," say) into the file where you want the printout to stop. The program waits there until you tell it to go on. This deserves a quarter point.

A related but much more important feature is the ability to start printing from the middle of a file. Let's say you're printing out a ten-page document and you discover you turned underlining on but forgot to turn it off on page 5. Since you don't want the last half of the report to be underlined, you stop the printer. (I assume that any program will let you stop a printout from the keyboard. If it doesn't, it loses two points.)

Since the first four pages of the printout are OK, you'd like to begin again at the top of page 5. Some programs won't let you do that; they make you start from the beginning of the file again. You can see what a pain this could be. So I give one point to programs that let you print from the middle of a file.

Can lines be justified to the right margin (one point)? Is there true **proportional spacing** (with i's getting less space than m's — not just microjustification between letters)? Proportional spacing, not justification to both margins, is what makes typeset copy so much easier to read than typewritten copy. In fact, if text isn't proportionally spaced, I find it harder to read when the right margin is straight than when it's **ragged** (not justified).

I give proportional spacing two points because it makes a really dramatic difference in how good a printout looks (as well as how easy it is to read).

On-screen formatting means that you can see on your screen how the printout will look without having to waste paper running off a draft of it. Although much touted by the programs that have it, I consider it an overrated feature, except on machines — mostly dedicated word processors — that have a high-resolution, 66-line screen.

Since on-screen formatting depends so much on hardware, I need to discuss it in two pieces. First I'll talk about it on regular microcomputer CRTs.

These screens can't really show you how a piece of text is going to look on paper, since they don't have the resolution to simulate what a printer with microspacing can do (e.g., boldfacing, proportional spacing).

Control characters which don't show up in the printout do show up on the screen (unless the program allows you to suppress them). They add spaces that won't be on the paper.

Since on-screen formatting on a normal screen can't show boldfacing and underlining, a mistake like starting to boldface and forgetting to turn it off can be hard to catch. You end up discovering it during the printout anyway. And, although line breaks and page breaks are indicated, actual placement on the page is difficult to judge.

If you want the document you're working with to be double-spaced, you'll halve the number of lines you can see on your screen the minute you format it. And you'll also reduce the amount of text you can fit into a file, since actually inserting blank lines — no matter how it's done — is bound to take up more space than a simple command that tells the printer to do that every time it moves down a line.

There's a way to substitute for on-screen formatting that's elegant in its simplicity — old ribbons. Paper costs a penny or two a sheet, and old ribbons you've already gotten your use out of cost, in effect, nothing. For a long time after a ribbon has become too faded to use on something someone else is going to see, it's still quite adequate for draft copies.

I'm talking about fabric ribbons, of course — which are all you need for most uses. For this use, they're essential, since film ribbons can't be reused once they've run out. I estimate that fabric ribbons produce perfectly readable images for about ten times longer than they produce images dark enough to send out, and for most of that time, you can make excellent photocopies of them — assuming you know about the ''light original'' button.

I just run off a draft with an old ribbon whenever I want to see how something looks, even though that's often forty pages or more long. After all, you always want a copy for yourself, and changing the ribbon is easier, faster, and cheaper than going to a copy machine, even if there's one right where you work. (If you need a better copy later on, just run one off with a new ribbon.)

Unfortunately, some printers, like the Centronics 737/739, won't let you put an old ribbon back in. But most letter-quality printers will.

The only thing I wish I had on-screen formatting for is checking page breaks, since when you change one page break, it affects other ones later. (Line breaks are no problem, unless you change your margins.) I could just make successive printouts, but then the cost of paper begins to be significant. What I do in fact is figure as far ahead as I can — let's see, all these pages will move up one line, therefore . . .

Of course, if I had a slower printer, I would probably want on-screen formatting more so I wouldn't have to wait around for printouts.

And that's what I have to say about on-screen formatting on a regular screen. But . . . on a 66-line, high-resolution screen, the story changes. Let's use the Dictaphone Dual Display word processor as an example. It will show boldfacing as it actually looks on paper, and the same for underlining. It can even show double underlining (which you can also get on the printout). It displays pica type or elite type, a ragged right margin or a justified right margin, regular spacing between letters or proportional spacing.

You can see how text will fall on the page, because the screen represents an entire page. You can call up one page after another in rapid succession. About the only thing you can't do is put two or more pages side by side.

On a screen like this, on-screen formatting is an excellent substitute for hard copy drafts and is therefore a *much* more useful feature. So I give *this* level of on-screen formatting (which I call **virtual representation**) seven points. (That puts me over 100, but no one's going to get all the points anyway.)

I give on-screen formatting on a typical low-resolution CRT a maximum of two points — it's a handy feature, but not, to my mind, a crucially important one. The two points break down as follows:

Display of:
- line breaks (half a point).
- page breaks (half a point).
- centering (half a point).
- other formatting information (half a point).

The five extra points for virtual representation break down like this:
Display of:
- full page (at least 54 lines) of text (one point).
- underlining (half a point).
- double underlining (half a point).
- boldface (one point).
- justified right margins (one point).
- proportional spacing (one point).

A few word-processing programs offer a sort of inexpensive substitute for some of the features of virtual representation. It's called **printing to disk** and it works like this: You format a file and proceed to print it, but instead of coming out on paper, the printed image becomes a new file on disk. Then you can bring it up on the screen and look at it — but you *still* can't see boldfacing, whole pages at a time, etc. Printing to disk gets the last half point of the two for on-screen formatting (as do other features).

If a program has some sort of automatic hyphenation capability (which means that it's smart enough to hyphenate a word when it's at the end of a line but not when it's in the middle), it gets a point. It does this by inserting conditional hyphens into every long word.

Conditional (or **soft**) **hyphens** break a word and print out when they're at the end of a line, but leave the word in one piece and disappear when they're not at the end of a line. Some programs won't insert conditional hyphens for you automatically but will let you put them in yourself. This is worth half a point.

Sometimes you want a hunk of text — like a table, for example — to be printed out all on the same page. Some programs let you do this, with a command called **conditional page break.** Let's say you have a table that has fifteen lines in it (counting the title and everything). Naturally, you don't want it split between two pages. So, on the line before it, you embed a command line that reads ''.cp 15'' (for example). When the program hits this line, it stops and counts the number of lines left on the page it's working on. If there are fewer than 15, it moves on to the next page. If there are more than 15 lines left, it just keeps on printing.

The conditional page command is also useful for preventing the first line of a paragraph from appearing alone at the bottom of a page (called an **orphan**). When you're finished editing a file but before you print it out, you do a global which inserts a .cp 2 command at the start of every paragraph. If there's only room on the page for the first line of a paragraph, the program will move on to the next page before printing it. I give half a point to programs that have conditional page break commands.

If you think about it, there are two kinds of spaces that occur in text: regular spaces between words, which should be allowed to fall at the end of a line, and spaces that occur within (and are part of) a name. These **no-break spaces** — like the ones in Osborne 1, Apple II, CP/M 2.2, and Louis XIV — look funny when split between lines. But it's a rare word-processing program that has a way to do that. I give the ones that do a quarter point for it.

Another handy feature is an **instant print** capability, which lets you use a word processor like an ordinary typewriter — that is, you hit a key, and the printer prints a character; you hit the next key, and the printer prints out the next character — immediately. Instant print is great for filling out forms, or writing a short note on an odd size of paper when you don't want to bother figuring out formatting parameters. It's worth half a point.

(Hang in there. I see light at the end of the formatting tunnel.)

Since many programs have unique formatting features undreamed of by most others, I reserve the last point and a half for them. One good example is the ability to do double underlining.

Another is a footnoting feature. This is more than just the ability to do footers. The program keeps the length of the footnote in mind, and stops printing out the main text when there's just enough room left at the bottom of the page for it. Then it spaces down, prints the footnote out, and resumes printing out the main text at the top of the next page.

And that, gentle reader, makes 25 points.

It must be obvious by now that, had I but world enough and time, I could have devised an evaluation scheme of a thousand, rather than a hundred, points. Word-processing programs are very, very complex products.

Here's the formatting chart:

FORMATTING POWER	Total Score	Margins?	Character spacing?	Line spacing?	Individual variable tabs?	Decimal?	Indents?	Outdents?	Page numbers?	Headers & footers?	Help w/tables?	Boldfacing?	Overstriking?	Sub & superscripts?	Continuous underlining?	Centering?	Two-column printout?	Single page or continuous?	Link files?	Multiple copies?	Embedded stop & wait?	Print from mid. file?	Justify right margin?	Prop. spacing?	On-screen formatting?	Auto. hyphenation?	Conditional page break?	No-break space?	Instant print?	Other special features?
DICTAPHONE DUAL DISP.	26¾		½	½	1	½	½	¼	1¾	1	½	¾	¾	½	½	½	¼	1	0	½	¼	1	1	2	7	1	1	¼	½	1½
CPT 8100	26¼		¾	1	1	½	½	¼	1¾	1	½	¾	1	½	½	¾	0	1	1½	½	¼	1	1	2	4	1	1	¼	½	1½
A. B. DICK MAGNA SL	25		¾	¾	1	½	½	¼	1¾	1	½	0	1	½	½	¾	½	1	0	½	¼	1	1	2	5¼	1	1	¼	0	1½
MICOM 2001	23½		1	1	1	½	½	¼	1¾	1	½	¾	0	½	½	¾	½	1	0	½	¼	1	1	2	3	1	1	¼	½	1½
PIE WRITER (W PRO/FORMAT)	22¼		1	¾	1	0	½	¼	1¾	1	½	¾	1	½	½	¾	0	1	1½	½	¼	1	1	2	2	0	1	¼	0	1½
WORD STAR	22		1	1	1	½	½	¼	1¾	1	½	¾	1	½	½	¾	0	1	0	0	¼	1	1	0	4	1	1	¼	0	1½
MAGIC WAND	20		1	1	1	0	¼	¼	1¾	1	0	¾	½	½	½	¾	¼	1	0	½	¼	¼	1	2	2	½	1	¼	¼	1½
NEW SCRIPT	19¾		1	½	½	0	½	¼	1¾	1	½	½	1	½	½	¾	0	1	1	½	¼	1	1	1	1½	½	1	¼	0	1½
MINCE & SCRIBBLE	17¾		¾	1	½	0	¼	¼	1¾	1	0	¾	½	½	½	¾	0	1	1½	½	0	1	1	2	0	0	1	¼	0	1½
WRITE	17½		1	1	1	½	½	¼	1¾	1	0	¾	0	½	½	¾	0	1	1	½	¼	1	1	0	0	½	1	½	½	1½
WANG SYSTEM 5	17¼	−1	¾	¾	1	½	½	0	1¾	1	½	0	¼	½	½	¾	½	1	0	0	¼	1	1	2	2	0	0	¼	0	1½
EASYWRITER	16¾		1	¼	1	0	0	0	1¼	1	½	¾	0	½	½	¾	0	1	1	½	¼	1	1	0	2	0	1	0	0	1½
SCRIPSIT	16¼	−1	½	¾	1	½	¼	¼	1¾	1	½	¼	½	½	½	¾	¼	1	0	½	¼	1	1	0	0	1	1	¼	0	1½
WANGWRITER	14½	−1	½	1	1	½	½	0	0	0	½	¾	½	½	½	¾	0	0	0	½	0	1	1	0	4	0	0	0	½	1½

This is one area in which dedicated word processors have a clear advantage (unless they're Wangs), although PIE Writer and WordStar do surprisingly well for microcomputer programs.

Many of the features the Wangwriter is missing are supposed to be coming in newer versions of the system.

RESPONSIVENESS AND SUPPORT — 4 POINTS

There's no question that it's the responsibility of the vendor — the company that actually sells you your program — to give you most, or all, of the support you need. That's part of what their markup is for.

But even the best vendor can't make up for an irresponsible publisher. Any complex program like a word processor is bound to have some bugs in it. In addition, the design for any such program is bound to have some limitations — some contingencies and user needs unanticipated by the programmer. You want a publisher who's going to constantly fix up and improve the product (you usually get these new versions at a reduced price, if you already own the program). WordStar is a good example of a program that is constantly being enhanced and improved.

(Some software publishers will sell their programs directly. If you want to buy from them, make sure they're willing to offer support at the level you have the right to expect from any other vendor. If a call to them is long distance, whatever you save may be wiped out by your phone bill — unless the documentation is a lot better than average.)

I should tell you a little about the typical way of numbering versions of computer programs. **Pre-release versions** are called 0.7, 0.8, 0.9, and so on. These are tested by people who work for the publisher (**alpha testing**) and then by a small, select group of customers, associates, colleagues, or friends who are willing to give detailed accounts of any problems they encounter (**beta testing**).

The **release version** — that is, the first version sold to the public — is usually labelled 1.0. Subsequent versions are numbered 1.1, 1.2, 1.3, etc., or sometimes 1.21, 1.22, 1.23, etc.

The reason for this decimal notation, rather than just talking about version 1, version 2, version 26, and so on, is to indicate how different from previous versions a new one is. Version 2.0 will be more of a leap from 1.0 than 1.5 was. (If you're only up to 1.4 and changing the program in some dramatic way, you call the new version 2.0 not 1.5.) Likewise, 1.26 will normally be more similar to 1.2 than to 1.3.

(I'm just speaking generally, of course. Programmers and publishers vary in how perfectionistic they are, so what one considers ready for release another wouldn't consider even adequate for testing. For example, Tony Pietsch didn't release his WRITE word-processing program until version 2.0, after having alpha- and beta-tested pre-release versions 1.0, 1.1, 1.11, 1.12, 1.13, 1.2, 1.21, 1.3, 1.4, 1.5, 1.51, 1.52, 1.6, 1.61, 1.62, and 1.7 over a period of two years. On the other hand, after various versions of its Selector information management program had been out for years, Micro-Ap came out with Selector *IV*, which *Info World* said was "introduced before it was ready. It was first advertised last July, but the first acceptable version was not until January.")

Obviously, something as intangible as the responsiveness of a software publisher is hard to rate objectively. (If that were not the case, I might have been tempted to give it more points than four.) I've had to rely on the publisher's reputation, my subjective impression of what they're like to deal with on the phone and by mail, and interviews with users of their software. (When I've been able to contact owners, I gave their comments more weight than the publisher's general reputation or my impressions.)

There's no need for a chart for this category, since most programs got the full four points. Here's a list of the ones that didn't:

- WRITE — 3½
- Wangwriter — 3¼
- Wang System 5 — 3¼
- Scripsit — 3
- Magic Wand — 0

(The notes on these programs in Chapter 6 explain the reasons for these ratings.)

COMPOSITE SCORES

Now that I've gone over each evaluation area in detail, it's time for the master chart. Remember that these evaluation scores can only be a rough approximation of the actual quality and usefulness of a product as complex as a word-processing program.

OVERALL SCORES	Version(s) (of software)	Operating system(s) &/or machine(s)	Price	Overall score	Safety & error handling	Documentation	Ease of use	Workfile in memory or on & off of disk	Editing power	Formatting power	Responsiveness & support
CPT 8100	G-2	ded. word proc.	$15,000	94¾	9	16¾	14¾	M	24	26¼	4
DICTAPHONE DUAL DISP.	D	ded. word proc.	13,500	85¼	7	16¾	12	D	18¾	26¾	4
PIE WRITER (W/ PRO/FORMAT)	2.1 (2.2)	Apple II, Flex, IBM PC, TRS-80 Color Computer	200	84¼	9½	15	13	M	20½	22¼	4
A. B. DICK MAGNA SL	7	ded. word proc.	14,500	83	8	16½	9¾	D	19¾	25	4
WRITE	1.4	CP/M	400	82¼	10	15½	16¾	M	19	17½	3½
MICOM 2001	5.1R	ded. word proc.	12,000	82¼	7¾	15¾	10¾	M	20½	23½	4
WORD STAR	3.0	CP/M, Apple II, IBM PC	500	80	7½	11¾	13	D	21¾	22	4
NEW SCRIPT	7.0	TRS-80 Models I & III	125	79¼	8½	15½	12¾	M	18¾	19¾	4
WANGWRITER 5503A	3.1	ded. word proc.	6,400	74	8	16	13½	D	18¾	14½	3¼
WANG SYSTEM 5, MODEL 3	3.2	ded. word proc.	11,500	70	6	14¾	10¾	D	18	17¼	3¼
MINCE & SCRIBBLE	2.6 + 1.3	CP/M, UNIX, PDP-11	275	67¼	7	12¼	8	D	18¼	17¾	4
SCRIPSIT	2.0	TRS-80 Model II*	400	61½	2	14¼	7¾	D	18¼	16¼	3
MAGIC WAND	1.11	CP/M	400	61¼	3¼	12¾	8	M	17¼	20	0
EASYWRITER	1.0	IBM PC**	175	35	−24	14½	11¼	M	12½	16¾	4

*Similar Scripsit program also available for Models I & III
**Very similar program called Easywriter Professional, available for the Apple II.

CPT emerges as the clear winner, 9½ points in front of the second-place Dictaphone. PIE Writer is fast upon Dictaphone's heels, and five other programs and systems are within five points of it.

Two things strike me about these scores. The first is the exceptional showing of PIE

Writer — third from the bottom in price and third from the top in performance. The second is the fact that, although dedicated word processors tended to do better than microcomputer programs (an average ranking of about fifth place, as opposed to an average ranking of about ninth place), there was a lot of overlap. PIE Writer beat four out of six dedicated word processors, WRITE beat two and tied a third, and WordStar and NewScript beat both Wangs.

This means that dedicated word processors and microcomputer word-processing programs are comparable in their abilities, and it is *not* the case, as it is sometimes claimed, that dedicated word processors represent a whole level of word-processing capability above and beyond what a microcomputer can do.

SOFTWARE CHECKLIST

On the following pages you'll find a blank checklist you can use to evaluate word-processing programs that I haven't covered. Feel free to make copies of it for your own use (although copying it for any other purpose is illegal, of course).

All items have been given the weightings I used above; you should alter them to fit your own needs. Don't be afraid to make drastic changes. If you do a lot of work with numeric tables, for example, you might want to give individual tab settings five points, instead of half a point, and do the same for decimal tabs. If you publish a newsletter, you'll want to give more weight to on-screen formatting and proportional spacing, among other things. And so on.

I could spell out the different requirements of the various jobs word processors get used for — business letters, articles, memos, reports, and so on. But although that's what most books like this do, I don't think it really makes a lot of sense. You know what's involved in what you do better than I ever could. Since you now also have a pretty good idea of what word processors can do, just tailor a set of weightings to your own individual needs. This self-customization is bound to be a lot more accurate than my trying to lump you into a category.

It's a good idea to make a copy of the checklist before you alter it, so you'll still have a clean one in the book to work off of if you change your mind about the importance of various items. You can also use your own weightings to go back and re-evaluate the programs I rated in this chapter on the basis of the detailed information in the next chapter.

One important consideration that isn't included on the checklist is the company that sells you the program — the vendor. (Reread the first section of Chapter 4 if you're not sure why that is.) Sometimes the vendor and the publisher will be one and the same, but more usually, you buy programs from a retailer or distributor.

In either case, ask for the names of a couple of satisfied customers you can call, especially if you came to the vendor out of the blue rather than through a friend's recommendation. And trust your feelings — life is too short to do business with people you don't feel comfortable with.

100-POINT CHECKLIST FOR EVALUATING WORD PROCESSING PROGRAMS

PROGRAM NAME: Version #:

Operating system(s) it runs under and/or machine(s) it runs on:

Price: $

Publisher:

Vendor(s):

Overall score:

Scores in specific areas:
  Safety and error handling (10):
  Documentation (18):
  Ease of use (18):
  Editing power (25):
  Formatting power (25*):
    (*With virtual representation, a total of 30 is possible)
  Publisher support (4):

Special notes:

HOW TO KEEP SCORE

In the case of all yes/no questions, yes is the answer that earns the points.

When keystrokes are being counted, control characters count as a stroke and a half. So do shifted characters. Shifted control characters — or any other combination of three keys you have to hold down at once — count as two keystrokes. If a program can't do the function at all, it gets a five-keystroke penalty.

Count cursor arrows with auto-repeat for a minimum of 3 (it takes a while to get started) and a maximum of 10 (to move from the top to the bottom of the page or from one end of a line to the other).

If a question asks, "Is there a one-stroke command to . . .," count control characters (but not shifted control characters or other three-key commands) as one stroke.

Since some microcomputer keyboards have special function keys like those on dedicated word processors, and since certain word-processing programs have been designed to work with them, such programs may get different scores below, depending on the system they're used on. But for dedicated word processors (which always use the same hardware), and for word-processing programs that can't take advantage of special function keys, the score won't vary.

If a file name is required, assume it consists of eight characters. Be sure to include *every* keystroke — RETURN, ENTER, etc. Remember that you can give partial points (for partial performance) on any item.

Since the checklist is so long, I've boldfaced certain key words throughout, to help you find particular items more quickly and easily.

Safety and error handling — 10 points

How hard is it to **lose text**? (4)
Are there hard-to-avoid fatal error(s) that are likely to occur:
   about 1% of the time? (-25)
   about 2% of the time? (-50)
   about 3% of the time? (-75)
How well are **errors documented**? (2)
How clear are the error messages? (1)
Is verification of **saves** automatic? (1)
Are backup copies automatic? (1)
Can you save to either disk, or switch disks without exiting the program? (1)

Subtotal for safety and error handling:

Documentation — 18 points

Is the **training manual:**
   well-organized? (3)
   readable? (3)
   complete? (1)
Is the **reference manual:**
   complete? (3)
   well-organized? (2)

understandable? (2)

Is there a good, complete **index**? (1)

Are the manuals **typeset**? (1)

    If not, is the text proportionally spaced? (½)

Is the layout intelligent and the **design** graceful? (1)

Are there **special kinds of documentation,** other than manuals (like a reference card, on-screen tutorial, training tape, etc.) that you find useful? (1)

Subtotal for documentation:

Ease of use and human engineering — 18 points

Is the **workfile held** in **memory** or **on-and-off disk**?

    (no score, but an important consideration)

How many keystrokes does it take to go through the following

    sequence of 23 commands? _____

  1) open a new text file (don't count the characters in the file name itself);

  2-4) center, boldface, and underline a title;

  5) skip a line;

  6) indent the next line of text 5 spaces;

  7) indicate the end of that paragraph;

  8) skip a line;

  9) indent the next paragraph 5 spaces;

10) put a page break at the bottom of that paragraph;

11-14) reset the top, bottom, left and right margins

        (just count the commands, not the numerical values);

15) order the file to be double-spaced (if single-spaced is the default), or vice versa

        (again, not counting the numerical values);

16) save the file;

17*) print it out;

18*) stop in the middle of printing out;

19) return to the text;

20) delete a word (5 characters and a space);

21) delete a line (60 characters or more);

22) save this new version of the file, keeping the old version for backup; and

23) begin printing out again at the top of the page.

    [*Systems with virtual representation can skip these two steps (17-18), since it's just as likely that a mistake will get caught on the screen as in a printout.]

Fewer than 55 strokes — 5 points

    56–60 strokes — 4½ points

    61–65 strokes — 4 points

    66–70 strokes — 3½ points

> 71–75 strokes — 3 points
> 76–80 strokes — 2½ points
> 81–85 strokes — 2 points
> 86–90 strokes — 1½ points
> 91–95 strokes — 1 point
> 96–100 strokes — ½ point
> more than 100 strokes — no points

How **easy** is it **to remember commands** (thanks to mnemonics, cursor diamond and other logical key placement, menus, logical command structure, reference card, key tops, dedicated keys, reconfigurable commands, etc.)? (3)

Is the main editing **menu suppressible,** or not normally on the screen with the text? (½)

Is there a way to know:

> what **page** of the printout you're on? (½)
>
> your **location** with respect to the entire file (what percentage of it is behind you, for example)? (¼)

Can you **find** out the **total size of the file** you're editing without exiting the program? (½)

Can you do that and return to where you were in the file in less than 3 keystrokes (or two control characters)? (¼ additional)

Can you **copy the program** as often as you need to? (2)

Total program size:

> Less than 25K? (1)   25-35K? (½)

Or — on dedicated word processors, and other systems where the software and hardware are integrated —

> **Workspace** more than 30K? (1)
>
> Workspace more than 20K? (½)

Are the **editor and formatter** loaded **together**? (1)

> If not, can you keep the workfile in RAM while switching from the editor to the formatter? (½)

How often does the **program** have to go to the disk to access **overlays**? (never, because whole program resides in memory — 1; only goes to overlays occasionally, for special jobs — ½; overlays are essential part of program — 0)

Can you:

> **rename** the file you're working on without abandoning the edit? (¼)
>
> rename a file other than the one you're working on without leaving the program? (¼)
>
> **delete** a file other than the one you're working on without leaving the program? (¼)

Can you get a **directory** of files on the disk without exiting the word-processing program? (− 1 if not)

> Does this directory also give you the size of each file? (½)
>
> Can you ask for just part of the directory? (¼)

Is there a **type-ahead buffer (keystroke storage)**? (1)
Will this program run **memory-mapped**? (½)

Subtotal for ease of use:

Editing power — 25 points

What is the **total number of commands** this program offers you
(for editing, formatting — everything)? [Count every possible option]_____
more than 170 — 4 points
150–170 — 3½ points
130–149 — 3 points
110–129 — 2½ points
90–109 — 2 points
70–89 — 1½ points
50–69 — 1 point
30–49 — ½ point
fewer than 30 — no points
Is there **word wrap**? (1)
Ease and power of **basic** cursor movement, insertion and deletion **commands** (6)
[The next 16 questions will give you a reasonable score for this item for programs
that use conventional techniques. For other programs, you have to make
this judgment subjectively.]
Is there a one-stroke (or one-control-character) command to **move the cursor**:
right one character? (− 1 if not)
left one character? (− 1 if not)
up one line? (− 1 if not)
down one line? (− 1 if not)
(two-stroke or two-control-character commands count half for the next 11 questions)
forward one word? (½)
backward one word? (½)
to the end of the line? (½)
to the beginning of the line? (½)
to the top of the screen? (½)
to the bottom of the screen? (½)
to the beginning of the file? (½)
to the end of the file? (½)
Is there a one-stroke (or one-control-character) command to:
delete a whole word? (½)   delete a whole line? (½)
switch between insert and writeover mode? (1)
either mode missing (− 5)

Is there continuous and unlimited:

   forward **scrolling**? (½)

   backward scrolling? (½)

Can the **scrolling speed** be altered? (¼)

Can you **call** up any **page** in the text **by number**? (1¼)

Can you **move** the **cursor where** there is **no text**? (½)

Can you:

   copy **blocks of text**? (¾)

   move blocks of text? (¼)

   delete blocks of text? (1)

   make a new file out of a block of text without having to stop editing the file you're
      working on? (½)

   insert another file into the one you're editing? (½)

Can you:

   find a string anywhere in a file? (1)

   replace a string anywhere in a file? (1)

   search **backwards** as well as forwards? (¼)

   do many substitutions **all at once,** without having to approve each one? (1)

Can you **see each change** for approval if you want? (− 2 if not)

In doing finds or substitutions, can you tell this program to **ignore** caps/**lowercase**? (½)

Look for **whole words only**? (½)

Can you:

   make substitutions that affect more than one file at a time? (½)

   store stock phrases in memory and insert them with a coded command while typing?
      (½)

Are there **other** special **global capabilities**? (¼)

Is there a command that **moves** the **cursor** to **where it was before** the **last command**
      was executed? (¼)

Is there a **split-screen** feature? (1)

Can you **edit** one file **while printing out** another? (1)

Are there **other** special **editing features** that appeal to you? (1½)

Subtotal for editing power:

Formatting power — 25* points

[*With virtual representation, possible total of 30]

Can you vary:

   the top and bottom **margins**? (− 1 if you can't)

   the side margins? (− 1 if you can't)

   character **spacing**? (1)

   line spacing? (1)

   the **tabs**? (½)

each tab setting individually? (½)

Are there decimal tabs? (½)

Are there automatic **indents**? (½) outdents? (¼)

Automatic **page numbering**? (1)

Can you choose:

where on the page the page numbers go? (½)

what text (if any) accompanies them? (¼)

Can you get **headers** and **footers** printed automatically on each page? (1)

Are there special features like horizontal scrolling to help with formatting **extra-wide text** or **tables**? (½)

Will the program allow you to **boldface** on printers that are capable of it? (¾)

Is there **overstriking**? (1)

Are there **subscripts**? (¼) superscripts? (¼)

Can you **underline** continuously, i.e., under spaces and punctuation as well as letters and numbers? (½) (− 1 if program can't underline at all)

Can you automatically **center** lines? (¾)

Is there automatic **two-column printout**? (½)

Do you have a choice of **single-page or continuous** printout? (1)

Can you **link files** during printout, either by embedding a line at the end of each file or by specifying the files to be linked when you give the print command?

Either (1)   Both (1½)

Can you have **multiple copies** of the same file printed out with one command? (½)

Can you embed a command that makes the printout **stop and wait** for your instructions? (¼)

Can you stop printout from the keyboard? (− 2 if can't)

Can you **print from** the **middle** of a file? (1)

Can you **justify** the **right margin**? (1)

Is there true **proportional spacing** on printers that allow for it? (2)

Is there **on-screen formatting**? (2)

(line breaks — ½; page breaks — ½; centering — ½; other formatting information displayed — ½)

[An extra 5 points is given for **virtual representation** (which is machine dependent). To qualify, the screen must display all of the following (partial points as indicated):

full page (at least 54 lines) of text (1)

underlining (½)

double underlining (½)

boldface (1)

justified right margins (1)

proportional spacing (1)]

Is there automatic **hyphenation**? (1)

If not, are there conditional hyphens? (½)

Is there a **conditional page break** feature? (1)

Can you ask for a no-break space? (¼)
Is there an **instant print** feature? (½)
Are there **other** special **formatting features** that appeal to you? (1½)

Subtotal for formatting power:

Responsiveness and support — 4 points

(Based on reputation, users' comments, what the vendor says, etc.)

6

Notes On 104 Word-Processing Programs And Dedicated Word Processors

In this chapter, I've tried to give you the most comprehensive list possible of all the word-processing programs available — both for microcomputers and for dedicated word processors — at the time this book was written. It certainly isn't a complete list, but it is much more complete than any other list I've seen.

Given the number of programs I cover, I can't provide an exhaustive description of all of them; that would be a book in itself. Here's what you'll get (assuming I have it):

- the publisher's name and address;
- the price of the program (as of this writing, with $95 and similar nonsense rounded to the next hundred); and
- the machines and/or operating systems required to run it.

If I know of other programs related to word processing that are published by the same company, I list them too.

If a program was evaluated in Chapter 5, the entry on it in this chapter explains why it got the points it did. In some cases, I include actual commands in the explanation, to give you a feeling for what it's like to use the program. For some programs, I also give a little history or my subjective impression of them.

When a score is self-explanatory, I don't comment on it. For example, if a program gets two points for being copyable, the program is copyable and what else is there to say about it? If it gets no points, the program isn't copyable and what else is there to say about it?

If a program wasn't evaluated in Chapter 5, I simply give whatever additional information, if any, I have on it. If I wrote the publisher, I tell you how helpful they were to me. It seems to me that this is at least an indirect measure of how helpful they're likely to be to you. If I don't mention writing, I learned of the program too late to send a letter and whatever information I provide comes from an ad or a magazine article.

Be aware that a few of the programs listed below are only editors, or only formatters, rather than integrated word-processing programs with both those capabilities.

A.B. Dick Magna SL, Software Version 7

Dedicated word processor.
$14,500 for one work station with word-processing software, sort program, statpack, etc., plus free updates (since the Magna SL is a shared-logic system, configuration with one work station doesn't make a lot of sense).
A.B. Dick Company
5700 West Touhy
Chicago, IL 60648
(sales offices in most cities)

The Magna SL is the only multi-terminal system evaluated in this book. It consistently scores among the highest in this category in the Datapro reports. It's particularly strong in the area of training and support.

Safety and error handling

It's just about impossible to lose text on a Magna SL. Each page is saved automatically when you're finished with it. Before you can delete a page, you must respond to an ''Are you sure?'' question. It's also very hard to accidentally erase a file. And you can recover one full page or even a whole disk.

The Magna SL also has absolutely the best error documentation I've ever seen. It's a whole book, entitled *What If?*, that lists every possible contingency, its probable cause (or causes), and what to do about it. I wish I had more than two points to give for documenting errors; this manual is outstanding.

Eight points total for safety.

Documentation

The training manual would be fine if it didn't favor lists of items and numbered, unindented paragraphs. Both these lose it half a point for what would otherwise be perfectly readable text.

The reference manual is organized like a dictionary, in straight alphabetical order —a simple and effective approach. Unfortunately, the reference manual could be more complete and loses half a point for discussing only commands, not default values and other relevant information.

There's a pretty good index, but it's missing some items (minus a quarter point). The design of the manuals could be better, and the brown ink is unattractive (minus another quarter point).

There's a very useful reference guide to the Magna SL, but after the training you get you may not need it. The training lasts for up to three days, with a maximum of four people in each class. You get two free trainings per keyboard, advanced seminars, and unlimited free support (no support contracts).

All this gives the Magna SL a total of 16½ points for documentation.

Ease of use

The Magna SL has one clumsy feature — it requires you to reform every paragraph you want doublespaced. Fortunately, there's a way to make the computer automatically repeat the necessary series of commands until it reaches the end of the file. Nevertheless, this flaw, and the absence of automatic backup — which forces you to make a copy of the file before re-editing it — gives the Magna SL a total of 103½ keystrokes for the 23-command sequence. But since the system displays just about everything but proportional spacing on the screen, I subtract ten keystrokes, for a total of 93½.

It's easy to remember commands on the Magna SL, both because of all the dedicated keys and because many of the other keys are labelled with their control functions.

The program is not copyable, but many local sales offices will give you new systems disks free. I only give half a point here, however, because some sales offices charge the official $30 for replacing them.

The size of the workspace is 11K. A.B. Dick gets 9¾ points in this area; the rest of the reasons are obvious from the chart.

Editing power

There's a cursor movement feature: if you press the down and right arrow keys simultaneously, the cursor will move diagonally. (The same is true for the other three combinations, of course.) I have the feeling that this could be quite a useful feature.

Most systems search only for capitals if you type capitals or lowercase if you type lowercase. Others let you specify. The Magna SL always looks for both, which is better than the former but not as good as the latter, and thus earns it a quarter point. Bypassing a substitution and going on to the next is very easy on this machine, and that's worth another quarter point.

The Magna SL easily gets the additional point and a half for the following special editing features. For one thing, it has an ''undo'' command (called ''restore'') that lets you recover up to a page of deleted text. For another, it has **executable command files** (which allow you to put together a bunch of commands and save them as a file; when you give the system the name of that file, it executes every command in it). Executable command files have many uses — a common one is converting files produced by one program so that they can run under another.

The Magna SL also lets you move columns of text and will automatically delete text by sentence or paragraph. It gets a total of 19¾ points for editing power.

Formatting power

The Magna SL can't boldface or link files; otherwise, it can do pretty much everything on my list. (It won't show proportional spacing on the screen, but will show pica or elite characters — a quarter point.)

It gets the extra point and a half for a whole slew of special features:
- typing Greek, scientific symbols, and English all on the same line
- displaying them all on the screen
- being able to encode a whole file into Greek with a couple of keystrokes (and decode it the same way)
- showing different fonts in different levels of intensity on the screen
- letting you queue files for the printer
- letting you prioritize files on that queue after you've put them there
- giving you a list of the last hundred jobs sent to the printer

The Magna SL gets an outstanding total of 25 points for formatting power.

Responsiveness and support

This is A.B. Dick's strongest area. They got an outstanding 3.5 in training and maintenance responsiveness in the *Datapro* reports, 3.3 for troubleshooting, and 3.2 for maintenance effectiveness. My personal experience tells the same story. Kim Speer was extremely helpful, as was Maxine Bolf, and I was impressed by how well Kim understands the machine; she really knows it backwards.

A.B. Dick gets the full four points for this category, and probably deserves five. This gives the Magna SL an impressive total of 83 points overall.

All-In One

6800 and 6809 machines.
$35.
AAA Chicago Computer Center
120 Chestnut Lane
Wheeling, IL 60090

Alphaview

Alpha Micro machines.
Alpha Micro
17881 Sky Park North
Irvine, CA 92713

I wrote Alpha Micro for information, but got no response.

Apple Writer

Apple II.
$75.
Apple Computer
10260 Bandley Drive
Cupertino, CA 95014

I wrote Apple for information on this program and on their machines, but got no response.

Apple Writer III

Apple III with SOS and 128K of RAM.
$225.
Apple Computer
10260 Bandley Drive
Cupertino, CA 95014

InfoWorld rated this program good in all categories except error handling, where it was rated excellent.

Atari Word Processor

Atari 800 with 48K of RAM.
$150.
Atari
1265 Borregas Avenue
Sunnyvale, CA 94086

Autoscribe

North Star and other CP/M computers.
$400.
Microsource
1425 West 12th Place
Tempe, AZ 85281

I wrote this publisher for information but got no response. *InfoWorld* reviewed Version 5.0 of Auto Scribe II (for the Heath-Zenith Z/89 computer) and gave it a mediocre review — good in documentation and error handling, only fair in performance and ease of use.

AXE (Advanced X-Tended Editor)

Apples with 48K, Applesoft, and DOS 3.3.
$70.
Versa Computing
Suite 104, 3541 Old Conejo Road
Newbury Park, CA 91320

Bare Bones

OSI with 8K.
$10 (on cassette).
Elcomp Publishing
3873L Schaefer Avenue
Chino, CA 91710

The Benchmark

CP/M.
$500 (Mail List program $400 extra).
Metasoft
Suite E
711 East Cottonwood Lane
Casa Grande, AZ 85222

This word processor was designed to be easy to learn and easy to use. Its documentation is quite good and most commands are mnemonic. The Benchmark has most of the features on my 100-point score sheet, including some of the rarer ones — like the ability to select up to 52 stock phrases and insert them with a coded command and a directory which displays (in addition to file names and numbers) the author's initials, the operator's initials, and the date and time of the last revision.

Metasoft was quite helpful and responded to my request for information quickly and fully. I wish I'd had the time to give The Benchmark a full evaluation.

Capdoc

CP/M machines, with CBASIC and 48K RAM or more.
$300.
Monoson Microsystems
51 Main Street
Watertown, MA 02172

Connecticut Micro Word-Processing Program

Commodore PET.
$30-40, depending on the version.
Connecticut Microcomputer
34 Del Mar Drive
Brookfield, CT 06804

Both an editor and a formatter, despite its low price.

Copywriter +

CP/M machines with at least 56K.
$600.
Digital Marketing
2670 Cherry Lane
Walnut Creek, CA 94596

I wrote this publisher for information but got no response. When *InfoWorld* reviewed this program, they gave it excellent for usefulness and error handling, good for documentation, and fair for ease of use.

CPT 8100, Software Version G-2

Dedicated word processor.
$14,000 for whole system (plus or minus a couple of hundred dollars depending on which printer you choose). The price includes all updates of word-processing software and also, at the time of this writing, the mathpack, spelling checker and sorting software, which normally cost an additional $500 each.
CPT Corporation
8100 Mitchell Road
Minneapolis, MN 55440
(sales offices in most cities)

This is a superb system, with many virtues that don't even show up on my evaluation scale. For example, while some manufacturers of dedicated word processors have finally realized that their customers deserve access to other software and are therefore finally offering CP/M, CPT has supported CP/M on their machines for years.

CPT has good communications software and a choice of two spelling checkers: one provides you with a 100,000-word dictionary (which is *very* large) and lets you add 20,000 words of your own; the other is smaller and less powerful, but it's built-in — that is, it actually checks your spelling while you're typing.

Whatever CPT does, they seem to do right. Their word-processing software is no exception.

Safety and error handling

The only thing CPT doesn't give you is automatic backups of your files, but it has some special features — for example, their floppy disk unit is set up so it *can't* crash; the head is shimmed so that even if the power goes off, it won't fall onto the disk.

CPT gets nine points for safety and error handling.

Documentation

About the only problem with the CPT manuals is that the training manual could be more readable. The style is somewhat stiff and the paragraphs are not indented. The index is adequate but could be better; it leaves out some terms (''proportional spacing,'' for example).

CPT provides a plethora of special kinds of documentation — audio cassettes, three training disks, a good reference card, and a series of workbooks. And that's all in addition to the free training sessions you get.

CPT earns an impressive 16¾ points for documentation.

Ease of use

CPT gets through the 23-command sequence in 61½ keystrokes, and I subtract five keystrokes because the system displays underlining (as underlining) on the screen, thus eliminating the risk of one common mistake — forgetting to close underlining.

The 8100 will hold a workfile of up to 12K in memory; you can also choose to have it automatically swap the file on and off of disk in chunks of various sizes (every 256 bytes, for example). A combination of dedicated keys, mnemonics, and a good reference card makes commands easy to remember.

As with most dedicated word processors, the program is not copyable, but CPT will give you extra disks at $7 a pop (or free if the old one was faulty). Since they have offices all over and since $7 is not much more than what a blank disk costs, I consider this setup almost as convenient as being able to copy the program, and I give one point for it.

In addition to a ten-character file name, you can add a description of up to 240 characters to help identify a file. CPT gets a total of 14¾ points for ease of use.

Editing power

CPT's word wrap works with hyphenation. That is, the program will hyphenate words as you type them in and move any *syllable* that doesn't fit at the end of the line down to the next line. That's really incredibly sophisticated.

CPT approaches cursor movement in an unusual way. Basically, the cursor always stays on a ruler line which extends across the page and has the margins and tabs indicated on it. You scroll the text up and down past this line; when you have the line of text you want positioned just above the ruler line, you move the cursor across to where you want to make a change. This works pretty well, when you get used to it, but it isn't as fast or efficient as actually being able to move the cursor all over the screen.

CPT lets you move the text up or down, delete, or reform by characters, words, lines, paragraphs or pages. You can also vary where the ruler line appears on the page. These are more choices than you're probably ever going to need, but it's nice to have all of them. I give CPT five and a half points for basic commands, and would give it six but for the somewhat clumsy cursor movement setup.

You can call pages up by number and also scroll down through the workfile. You can move ten blocks of text at one time (that is, you can hold ten separate hunks of text in different move memories and pop any of them in wherever you want it). CPT's global editor can find any sort of character and will find a string regardless of whether it's underlined or hyphenated. It will hold a thousand separate phrases on disk, and you can load ten of them into move memories and insert them into the text as stock phrases.

Not only can you edit one file while printing out another, but the 8100 will drive *three* printers while you're working on a fourth file.

CPT easily gets the extra point and a half for special editing features, because it moves columns, automatically checks spelling and hyphenation as you go along, lets you release the margins, lets you design your own command sequences and assign them to keys, and offers a shift-lock function which automatically capitalizes just letters (not numbers or symbols).

It can even reverse case automatically — so, for example, if you accidentally typed something with the shift-lock in and don't want it to be all capitals, or if you decide that you want something you typed in lowercase to be all caps for emphasis, you don't have to retype. You just mark the text involved and order reverse case; all the capitals become lowercase and all the lowercase letters become caps.

The CPT 8100 gets a remarkable 24 out of 25 points for editing power.

Formatting power

You get only limited choices for character spacing (10, 12, or 15 to the inch or proportional spacing); since this is a pretty good selection, I deduct only a quarter point. The CPT will do everything else I list, except for two-column printout. It doesn't have virtual representation, but it does display underlining, double underlining, and a full page of text, thus gaining two extra points (in addition to the two it gets for on-screen formatting).

CPT earns the extra point and a half for the following features: graphics; black on white display; ability to feed wide sheets through the printer; support of a dual-head printer; triple-bin cut-sheet feeding in a software-controlled pattern; and special symbols, including scientific notation, Greek, Arabic and thirteen other languages (special keyboards are required for this last feature).

This gives it an incredible total of 26¼ points for formatting power.

Responsiveness and support

Many of the people I contacted when writing this book were very helpful, but none were as helpful as Jackie Alexander. She sent me tons of material, called to ask if I needed more, and provided the additional information I requested. The other people who demonstrated the CPT 8100 for me — James Thomas and Don Short — were also top-notch. The company's main office responded to my letter promptly and in detail.

In the *DataPro* reports, CPT got 3.3 for maintenance service, 3.1 for troubleshooting, and 3.0 for training. It gets all four of my points for responsiveness and support, which gives it an amazing total of 94¾ points overall.

Dictaphone Dual Display, Software Version D

Dedicated word processor.
$13,500 for whole system, including all software and all updates.
Dictaphone Corporation
120 Old Post Road
Rye, NY 10580
(sales offices in most cities)

Dictaphone makes much of the fact that this system has two displays — a full-page CRT and a single-line thin-window display on the keyboard. While it is nice to have all the system prompts appear on the thin display, leaving the screen clear for text, I don't think it's really such a big deal. I'm much more impressed with the virtual representation (the screen shows your text *just* the way it will appear on paper) and with some of the human engineering touches, like the little lights on dedicated keys to tell you if they're engaged or not.

The Dual Display tends to do quite well the things it can do; it falls down in terms of the things that it can't do.

Safety and error handling

The Dual Display has several ways to protect you from losing text. For example, if you try to erase a bunch of different files, the machine requires that you verify each deletion individually. But you can run into trouble with full disks, so I give it three and a half points.

Errors are generally well documented, but the disk-full error isn't explained clearly enough, so I deduct half a point here. Dictaphone gets a total of seven points in this category.

Documentation

The training manual could be warmer and more colloquial (minus half a point). The reference manual could be better organized — for example, new material is presented in a separate section rather than integrated into the text (minus half a point). The index is pretty good, but there are several terms missing from it (''proportional spacing,'' for instance) — minus a quarter point. Other than this, Dictaphone gets all the points for documentation.

It has several nice features worth noting. The binder for the main manual converts into a stand. Colored tabs in the manual make it easy to find the sections you're looking for. Prompts appear on the single-line display, leaving the screen clear to display the text. There are also help menus, and Dictaphone provides training, of course.

The total score for documentation is an impressive 16¾.

Ease of use

Extensive dedicated keys, including a cursor diamond, and the use of mnemonics for other commands earns this system the full three points for command recall aids. The thin-window display functions as a suppressible main menu, in effect. You don't have to leave the program to find out the total size of the file you're editing, but you do have to close the file, so I give a quarter point for this.

You can't copy the program, and a new disk with the program on it costs $18. This is too expensive, but since the Dictaphone office is likely to be near you, it's not too inconvenient. So I give half a point on this item, which gives the Dual Display twelve points for ease of use.

Editing power

The Dual Display is missing many of the specific basic commands I mention in my list; for example, it can't move forward or backward by words or to the beginning or end of a line with a single command. But, as I mentioned in Chapter 5, it uses searches to accomplish the same ends. Since you're in the search mode by default, all you have to do to find the end of a sentence, for example, is type a period and hit the CONTINUE key. This unusual but interesting approach — combined with the convenience of cursor arrows — earns Dictaphone five points for basic commands.

You can scroll (somewhat slowly and inefficiently), but it's much easier just to call up pages by number. You can make blocks of text into new files, but they can't be longer than a page. That's also the length limit for blocks of text you can insert into a file (half credit on both items).

The global editor is similarly limited. Because the Dual Display is page oriented, it can't find (or find and replace) a string that falls across a page break (that is, when the first part of the string is at the bottom of one page, and the second part is at the top of the next). It will, however, prompt you with the phrase ''incomplete string'' (minus half a point).

Since the Dual Display is in search mode by default, searches and substitutions are extremely easy; I give the extra quarter point for this ease. After a search, you're *automatically* returned to where you were when you began it.

Deleted text is saved in a temporary buffer until the next delete, so you can retrieve it if you make a mistake. Zoom video doubles the size of the characters on the screen. These two features, combined with the dual display, earn this system the extra point and a half, for a total of 18¾ points for editing power.

Formatting power

Your choices for character and line spacing are both limited (minus half a point for each). There is overstriking, but it's clumsy; you have to hit a key for each character you want overstruck (minus a quarter point). Centering is also somewhat clumsy; you have to move the cursor to either end of the text you want centered (minus another quarter point).

There is two-column printout, but it doesn't work the easy way (the first line of each column printed out, one after the other, then the second line of each column, and so on); instead, one column is printout in its entirety, then the printer moves back up to the top of the page and prints out the second column in its entirety.

The Dual Display has complete virtual representation — boldfaced text, proportional spacing and all. It gets the extra point and a half for the following features: footnoting (one of the few systems to offer this), double underlining, centered or flush right text within columns, special forms to fill in for various functions, the ability to embed different page formats, and footers that alternate sides from one page to the next.

All this gives Dictaphone a preternatural score of 26¾ on formatting power.

Responsiveness and support

Dictaphone scored 3.4 for maintenance service, 3.0 for trouble shooting, and 3.1 for training on the *DataPro* user's surveys. Their national office responded promptly to my letter, and Al Jacobsmeyer of their Oakland office was quite helpful. Dictaphone gets the full four points for support and responsiveness, giving their Dual Display an outstanding overall score of 85¼.

The Correspondent

Apple II.
$35.
Southwestern Data Systems
Box 582
Santee, CA 92701

The Correspondent is a pretty basic program, without many formatting features or even word wrap and global replacement. *InfoWorld* rated it excellent in error handling, good in usefulness, fair in ease of use, and poor in documentation.

Datacope Scribe

Apple II.
$80.
Datacope
Drawer AA
Hillcrest Station
Little Rock, AR 72205

Docuwriter

Apple II.
$150.
Charles Mann and Associates
7594 San Remo Trail
Yucca Valley, CA 92284

The program lets you do file linking, global replacements, block moves, scientific notation, merge printing (for form letters), and even footnotes.

Dravac WPS

Alpha Micro.
Dravac Ltd.
53 Deerhaven Road
Mahwah, NJ 07430

EasyWriter Version 1.0 for the IBM Personal Computer

$175.
IBM
Personal Computer Division
Box 1328
Boca Raton, FL 33432

Apple version (EasyWriter Professional):
Information Unlimited Software
281 Arlington Avenue
Berkeley, CA 94707

It's hard to understand why IBM would choose EasyWriter for their Personal Computer when so many better word-processing programs are available. EasyWriter is far and away the worst program I evaluated — inconvenient, poorly thought out, and full of bugs. That the largest computer company in the world should offer it as the first (and, for a time, the only) word-processing program on its personal computer is, in a word, disgraceful. It just goes to show you — you can't trust a name.

A debugged and enhanced version of EasyWriter (1.1) is planned and will doubtless be out before this book is. In IBM's corporatese, this new version "improves the usability and function of the product" — as well as it should. They figure Version 1.1 will score 80¼ on my checklist. *I* figure they should provide a free copy of it to every purchaser of Version 1.0.

Information Unlimited Software (but not IBM) also has another new product. Called **EasyWriter II,** it's a completely different program, written in C (a high-level language) by a software group up in Vancouver. Because C is machine independent, EasyWriter II will run on many different systems. It's a page-oriented program that swaps the workfile on and off of disk. IUS figures it will score 92 on my checklist.

Neither IBM nor IUS responded to my initial letter, but both sent copies of the documentation when contacted on the phone. Jeanette Maher of IBM was quite helpful after we had made contact.

Safety and error handling

Although EasyWriter is weak in many areas, this is clearly the weakest. There are several ways to lose text; one of them is inserting without pressing INS (which is easy to do, since generating blank lines is the only way to insert without waiting forever for the program to catch up with you). The most serious bug comes if you try to align when there are extra lines at the end of the file (this can happen quite easily). The result is a fatal error that locks up the keyboard.

I believe this error is likely to occur at least one percent of the time and therefore I deduct 25 points for it. Certainly IUS will clear up this bug — by the time you read this, it probably will already have been done — but I think programs should be debugged *before* they're released, not after thousands of hapless souls who've never used a computer before spend hours trying to figure out what *they* did wrong.

The EasyWriter manual has no list of error messages, and the ones that appear on the screen aren't terribly clear. For example, another bug causes the program to falsely issue a message that reads "DISK NOT INITIALIZED. DO YOU WISH TO FORMAT?" when you haven't changed disks. If you answer yes (by typing Y) to this question, you'll erase everything on that disk. An adequate error message would warn you about that. (Of course, an adequate program wouldn't give you this message about a disk that has been initialized.)

The only point EasyWriter gets in this category is for letting you save to either disk (or switch disks), giving it a total of − 24.

Documentation

EasyWriter has one manual, which functions better for training (five and three quarters points) than for reference (five points). It's reasonably well organized, although things get repeated in unlikely places. It's also reasonably well written, although there are flukes. The main problem with the manual is its incompleteness. Many questions are left unanswered and information is missing; for example, it tells you that "it is possible to set your margins so that they exceed the 80 columns that can be seen on the video display," but it doesn't tell you how wide you can set them.

The index could also be better. It's missing key words (like "paragraph") and needs to be more hierarchical. The manual is quite well designed, however, and I wish I had an extra point to award for the fact that the binder is not only pretty, but doesn't stink of vinyl fumes.

EasyWriter provides you with a reference card which, given the skimpiness of the program itself, is all the special documentation a user will need. EasyWriter gets a total of 14½ for documentation.

Ease of use

As other reviews of this program have noted, EasyWriter doesn't live up to its name. The ENTER key, which inserts line breaks, also turns off insertion mode, so you have to keep hitting INS to get back into insertion mode again. Moving a block takes at least *21* keystrokes! Centering a line takes at least 11, assuming you want the line to stay centered when you align the text. (It turns out there's a way to center a line in four keystrokes, but the manual doesn't tell you how to do it.)

EasyWriter lets you make one (and only one) copy of the program, for which I give it a quarter point. The rest of the items are obvious from the scores on the chart. EasyWriter's total for ease of use is 11¼.

Editing power

This is another weak area for EasyWriter, in which it gets less than half the available points. I give the program four and a half points for basic commands, since it has one-stroke commands for every function I list except moving to the end and beginning of a line and to the bottom of a screen. But if I were making a subjective judgement, EasyWriter's clumsy insertion mode and other inconveniences would earn it a lower score.

There is, officially, a block move capability, but the blocks are limited to 3500 characters and the whole procedure is so incredibly clumsy and buggy that it's virtually useless. Giving it half credit (a point and a half out of three) is quite generous.

The global editor is no winner, either. You can find a string anywhere in the file — as long as it doesn't contain a control character, isn't split between lines, and isn't right justified. EasyWriter does get the extra quarter point for its selective search and replace, however; it lets you choose, at each occurrence of a string, whether to make the change or to move on to the next occurrence.

EasyWriter also gets an extra half point for a special editing feature I would like to have — reverse tab. And it also gets half a point for its rather limited ''undelete'' feature. This makes the total score for editing power 12½.

Formatting power

EasyWriter lets you insert whole lines only between lines of text and so gets a quarter point for this limited sort of variable line spacing. Moving the location of the page number around is clumsy, since you must specify, in numbers, the line and column where you want it (although IUS claims that this feature has received ''much positive feedback'').

The print-to-screen feature gives the equivalent of on-screen formatting. Special features like the ability to generate two headers or footers (or even three), to print without saving, and to define your own commands for special printer functions earn the program the extra point and a half. Its total in this area is 16¾.

Responsiveness and support

Despite the lack of concern for users that EasyWriter demonstrates at every turn, individual users speak very highly of IUS's responsiveness. And, in any case, buyers of this version of EasyWriter will turn to IBM with their problems first. I can testify from personal experience that IBM *really* knows how to provide service. It's too early to say how well they'll support EasyWriter, but if it's anything less than superbly, they'll be departing from a fifty-year tradition.

So EasyWriter gets the full four points for publisher support, giving it an overall score of 35. This is perfectly wretched, of course; even if the program hadn't lost 25 points for being unsafe, it would *still* score only 60 and would still be the lowest-rated program. IUS, and IBM, should be ashamed.

The Electric Blackboard

CP/M with 48K.
$200.
Santa Cruz Software Services
1711 Quail Hollow Road
Ben Lomond, CA 95005

Edit

TRS-80 Models I or III.
$40.
Allen Gelder Software
Box 11721, Main Post Office
San Francisco, CA 94101

This is an editor (no formatter) written in BASIC.

Electric Pencil

TRS-80 Models I, II, and II; CP/M systems with memory-mapped video.
$90 (disk); $80 (tape or stringy floppy).
IJG
1260 West Foothill Boulevard
Upland, CA 91786

Electric Pencil was the first full-powered word-processing program for micro-computers and therefore made quite a big splash a few years ago. Unfortunately, according to some people I've talked to, the publisher's attitude seemed to be: "You already have your money's worth out of this program. If there's something wrong with it, *you* fix it."

They unlisted their telephone in Palm Springs and sold the rights to distribute Electric Pencil to IJG, who reworked the program extensively and put some energy into debugging it. As they put it in their brochure:

"QUESTION: The 'old' Pencil would do some 'funny' things. Have you corrected all of the problems the 'old' Pencil had?"

"ANSWER: Yes; in fact, you could even say that the 'new' version is 'bulletproof.' "

Well, that's good, because "bulletproof" is something the old Pencil certainly was not.

Electric Pencil was an advanced program for its time. Whether this revised version can compete with today's programs I don't know, since I didn't get a response to my letter until four months after I sent it.

Executive Secretary

Apple II with 48K or more of RAM; IBM Personal Computer.
$250.
Sofsys
4306 Upton Avenue South
Minneapolis, MN 55410

I wrote Sofsys about this program, but they didn't respond with the information I requested. *InfoWorld* rated Executive Secretary good in performance and ease of use, excellent in documentation, and fair in error handling (*InfoWorld's* reviews tend to be less critical than mine). The only Executive Secretary user I know doesn't think much of it.

Sofsys' ads annoy me. Under the guise of comparing Executive Secretary with other word-processing programs, they make a series of claims that are as grandiose as they are untrue. For example, ''nobody else's manual even comes close'' (has Sofsys, in fact, read every one of the hundreds of manuals published by their competitors?). Or, ''only one [other program] has an index-maker available.''

They summarize their competition like this: ''Dozens [of other programs are] on the market. Some cost a little less, but do much less. A few cost more, but they also do less.''

How's that for blithe, supercilious smugness? I don't know about you, but I don't trust companies that come across like this.

The Finalword

CP/M (with 56K or more), including TRS-80 Model II; also, the IBM Personal Computer.
$300.
Mark of the Unicorn
Box 423
Arlington, MA 02174

This is the new word processor from the publishers of Mince and Scribble. Since it's written in C (a high-level programming language), it's relatively machine independent and can be adapted to run on any new machine very quickly. It has several advanced features; for example:
- automatic generation of indexes and tables of contents
- automatic footnoting
- proportional spacing
- moving or deleting by words, sentences, paragraphs, or pages
- user-defined commands
- the ability to alter file names by directly editing the directory
- the ability to leave the editor and use another program without dumping your workfile
- recovery of text deleted by mistake
- recovery from hardware crashes

Mark of the Unicorn is a *very* responsive and helpful publisher and a real pleasure to deal with.

Hesedit

Commodore PET.
$16.
Human Engineered Software
3748 Inglewood Boulevard
Los Angeles, CA 90066

This is just an editor; it doesn't do formatting.

IBM Displaywriter with Textpack 1, 2, 3, and 4 software

Dedicated word processor.
$8000 and up.
IBM
Parson's Pond Drive
Franklin Lakes, NJ 07417
(sales offices in most cities)

IBM didn't answer my letter, but I figured I should mention the Displaywriter anyway. It's their general-purpose word processor, positioned to compete head-to-head with Wang, Lanier, and the like.

Despite its reputation, IBM does less well in the *DataPro* reports than many other manufacturers. Almost a quarter of the people responding said they wouldn't recommend the IBM word processor they were using to someone else with the same needs. Overall satisfaction with IBM word processors is 3.2, with the weakest areas being training (2.8) and documentation (2.9).

IDS Word

CP/M, TRS-80 Model II.
$125–320.
CW Applications
1776 East Jefferson Street
Rockville, MD 20852

I wrote CW for information on IDS Word, but they didn't respond.

Lanier Super No Problem ($13,000), Typemaster ($8000), and EZ-1 Word Processor ($6000)

Dedicated word processors.
Lanier Business Products
1700 Chantilly Drive N.E.
Atlanta, CA 30324
(sales offices in most cities)

Although Lanier did respond to my letter, the information they supplied was skimpy, and I never did get around to evaluating one of their machines. Lanier gets good grades from their users. Ninety-one percent say they would recommend a Lanier like the one they have to someone else in the same situation, and the overall satisfaction score in the *Datapro* reports is 3.4. Weak areas are troubleshooting (3.0), training (3.0), and documentation (2.9).

Lazy Writer

TRS-80 Model II.
$125.
Soft Sector Marketing
6250 Middle Belt
Garden City, MI 48135

Lettergo

North Star.
$500.
Datek Systems
4786 Lee Highway
Arlington, VA 22207

Letter Perfect

Apple II with DOS 3.3.
$150.
LJK Enterprises
Box 10827
St. Louis, MO 63124

I wrote LJK for information on this program but got no response.

Letteright

CP/M.
$200.
Lifeboat Associates
1651 Third Avenue
New York, NY 10028

Letter Writer

TRS-80 Model I or III.
$38.
Astro-Star Enterprises
5905 Stone Hill Drive
Rocklin, CA 95677

Magic Typewriter

Version 2 — CP/M and North Star — $175.
Version 3 — CP/M — $350.
California Digital Engineering
Box 526
Hollywood, CA 90028

Magic Wand Version 1.11

CP/M.
$400.
Peachtree Software
Three Corporate Square
Atlanta, GA 30329

Related programs available from the same publisher: Spelling Proofreader, Peach-Calc, Mailing List Manager, and Telecommunications.

A couple of years ago, Magic Wand was considered to be the main competition to WordStar. But the program has major flaws and has failed to evolve at the same rate as other word processors. Today, most other programs offer better value.

A new version of Magic Wand (2.0, now known as **PeachText**) came out too late to be reviewed in this book. Among other things, it offers a new main menu, much more on-screen help, and new documentation. According to Peachtree, ''it is a major upgrade of the product and corrects all known bugs in the program.''

Safety and error handling.

This is a particularly weak area for Magic Wand. There are some precautions to prevent loss of text — like a safety question when you delete a block — and the machine beeps at you several hundred times before you can overflow memory. But you can lose text by switching disks, typing too fast while background printing, and also by overflowing memory, if you're persistent enough. Working saves are discouraged, since you can't save a file without terminating your edit of it *and* exiting the program.

Worse, there's an undocumented error that works like this: if you run out of space on a disk when a file has been almost completely written to it, you will lose some lines at the end of that file when you go to save it again (after making room for it on the disk by deleting some other files). You won't even know this till the next time you go to edit it.

Errors are reasonably well documented (except for this last one) — once you find the place where they're discussed. There's no special section on errors, nor is that word (or ''problems,'' ''warnings,'' ''cautions'') mentioned in either the table of contents or the index. Even the discussions themselves are sometimes a little vague.

Error messages on the screen vary from clear to fairly clear. There is no list of them in the manual.

Magic Wand gets three and one quarter points overall in this area.

Documentation

Once considered the best training manual around, the Magic Wand User's Manual today seems good, but not great. The main problem is that it's too lesson oriented; there aren't enough general statements of the form: "to accomplish that, you do this." People quickly grow impatient with specific lessons. Also, each sentence is numbered (or lettered) and not indented. And the black shapes which are supposed to represent what gets displayed on the screen are virtually unreadable.

Still, the training manual gets six out of seven points. The reference manual (a section of the same book called "Notes") only gets four and a half out of seven. For one thing, it's far from complete; for example, I couldn't find anything about word wrap, and the section on line length tells you can vary it but doesn't say what the maximum is.

Items are listed in the order you would use them, which makes sense for teaching, but not for reference. It's very hard to find what you're looking for in this section of the manual. A good index would solve the problem, but the index provided is quite minimal, with many items missing.

Another maddening thing about the manual: there are no chapter headers at the top of the page. Each page says "MAGIC WAND User's Manual" and nothing else, so if you leaf through the book, you quickly lose track of where you are.

I take off a half point for design, because of the unreadable "screens." Although there is a decent reference card, there should also be more menus — a deficit presumably corrected in version 2.0 (minus a quarter point under special kinds of documentation). This gives Magic Wand a total of 12¾ in this category.

Ease of use

This is another weak area. Commands tend to be either mnemonic or the whole name itself (e.g., to enter the editor, you type the word "edit"). This makes them easy to remember but costs keystrokes.

You can swap pieces of the workfile on to and off of disk as much as you want, but the part of it you're working on at any given time resides entirely in memory. The editor part of the program is 15K and the formatter 41K. You have to issue special commands to use all of the work space; otherwise, your text only fills up half of it.

Magic Wand gets a total of eight points for ease of use.

Editing power

Aside from the absence of automatic scrolling, Magic Wand has a reasonably powerful editor. Its global editor can't do anything fancy (backward searches, whole words only, etc.), but it does get an extra point for its ability to automatically repeat the last command given.

It can edit one file while printing out another, but it does it somewhat sluggishly. Magic Wand gets the extra point and a half for a special screen display mode for programming and for the ability to control (down to a single page) how much of a file gets loaded into memory.

This gives it 17¼ points for editing power.

Formatting power

This is the strongest part of the Magic Wand program. The chart pretty much tells the story, but the following items deserve special attention.

You can automatically indent only the left margin. It's possible to do overstriking, but the method is quite clumsy. You can choose the intensity of boldfacing, from one overstrike to *nine!* (Nine overstrikes — including, of course, moving the print head progressively farther right each time — should be useful for producing completely illegible text.)

There's no direct command for double-column output, but it can be done with a little ingenuity. You can print from the middle of a file, but there are a lot of bugs in this part of the program; very frequently, in bi-directional mode, you'll get bad margins and other problems. There is an instant print feature, but it's clumsy; you have to re-invoke it for each keystroke you want to send to the printer.

Magic Wand has on-screen formatting, although its ways of displaying things is characteristically awkward. Let's say, for example, that you wanted the word INTRO-DUCTION boldfaced and you choose to have it overstruck three times. It would show up on your screen as IIINNNTTTRRROOODDDUUUCCCTTTIIIOOONNN.

There's also a print-to-disk feature that will show you the pages as they'll appear on paper, complete with headers, footers, and page numbers.

Magic Wand easily gets the extra point and a half for special formatting features; its extensive system of variables and if/then statements — a virtual programming language for formatting — would earn them all by itself. There's also merge printing, headers and footers with more than one line in them, the ability to generate an index, and kerning (reducing the space between two letters — like a capital W and a small e — so they look better together).

Magic Wand gets 20 points for formatting power and would score even higher if I had reserved more points for special features.

Responsiveness and support

I had more trouble with Peachtree than with any other company I dealt with while writing this book. I probably had to call them ten times to get the materials and information I requested. Since my impression of them was so unfavorable I knew there was no way it wouldn't distort my scoring in this area, I asked them for the names of some local dealers I could call. They gave me three.

The first dealer said that, while they carried other Peachtree Software, they didn't support Magic Wand; they sold Memorite and WordStar instead. The second said that they used to sell Magic Wand but had switched over to WordStar because they thought it was a better program. The third dealer also said that they had stopped selling Magic Wand because there were several bugs in it that never got fixed. Remember — these are dealers Peachtree *themselves* told me to call.

So I feel perfectly justified in giving Peachtree no points at all for its support of (and responsiveness to problems with) Magic Wand. This gives the program a total of 61¼ points overall.

Magic Window

Apple II.
$100.
Artsci
10432 Burbank Boulevard
North Hollywood, CA 91601

Artsci sent only skimpy information on this program, so I can't tell you much about it. *Creative Computing* reviewed it and liked it.

Manuscripter

CompuSystems
2301 Devine Street
Columbia, SC 29205

I wrote for information but got no answer.

Maxi-Pros

OSI.
$40.
Aardvark Technical Services
1690 Bolton
Walled Lake, MI 48088

This program includes formatting, even at this low price. It's written in BASIC and can be modified by the user.

Memorite III

Vector Graphic.
$450.
Vector Graphic
31364 Via Colinas
Westlake Village, CA 91361

This program includes spelling checking, list processing, and merge printing. I'd tell you more about it, but they never answered my request for information.

Metatype

CP/M 2.0 or above, with 56K RAM and at least 175K on the disk.
G & G Engineering
13708 Doolittle Drive
San Leandro, CA 94577

Jim Rosenberg, Metatype's author, sent me the program's documentation and, although its organization is a bit strange, it seems generally well thought out and clearly written. Unfortunately, I didn't have the time to fully evaluate the program. I can tell you, however, that it seems to have most of the basic features plus some rarer ones; just to pick one example, you can recover small-scale deletions up to 1920 characters and large-scale ones up to the capacity of the disk.

Micom 2001, Software Version 5.1R

Dedicated word processor.
$12,000 for whole system, including word-processing program and all updates.
Philips Information Systems
4040 McEwen
Dallas, TX 75234
(sales office in most cities)

This is an impressive system which does a great number of things well, which probably accounts for its high scores in user satisfaction.

Safety and error handling

About the only way you can lose text is if the power goes out. Otherwise you're protected by the fact that all deleted text is saved (up to the amount of room left on the disk) and by the program's generally crash-proof design.

Possible errors are well documented. Error messages are usually clear, and the ones that aren't are clearly explained in the manual.

The 2001 gets a total score of seven and three quarter points in this category.

Documentation

The training manual is fine; unfortunately, unindented, numbered paragraphs make it somewhat difficult to read. The reference manual has the same problem. It could also be more complete (it doesn't list the default value for tabs, just to pick one example).

The index is pretty thorough and makes good use of boldfacing. But it's missing several items; for example, the phrase ''top margin'' isn't listed.

The closest thing the 2001 has to a reference guide is several typed pages listing commands (in alphabetical order, rather than grouped by what they do). The system definitely needs a real reference card, and I penalize it half a point for not having it.

The total score for documentation is 15¾.

Ease of use

It takes the 2001 93 keystrokes to complete the 23-command sequence, but since it shows underlining, subscripts, and superscripts as such on the screen, I give it five keystrokes credit. Lots of dedicated keys and the extensive use of mnemonics make commands quite easy to remember.

The program is not copyable, and replacement disks cost $25, so I only give a quarter point out of two on this item. The workspace is 8K. Micom gets a total of 10¾ points for ease of use.

Editing power

The 2001's global editor can search for (or substitute) up to 94 strings and a total of 1200 characters *per page* and can do that all *in one pass* (this is global substitution with a vengeance!). It earns the extra quarter point for this.

The 2001 easily gets the extra point and a half for special editing features. Aside from being able to save unlimited amounts of deletions, the system has an advanced merge-print capability, can move columns of text, has vertical tabbing within columns, and can move the cursor or delete text sentence by sentence. It gets a total of 20½ points for editing power.

Formatting power

Micom gets most of the points in this area. Aside from what's listed on the chart, it can subscript or superscript to any level (so, for example, you can put a superscript on a subscript's subscript). It does horizontal scrolling the right way — moving the screen right one character at a time. You can print from the middle of a file and even from the middle of a page.

The Micom will do proportional spacing with an additional program that costs $200. I've assumed that the system I'm reviewing has this software on it. (You lose graphics and some statistical capabilities when you use it.)

There is a whole slew of features that earn Micom the final point and a half:
- It has codes for special characters like the trademark symbol (™).
- It can display Greek and scientific symbols.
- You can set several independent sets of margins, as you might want to do to produce newspaper columns on a single page.
- It has "true double underscoring" — that is, the lines are close together.
- You can center text on less than the full line.
- You can format math output.
- There's an excellent forms-handling capability.

The 2001 gets an outstanding 23½ points for formatting power.

Responsiveness and support

My personal experience with Micom has been good. Robert Silver of their San Francisco office was very responsive, as was his staff. The *Datapro* reports bear this impression out. Micom got 3.4 for how well it responded to maintenance calls, 3.3 for how effective they were once they got there, and 3.1 for troubleshooting and training.

Micom gets the full four points for this category, which gives the 2001 82¼ points overall.

Mince, Version 2.6 & Scribble, Version 1.3

CP/M with 56K RAM or more, UNIX and UNIX look-alikes, PDP-11s.
$275 for the two programs together.
Mark of the Unicorn
Box 423
Arlington, MA 02174

Mark of the Unicorn is one of those companies that makes me wish I gave more than four points for responsiveness and support. And the program they've written — I'll treat it as one program, Mince being the editor and Scribble the formatter — is no slouch, either; it has many advanced features that I don't give points for. Unfortunately, it lacks many simpler capabilities and thus didn't score particularly well.

Here (as elsewhere), you should customize your evaluation. If you have a use for Mince & Scribble's advanced features, this might be the program for you. If you have no use for them, it probably isn't.

Safety and error handling

Mince has many ways to prevent the loss of text, and one of the most useful is the "yank" command that allows you to pull deleted text back from wherever you sent it with the last command (i.e., restore it). The program also handles full disks and full directories quite well. But there are some ways you can get in trouble — by switching disks when you shouldn't, for example, or by ignoring the "swap file full" error message. So I give Mince three and a half points for this item.

Both the Mince and Scribble manuals tell you about possible errors clearly and in the appropriate places, and the Scribble manual has a complete list of error messages. Since the Mince manual is missing such a list, I subtract half a point.

Mince & Scribble gets seven points for safety.

Documentation

These are some of the best written manuals I've ever read; not only do they present material in an understandable way, they're actually a pleasure to read (although they do tend to get a bit too cute at times). Unfortunately, they have other defects, the most important of which is the absence of an index. Basically, both are designed as training manuals and don't serve particularly well for reference.

Even a training manual needs an index, so I take off half a point for completeness. And the fact that certain terms are introduced before they're adequately explained costs another quarter point. Otherwise, the training manual is fine.

The lack of an index is more important in a reference manual, so I subtract a full point in that section. And since the manual is organized entirely for training and not at all for reference, I give it no points for organization.

The manuals tend to present a grey sea of text that swims before your eyes, although it's well designed from a logical point of view. The Mince manual has an excellent collection of quick reference guides; the Scribble manual's command summary is less impressive. There are also tutorials on disk. All this earns the program one point for special kinds of documentation, for a total of 12¼ in this category.

Ease of use

Scribble's commands are *very* easy to remember since many of them consist simply of the name of what you want to change. For example, to reset the top margin, you type "topmargin," followed by the new value. This, along with excellent command summaries and lists, earns Mince & Scribble the full three points for command recall aids but plays hell with keystrokes on the 23-command sequence.

I should mention that it is possible to print directly from Mince, without entering Scribble, but this defeats the intention of the command sequence and would end up costing even more keystrokes in the long run.

Mince and Scribble are large programs, 30K and 34K respectively. They don't have an integrated directory function; you have to go out to the operating system to get a list of the files on a disk. The program can be installed to run memory-mapped if your video board emulates a terminal.

Eight points is the total for ease of use.

Editing power

Mince lets you delete the word behind the cursor, as well as the word in front of it, with one (two-stroke) command. You can move the cursor where there is no text if you're in "page mode." Making a new file out of a block of text or inserting another file into the one you're working on require moving the text to an intermediate buffer.

The global editor will ignore case if you type the string to be found in lowercase letters and will find caps only if you type it in caps. It will let you begin a series of substitutions in the approve-each-change mode, and then switch to the bulk substitution mode in the middle.

Mince has a great split-screen feature. You can have different portions of the same file (or the same portion, for that matter) in the two screens, and you can move text back and forth between them. Mince easily gets the extra point and a half for special editing features; it probably deserves an extra ten points. Here are just a few of the features:

- Any command that affects one character can be made to do the same thing to a word, a line, a sentence, or a paragraph.
- You are provided with source code, so you can modify the program to your own needs. The manual explains how to do it.
- As I mentioned above, you can recover text deleted in a previous command, up to a huge amount (the rest of the space left on the disk). Anything larger than a character is automatically saved for recovery.
- Mince can be instructed to support any size screen up to 66 lines.
- There are multiple buffers for storing blocks of text.

All this adds up to a total score of 18¼ for editing power.

Formatting power

Scribble gives you a choice of ten pitch, twelve pitch, or proportional spacing. Although indenting is somewhat clumsy, you can make it automatic, and you can nest progressive indentations. Headers and footers can be set to automatically alternate from page to page (so that they're always on the outside, for example).

Overstriking is handled in an unusual way — you can set any character to *always* overstrike (a tilde, for example, or an umlaut). You can have only letters underlined, letters and punctuation, or everything, including spaces. You can print from the middle of a file, and *to* the middle of a file.

Just as Mince got the extra point and a half for special editing features, and probably deserved ten, so Scribble gets the extra point and a half for special formatting features, and probably deserves twenty. It lets you:

- specify print parameters in inches, centimeters, picas, points — everything down to micas, which are 1/2540 inch.
- do footnoting.
- automatically generate a table of contents.
- automatically generate an index.
- customize the proportional spacing program by reassigning the spacing given to any letter you specify, or to all the letters.
- nest one piece of boilerplate into another piece of boilerplate.

- request that all paragraphs be automatically numbered.
- adapt the program to any printer.
- insert whatever formatting commands you want into the text, regardless of whether the printer you end up using can do those things. Scribble will automatically make the printer do the best it can.

Basically, Scribble lets you set variables to do just about anything and then call them back with a coded command. But since it's missing many simpler capabilities (on-screen formatting, automatic hyphenation, tabs you can set individually), it only scores 17¾ points for formatting power.

Responsiveness and support

Mark of the Unicorn was the most helpful and prompt of all the software publishers responding to my request for information. It was also a real pleasure to deal with them on the phone. And I'm not alone in finding them impressive — a complete stranger who happened to learn, in the course of a conversation, that I was reviewing Mince & Scribble in this book raved about how incredibly responsive Mark of the Unicorn had been in his dealings with them.

I award the whole four points here and wish I had more to give. This brings Mince and Scribble up to a total of 67½ points.

MWP/SEL

The Software Store
706 Chippewa Square
Marquette, MI 49855

Since this publisher didn't respond to my letter, I have no other information on their program.

NewScript, Version 7.0

TRS-80 Models I and III with 48K.
$125 (special proportional spacing program for common formed-character printers available for $50 or more).
Prosoft
Box 839
North Hollywood, CA 91603

This is a good, solid, all-around program with no weak areas and great support. It's also quite a bargain.

Safety and error handling

I wish NewScript asked a safety question ("Are you sure?" or the equivalent) when you go to delete a file or a block of text. But since its "whoops" command restores up to a screenful of lost text, and since there's another program to recover whatever was in memory before a system crash, I have to give it full credit for making it hard to lose text.

Error messages are generally clear and errors generally well documented, but sometimes an error message refers to terms not in the index, and the explanation of them in the manual doesn't clarify what's meant.

NewScript gets an impressive eight and three quarter points for safety.

Documentation

NewScript's documentation is generally excellent, but the manual tends to use terms before they're defined. This is more of a problem for someone learning to use the program than for an experienced user looking something up, so I deduct a full point for it under training and only a half point under reference.

The index is good, but there are a number of terms not listed in it. The design of the manual is generally well thought out, but the dot-matrix text is sometimes a bit hard to read (the very long lines don't help). The reference card could be better, but it's supplemented by alphabetical lists of commands in the manual.

NewScript gets a respectable 15½ points for documentation.

Ease of use

Many NewScript commands are the full name of what you want to do — QUIT, GET, END, etc. Once you've learned their names, you can call them up more quickly by just typing the first two letters. Mnemonics are used to help with other commands too.

The FR command ("how much workspace is FRee?") gives you the workfile length in both lines and characters (total workspace size is 14K). The type-ahead buffer is quite extensive, holding up to 128 characters.

The total for ease of use is 12¾.

Editing power

NewScript doesn't do automatic scrolling, but it can move a specified number of lines or screenfuls in either direction (and, of course, you can hold the cursor arrows down). The program lets you insert up to two stock phrases from memory by defining the two wildcard keys to do so. It will also let you run a negative search (''locate not''); for example, you can ask it to find every occurrence of the phrase ''first-strike capability'' that *isn't* preceded by the phrase ''senseless desire for.''

The following special features earn the extra point and half:
- Three places markers can be set.
- There are two user-definable (''wildcard'') keys.
- 255 characters can be defined (instead of the usual 128), giving you access to the Greek (or some other) alphabet, lots of symbols, etc.
- Commands can be repeated (there are many ways to do this).

The total for editing power is 18¾.

Formatting power

Line spacing is limited to half spaces. Tabs can be set individually, but are not displayed.

NewScript can't do a shadow-printed boldface, but its author tells me this was a conscious decision, because on many proportional type elements, moving over and reprinting the letter will result in a double image. His solution is to offer double-striking (you select how many times — up to four — you want the text double-struck). He says this produces a nice, strong boldface and doesn't run into problems. Since he has thought through this issue and even polled users on their preference, I give him half a point for boldface.

NewScript can link files not only at the end, but in the middle (so you can insert one file into another during the printout). The program lets you do proportional spacing on most dot-matrix printers. As I mentioned above, there's an optional program that lets you do proportional spacing on most formed-character printers.

Although NewScript has a print-to-screen feature, it can't show lines wider than 64 characters. It gets a point and a half for on-screen formatting. Conditional hyphens are standard, and there's a separate program you can use to get automatic hyphenation.

NewScript gets the extra point and a half for special formatting features because it can:
- merge print.
- generate indexes and a table of contents.

- automatically number lines or paragraphs.
- switch headers and footers from side to side on alternating pages.
- directly select from its own menu the Microproof spelling-checker program (and their automatic hyphenation sub-program).
- fully support italics, double-width characters, and similar features on eighteen different printers, including the Epson MX-80, TRS-80 Line Printer IV and Daisy-wheel II, and the Centronics 737 and 739.

The total score for formatting power is 19¾.

Responsiveness and support

NewScript's author, Chuck Tesler, was very responsive to my questions and requests for information. I've also read about Prosoft's support in letters to microcomputer magazines and talked to satisfied users. The four points in this category gives NewScript an overall score of 79¼.

NHS

TRS-80.
Real Computing
23727 Hawthorne Boulevard
Torrance, CA 90505

Since this publisher didn't respond to my letter, I have no other information on their program.

Northword

North Star.
North Star Computers
14440 Catalina
San Leandro, CA 94577

I found North Star the hardest of all hardware manufacturers to deal with. I was unable to get any information out of them, although I sent them the standard letter and followed it up with two phone calls.

Omniwriter

CP/M.
Omnigraphics
208 Diamond Street
San Francisco, CA 94114

Another non-responder.

Palantir

CP/M.
Designer Software
Suite 718
3400 Montrose Boulevard
Houston, TX 77006

When Designer Software didn't respond to my original letter, I called them. They send me a pre-release copy of their manual, which struck me as awfully skimpy.

Paper-Mate Command 60

Commodore PET.
$30
A B Computers
115 East Stump Road
Montgomeryville, PA 18936

Despite its low price, this program offers both editing and formatting, and even has some unusual features like file-linking and graphics.

Peachtext

This is the new name for **Magic Wand,** Version 2.0 and beyond.

Pencil Sharpener

Add-on to Electric Pencil (TRS-80 and CP/M).
Software Services
18323 Vanowen Street
Reseda, CA 91355

A few years ago, this program brought Electric Pencil's capabilities up to snuff. But they didn't answer my letter, so I don't even know if they're still publishing it.

Perfect Writer

Apple II, TRS-80 Model II, CP/M.
$290.
Related programs available from the same publisher:
Perfect Speller — $190.
Perfect Mailer — $190.
Perfect Sort — $190.
Computer Services Corporation of America
71 Murray Street
New York, NY 10007

PIE Writer, Version 2.1 (pre-release), with PRO/FORMAT, Version 2.2 (pre-release)

Evaluated as it runs on Apple II. Also available on IBM Personal Computer, TRS-80 Color Computer, and FLEX operating system.
$200 ($150 without PRO/FORMAT).
Hayden Software
600 Suffolk Street
Lowell, MA 01853

PIE is one of the oldest word processors for the Apple, and this incarnation of it crams an incredible amount of power into a small ($23\frac{1}{2}$K) and inexpensive package — proving once again that, in word processing at least, you don't necessarily get what you pay for (or pay for what you get).

PIE Writer, running on a humble Apple II, outscored every other word-processing program for microcomputers and all but two dedicated word processors.

Safety and error handling

PIE Writer won't let you delete more than a single character with just one keystroke. Typically, you "push delete" text into a buffer, which holds up to a screenful for you to recover if you make a mistake.

The manual refers early on to a troubleshooting reference section, which I assume will do a good job of listing error messages and telling you how you can get into (and out of) trouble. But since I had only a preliminary version of the manual to look at, I felt I had to subtract half a point here. PIE Writer gets everything else, for an impressive total of nine and a half points.

Documentation

Although I didn't have the final, printed version of the documentation to review, I was able to get a pretty clear idea of the training manual from the galleys provided me. It's basically well organized but does introduce some terms (e.g., "update," "documentation") before they've been defined.

Although perfectly understandable, the training manual is not particularly well written. It talks to "the user," instead of talking directly to "you," and isn't even consistent in this. The word order is sometimes a bit clumsy.

I took one point off for the organization of the reference manual, which is set up for more teaching than for reference. Most of, but not all, the necessary information is included. I assumed that the index would be adequate but not perfect.

The reference card is clear and complete. PIE Writer gets a total of 15 points for documentation.

Ease of use

PIE Writer's score on the 23-command sequence — 75½ keystrokes — falls squarely between the ranges for two and a half points (76-80) and three points (71-75). This was a contingency I hadn't anticipated, so all I could do was give two and three quarter points. PIE Writer needs either more mnemonics or more menus to make commands easier to remember. (I'm told that the next version has an optional help menu which can be loaded into memory.)

PIE Writer uses overlays occasionally; the editor and formatter are loaded separately, and the workfile stays in memory when you switch between them. (On a 64K Apple II, or a 48K Apple II with a language card, you can load the editor and the formatter together and there are no overlays.) The total score for this category is 13 points.

Editing power

PIE Writer's global editor will hold one stock phrase in memory (half credit on that item) and lets you use wildcards in global searches and substitutions. You can edit one file while printing out another only if you have a separate program which lets you format the program you're printing to the disk first (a quarter point out of one).

PIE Writer gets the extra point and a half for the following special editing features:
- the ability to mark off a rectangle of text (and blank space) with the cursor and move it wherever you want.
- column moves and deletes.
- a two-stroke command to delete the rest of a line.
- the ability to have a bell (actually, a buzzer or beeper) sound near the end of each line (you can specify how many spaces away).
- compatibility with a large range of hardware — 40-column and 80-column Apple IIs, hard disk drives, shift-key modifications, lowercase adaptors, etc.
- a command to delete to the next specified character.
- the ability to shift text left and right between two cursor positions.

PIE Writer gets 20½ points for editing power.

Formatting power

Line spacing is limited to half lines. PIE Writer's horizontal scrolling, no-fill mode, and line lengths up to 132 characters help you with tables. You have four underlining choices: continuous, everything but spaces, just letters and numbers, or just letters.

Special formatting features include an integrated merge-print capability, the ability to save and reload tab settings, a special version for playwrights, and auto-indent mode for programming and outlines.

The total in this area is an impressive 22¼.

Responsiveness and support

Hayden has a good reputation for supporting their products. I also know the program's author, Tom Crosley, and I have confidence in his dedication to keeping users happy.

The four points for support give PIE Writer a remarkable total of 84¼ points.

Pmate

IBM PC, CP/M.
$200.
Lifeboat Associates
1651 Third Avenue
New York, NY 10028

This is just a text editor, not a formatter.

Polytext/80

Micro Concepts
731 East Harmony
Fullerton, CA 92631

Micro Concepts didn't answer my letter, so their address is all I can give you (and even that may not be correct).

Pro-Type

Apple (with SoftCard), TRS-80, CP/M.
$75.
Interactive Microware
Box 771
State College, PA 16801

Pro-Type features on-screen formatting and will do right justification. Since this publisher didn't respond that's all I know.

Screditor II

6800 and 6809 machines.
$150.
Sonex Systems   or: Alford and Associates
Box 238   Box 6743
Williamsville, NY 14221   Richmond, VA 23230

Scripsit, Version 2.0

TRS-80 Model II (a version of Scripsit also exists for the Model I and Model III).
$400 (spelling-checker program $200 extra).
Tandy Corporation
Fort Worth, TX 76102

This is Radio Shack's own word-processing program for their TRS-80 computers, and it has some good points. For example, you have total control of the size and shape of the cursor you use; you can also adjust the rate at which it flashes or have it not flash at all. File names can be up to 16 characters long and can have additional descriptions of up to 76 characters. You can customize the program to your preferences and have all your zeros slashed automatically (for example).

Despite these nice touches, if I had a TRS-80, I'd run NewScript on it or adapt it to run CP/M software. (By the time this book is published, Radio Shack will have come out with a newer version of Scripsit, called SuperScripsit. Use the checklist at the end of Chapter 5 to see how much of an improvement it is.)

Safety and error handling

This is Scripsit's weakest area. Although there is a safety question ("Are you sure?") on file deletes, the program will block delete up to a whole page of text without verification. If you switch diskettes when you shouldn't, you can lose up to a page of text. Something called a data-block control error can cause trouble. And disk overflow problems are also possible.

All these pitfalls wouldn't be so bad if the documentation clearly told you how to avoid them. But if they're mentioned in the training manual, I can't find them. There is a list of error messages in the reference manual, but the messages aren't in alphabetical order, and there are no warnings about losing text there either.

Scripsit gets a total of only two points for safety.

Documentation

Scripsit's documentation is pretty good, the training manual particularly. Its main failing is the extensive use of columns of numbers and bullets instead of running text. There could also be more representation of what the screen looks like at various points. The organization is good, but tends to be a little confusing in certain places. And it would be nice to be told what the actual default values are.

Default values are even missing from the reference manual, a serious omission.

There's also no alphabetical list of commands. The manual is organized more or less as a training manual and uses some terms before it defines them. Although the writing is perfectly understandable, I take a half point off for all the wading you have to do through lists of instructions in order to dig out the reference information you're looking for.

Boldfacing is used well in the index, but some important terms are missing from it. Scripsit comes with a quick reference guide, and several cassette tapes (for those of you who are auditory learners). The training manual's binder converts to a stand, and the reference manual makes good use of tabs.

The total score for documentation is 14¼.

Ease of use

Scripsit lets you edit one page at a time and puts it back onto disk when you're done with it. Commands would be easier to remember if mnemonics were used more extensively and if the quick reference were better organized. There are many menus, however, and they help.

There is a type-ahead buffer, but it runs into trouble when the program is accessing the disk or when you're printing one file while editing another. The total score for this area is seven and three quarter points.

Editing power

Although Scripsit does some limited scrolling, the main way of moving around is to call up pages by number. You can move the cursor where there is no text, but you can't type anything there. Moving (and copying) blocks of text is possible but clumsy.

Scripsit lets you store stock phrases in memory and insert them into the file you're editing; the way it does this — with user definable keys — is very well designed. The program has many special global capabilities: specifying which pages you want searched, global deletes, counting the number of times a string occurs, and returning the cursor to where it was before a search (only on a single page) are a few of them.

Scripsit also has outline mode and will let you restore the page you're editing to its original state. It can convert any ASCII file (a program, say, or a data file) to be compatible with it. As if these aren't enough special features, the program lets you define your own keys in a truly powerful way — assigning long strings of commands and/or text to them.

Scripsit gets 18¼ points for editing power overall.

Formatting power

You can't set the top margin directly. The only choices for character spacing are ten pitch and twelve pitch; for line spacing, just half lines. You can only indent from the left; to indent from the right, you have to reset the right margin.

There is no true boldfacing and the doublestriking that substitutes for it is time consuming — each character gets hit five times. Overstriking is possible, but only by defining your own print codes. Two-column printing is also possible, but only by invoking a reverse page feed (that is, the first column appears and then the printer goes back to the top of the page and prints the second column).

Scripsit easily gets the extra point and a half for special features. For one thing, merge printing is included in the program, and a whole slew of special symbols — like the trademark ™ — are built in. Headers and footers will automatically switch from side to side on alternating pages. And you can code the current date into either of them.

The total for formatting power is 16¼.

Responsiveness and support

Radio Shack didn't used to give a lot of support to its products, at least in terms of having knowledgeable personnel around to answer questions. But that seems to be changing. There's a special toll-free 800 number you can call with questions about Scripsit, and the fellow I spoke to there really knew what he was talking about.

There are also new Radio Shack stores that sell just computers, and their personnel are bound to know more than the workers in the general-purpose stores. Certainly the manager of my local store was friendly and helpful.

So I was inclined to give Scripsit the full four points for support, except for the fact that, despite many requests, I was never put in touch with any of their users. I feel that I have to take off a point for that. This gives Scripsit a grand total of 61½.

Secretary

North Star.
$100.
American Square Computers
Kivett Drive
Jamestown, NC 27282

Select

CP/M (also Apple).
$600 (with Superspell spelling checker).
Select Information Systems
919 Sir Francis Drake Boulevard
Kentfield, CA 94904

Select didn't respond to my letter, but did send me a manual when I called them to ask for one. There's also an extensive on-screen tutorial which leads you through the program. I can't say how well that works, but the manual is generally clear (although it would be a lot more readable without all the numbering and unindented paragraphs).

If your keyboard doesn't have cursor arrow keys, Select is likely to be quite clumsy to use. It only moves in one direction (forward or backward) at a time, and therefore you have to keep reversing directions to move freely around the screen.

I wish I'd had the time to do a full evaluation of Select, but my general impression from reading the manual is that it is somewhat less powerful and less carefully designed than many other programs.

Sequitur

UNIX Version 7 and look-alikes.
$3500.
Pacific Software Manufacturing Company
2608 Eighth Street
Berkeley, CA 94710

This is a combination data-base manager and word processor which repays its high cost in business applications involving large amounts of data. Among its advanced features is the ability to recover lost text (or earlier versions of changed records) with a single keystroke. The documentation is clear and readable.

Spellbinder

CP/M.
$400.
Lexisoft
Box 267
Davis, CA 95616

I had hoped to give Spellbinder a full evaluation, since they responded promptly to my inquiry and since a version of the program, called **Word 125,** is the official word processor on the HP 125 computer. Unfortunately, the manual lacks an index (which makes evaluation *very* difficult), and Lexisoft and I were unable to hook up together on the phone.

Spellbinder has a lot of powerful features, including true proportional spacing, automatic hyphenation, search with wildcards, integrated merge printing, sorting, two-column printing, and macros (command combinations), as well as most of the more ordinary capabilities of most programs. One problem with Spellbinder: it's possible to delete up to 1024 characters with one keystroke.

Star-Edit

CP/M, 32K or more.
$225.
SuperSoft Associates
Box 1628
Champaign, IL 61820

Star-Edit's split-screen option lets you edit several different files at once. The program does not include a formatter.

Star*Typist

North Star.
$500.
Micro Complex
25651 Minos Street
Mission Viejo, CA 92691

Stylograph

6809 machines.
$135–195, depending on the version.

FLEX version:
Sonex Systems
Box 238
Williamsville, NY 50304

OS-9 version:
Microware
Box 4865
Des Moines, IA 50304

Super Editor

TRS-80.
$100.
Donald R. Shroyer
29 Brinker Street
Latrobe, PA 15650

SuperScribe II

Apple II.
$130 (a spelling checker will be offered soon).
On-Line Systems
36575 Mudge Ranch Road
Coarsegold, CA 93614

For those of you who've forgotten where Coarsegold is, it's right between Fine Gold and Grub Gulch, just up the hill from Irrigosa and Notarb. Ah . . . the life of a programmer! You live out in the woods and rake in the millions — at least if your program is any good (which SuperScribe II seems to be).

It gives you:
- upper- and lowercase characters and 70-character lines on the screen without special hardware.
- printing of one file while editing another.
- a type-ahead buffer.
- access to commonly-used words, phrases, or commands with a single keystroke.
- proportional spacing.
- on-screen help menus.
- automatic hyphenation.

The information from On-Line Systems arrived somewhat late; even so, I wish I'd had time to do a full evaluation on SuperScribe II. As it was, my assistant Dan Donelly looked over the program, and I can give you his conclusions. In general, he felt that SuperScribe II is powerful but somewhat clumsy, particularly because it's often necessary to leave the change/insert mode and go to the command mode to do things.

The manual does a poor job of discussing errors, but otherwise it's written and organized very well. Unfortunately, it's hampered by an index that's not only incomplete, but uses categories so broad that they're virtually useless. The reference card, however, is excellent.

Dan counted 147 commands listed on the reference card but notes that some are duplications of the same function (one command for the insert/change mode, another for the command mode). SuperScribe II can copy and delete blocks of text and make new files out of them. It can also insert new files into the one being edited. Its global editor will search backwards, use wildcards, and store stock phrases in memory.

SuperScribe II has most of the formatting features on my list, including — in addition to the ones listed above — outdents, boldfacing, conditional page, right justification, and on-screen formatting. It also has a (not very crucial) option that, so far as I know, no other program offers — page numbering in Roman numerals.

SuperScript

TRS-80 Model I or III, with Model I Scripsit.
$30 (Model I), $52 (Model III).
Acorn Software Products
634 North Carolina Avenue
Washington, DC 20003

This is an add-on to Scripsit, in much the same way that Pencil Sharpener is an add-on to Electric Pencil. It lets you get a directory or kill a file without having to exit Scripsit and also gives you underlining, boldfacing, subscripting, and superscripting on printers that support those features. Since Acorn didn't answer my letter, that's all I can tell you about SuperScript.

Super-Text II

Apple II.
$150.
Muse Software
330 North Charles Street
Baltimore, MD 21201

Super-Text II offers a split screen, file linking for both global substitutions and at printout, a math mode for statistical reports, and limited on-screen formatting. I wrote for more information but got no response.

SuperVUE

Alpha Micro.
Micro Concepts
731 East Harmony
Fullerton, CA 92631

Micro Concepts eventually sent me a manual, about a month too late, but omitted the whole tutorial section as well as other basic information (like what the program costs). SuperVUE does on-screen formatting, has an integrated spelling checker, generates a table of contents automatically, and lets users create their own commands. The program seems to have a large number of commands.

The manual is somewhat stiff, with unindented paragraphs and extensive section numbering (e.g., "1.4.1.2 Display Mode Status"). But it seems to be reasonably well organized and complete, and the writing itself is clear.

Sword

Exidy Sorcerer.
$35 (on cassette).
Northamerican Software
Box 1173
Station B
Downsview, Ontario, Canada M3H 5V6

Telewriter

TRS-80 Color Computer.
$50 (on cassette).
Cognitec
704 Nob Avenue
Del Mar, CA 92014

This program expands the Color Computer's 16-line-by-32-character display to 24 by 51 and gives you lowercase letters in the bargain. Its editor provides most of the basic commands in my list (beginning and end of file, beginning and end of line, etc.), as well as scrolling, word wrap, block moves, and global substitutions. Its formatter lets you change all four margins, link files, and automatically number pages and center lines.

Tex 2.00

CP/M
$100.
Digital Research
Box 579
801 Lighthouse Avenue
Pacific Grove, CA 93950

This program, from the publishers of CP/M, can generate an index and table of contents, merge print, and do proportional spacing.

Text Wizard

Atari 400 or 800.
$100.
Datasoft
16606 Schoenbron Street
Sepulveda, CA 91343

InfoWorld liked this program a lot, giving it an excellent in all four categories (but bear in mind that their reviews tend to be less critical than mine).

Textform

Digital Deli.
80 West El Camino Real
Mountain View, CA 94040

I wrote this publisher but got no answer, so I can't tell you anything else about this program.

TSC Text Editor and Text Processor

6800 and 6809 machines.
$100.
Technical Systems Consultants
Box 2570
West Lafayette, IN 47906

Type-Righter

Apple III.
$200.
Imagineering
Suite 10
405 South Farwell
Eau Claire, WI 54601

I wrote this publisher for information but go no response.

VEDIT

CP/M.
$100–110 (depending on the version).
CompuView Products
618 Louise
Ann Arbor, MI 48103

Although CompuView sent me a manual (somewhat late), I didn't have time to give their program a full evaluation; however, my assistant Dan Donelly was able to look it over. In general, he felt that their assertion that no other editor approaches VEDIT's ease of use is grossly overstated and that its documentation, rather than being clear and slanted towards beginners (as they claim), is difficult and obscure. Here are some more specific comments:

VEDIT does a better than average job of documenting possible errors. But the manual's style is somewhat formal, almost academic, and is unclear on many points. It's organized more for reference than for training — although it can't be used for reference very well either, since there's no index.

VEDIT functions on two levels — visual mode and command mode. The former is quite easy to learn, the latter much more complex and powerful. The program itself occupies less than 12K. There are 71 basic commands, and many others that are not only not basic, but a little bizarre; for example, you can change every third occurrence of a word (try to think of a situation where you'd want to do that).

VEDIT has a fairly powerful global editor and can move blocks of text by specifying the lines involved. It also has an undo command. But probably VEDIT's strongest feature, and the one CompuView tends to stress, is the ease with which and the extent to which the program can be customized.

The version of VEDIT that we saw is basically a programmer's editor, with virtually no formatting capabilities. According to the publisher, a newer version will contain some ''primitive printing functions'' and ''new features oriented towards word processing and the novice user.'' The manual for this new version will also have a new section ''oriented towards the novice user'' consisting of a series of lessons.

CompuView sent me a list of thirteen satisfied users. Although I wasn't able to call them, the length of the list itself probably indicates that once people learn how to use VEDIT, they tend to like it.

Volkswriter

IBM Personal Computer.
$200.
Lifetree Software
Suite 342
177 Webster Street
Monterey, CA 93940

VTS/80

CP/M.
$550.
National Microsoftware Producers
3169 Fillmore Street
San Francisco, CA 94123

I wrote this publisher but got no answer.

Wang System 5 Model 3, Software Version 3.2

Dedicated word processor.
$11,500 for whole system, including word-processing software and sort program plus free updates.
Wang Laboratories
One Industrial Avenue
Lowell, MA 01851   (sales offices in most cities)

This system demonstrates how quickly the field of word processing develops. Although still in use as I write this, the System 5 — only a few years old — is clearly inferior in its capabilities to many microcomputer word-processing programs now available.

I chose to include the System 5 because a close friend operates one, and thus I knew I could get a good picture of how it works in actual use rather than just in a demonstration. This may be unfair to Wang; the other dedicated word processors might have fared worse in these ratings if I'd had more of an inside view of them.

Safety and error handling

There are several safety features to help you avoid losing text, but, most important, there's also a program that allows you to recover up to a diskful of text lost under various circumstances. Unfortunately, errors are not well documented and error messages could be clearer.

Not only is there no automatic backup of saves, there's not even a duplicate of the workfile on the disk (except for the page you're editing at the moment). When you finish it, it overwrites the equivalent page on disk, thus giving you no previous version to revert to if you change your mind, even if you change it during the very same editing session.

Six points total in this section.

Documentation

The training manual is well organized and complete, but it would be nice to be able to bypass the cassettes (or training session) if you want to. As it is, you can't really understand the manual without them; it just structures the information and supplements it.

The reference manual is not well organized and the index is terrible. These combine to make information pretty hard to find. The writing style is basic manualese. Fortunately, there's an excellent ready reference guide — a booklet with information presented graphically — in addition to the cassettes and training sessions.

The System 5 gets a respectable 14¾ for documentation.

Ease of use

The System 5 can't do boldface, and you can only alter the top margin by padding with blank lines and/or eyeballing how far down into the printer you put the paper. These deficiencies lose it ten keystrokes. But it picks up five for displaying underlining (as such) on the screen. With these penalties and rewards figured in, the total number of keystrokes for the 23-command sequence is 73.

Dedicated keys and the ready reference guide earn the System 5 the full three points for command aids. The program is copyable, but I can't give Wang the full two points for that item because they seem to create some weird mystification around the system disk. My friend who uses the system believed that the one thing you should never do is touch the system disk (until I told her otherwise). She thought that if it failed (due to age or some other reason), you had to call up Wang and have somebody come out and replace it.

Her training sessions somehow left her with the impression she couldn't even remove the system disk when the machine was off, much less make copies of it and pop them in and out as required. The person I spoke to at Wang was surprised at all this and said Wang tells its users that the system disk is copyable. In any case, I take half a point off for the unnecessary confusion.

There's a nice, and unusual, feature: At the same time you find out the size of the file you're editing, you're told how much time you've spent working on it in this particular session. The rest of the items in this category are obvious from the chart. The System 5's total for ease of use is 10¾.

Editing power

You can make a new file out of a block of text and insert another file into the one you're editing, but both processes are clumsy and get only half credit. Editing one file while printing out another is equally maladroit; the printer tends to stop all the time (minus half a point).

The System 5 allows you to set (and return to) one place marker, but much more significant is its glossary capability. By glossary, Wang means either a series of commands you execute simply by typing one coded command, a block of text you insert into a file with one command, or the two combined. This is an extremely powerful and useful feature, and it earns the System 5 the extra point and a half for special editing features.

At their most basic, glossaries allow you to store stock phrases in memory and insert them wherever you want. At their most complex, glossaries can contain long strings of interrelated commands, even including mathematical calculations, sorting, and if/then statements.

The System 5 gets 18 points for editing power.

Formatting power

I subtract a point for not being able to set the top margin. Character spacing is limited to ten pitch, twelve pitch, and proportional spacing (minus a quarter point). Line spacing is limited, but the choices are extensive (minus a quarter point).

The System 5 has a defect I didn't think to ask about in this rating scheme — although there is automatic page numbering, there is no automatic pagination. That is, you must indicate the end of each page yourself, and then the Wang will go back and number them for you (and renumber them each time you print out, if you wish). The System 5 gets the full point and three quarters for page numbering, but deserves to lose some points for not being able to create pages on its own.

There is no boldface on this machine, and overstriking is very clumsy — you need to put the characters you want to overstrike on a separate line, and you need to put a separate format line in front of it that calls for zero vertical space. This must then be followed by another format line that re-establishes line spacing (minus three quarters of a point).

There is on-screen formatting and even on-screen display of underlining (plus half a point), but if you choose proportional spacing, the line breaks won't show on the screen (minus half a point, for a total of two).

Glossaries again help Wang get the extra point and a half, since they can also affect formatting and printing out. For example, you could set up a glossary that closes a file, goes to the print menu, answers all the questions in a certain way, and prints out the file. The System 5 can also do merge printing, doublestriking, and double underlining; its total for formatting power is 17¼.

Responsiveness and support

This is an area in which Wang does significantly less well than other dedicated word processor manufacturers and even less well than many microcomputer software publishers. The *Datapro* reports give the company only 2.9 for maintenance responsiveness and 3.0 for maintenance effectiveness. Troubleshooting is even worse (2.7) and training worse than that (2.5).

These scores are born out by the experience of my friend who runs a Wang. I've already mentioned the mystification around the system disk. She also found some (although not all) of the Wang customer representatives fairly flaky. And there were many things about the machine's operation that her training either didn't teach her or taught her wrong.

I vacillated between giving Wang three and three and a half points in this category (since we're still talking about the level of support you expect on a dedicated word processor, with offices in every major city full of people whose job it is to help you). I finally compromised at three and a quarter points, which gives the System 5 a total score of exactly 70 points.

Wangwriter, Software Version 3.1

Dedicated word processor.
$6400 for whole system with single disk drive (Model 5503A), including word-processing software. CP/M — $200 extra.
Wang Laboratories
One Industrial Avenue
Lowell, MA 01851
(sales offices in most cities)

This system is well documented and reasonably easy to use, but it lacks a lot of features, many of which are promised for the future. One major limitation is the fact that files are limited to fifteen pages and can't be linked together during printout.

Safety and error handling

The Wangwriter has several excellent features to prevent the loss of text. For example, you can't remove a disk at a time when that might cause trouble because at such times the disk is *locked* into the drive; you have to move to another part of the program to unlock the latch on the drive door. And if you somehow manage to lose text, there's a program to recover it.

Errors are very well documented by a series of complete lists in each section of the reference manual, plus an overall index of every error message. The Wangwriter gets eight points in this category.

Documentation

The training manual is excellent and loses only a quarter point because its unindented paragraphs and san serif type make it hard to read. At the time I reviewed the system, the only reference manual available was an interim one. Although it outscored several actual manuals for other systems, the final version is likely to do even better. I had two basic problems with it: The organization is weak, and this problem is complicated by the absence of an index, and by a table of contents that isn't complete enough. (Only the training manual has an index, and even that one needs to be somewhat more complete.) Secondly, there are too many lists and not enough discursive text.

The Wangwriter has on-screen documentation and a reference guide; it could use a reference card or a shorter, more accessible ''ready reference'' like the one furnished for the Wang System 5. Other nice touches are tabs in the training manual and the fact that the manual cover converts into a stand.

The total for documentation is an impressive 16 points.

Ease of use

Since the Wangwriter displays both underlining and double underlining as such on the screen and uses reverse video to show boldface, I subtract eight keystrokes; this gives a total of 74 keystrokes for the 23-command sequence.

Although there are a couple of good help menus, the Wangwriter needs a reference guide or guide to make commands truly easy to remember. It gets 13½ points total for this category.

Editing power

Not only will this system let you insert one file into another, you can mark off just part of another file and insert that. This is helpful when there isn't room in the workspace for the whole file you want to insert text from and the work file together.

You can ask the global editor to prompt you as you go through a global substitution, and this earns Wangwriter the extra quarter point for special global capabilities. The extra point and a half for special editing features are earned by glossaries (explained under Wang System 5 above) and the unusual ability to edit a file while printing it (you can, of course, also edit a different file from the one you're printing out).

The total for editing power is 18¾.

Formatting power

As with the System 5, there's no way to set the top margin directly (minus a point). Character spacing is limited to 10, 12, or 15 pitch, although proportional spacing is promised for future versions. Lines can be up to 158 characters wide.

There's automatic overstriking with slashes, but if you want to overstrike with any other character, you have to use the clumsy, separate-format-line procedure described above for the System 5. Subscripts and superscripts, on the other hand, are quite convenient.

The Wangwriter insists on stopping printout after each page; if you want to use continuous form paper (which the printer isn't really set up to handle), you'll still have to give a separate command from the keyboard for each page.

The screen will display line breaks and page breaks (although you have to insert the latter yourself), centering, subscripts and superscripts, underlining, double underlining, and boldfacing (in reverse video). The extra point and a half for special features is earned by the following capabilities: removing all control symbols so you can get an idea of what the printed text will look like, printing out a directory of the files on a disk, centering text within columns, and preattaching glossaries so you don't have to manually do that each editing session.

The total for formatting power is 14½.

Responsiveness and support

See this section under the System 5 description above for the reasons why Wang gets three and one quarter points in this category. The Wangwriter's total score is 74.

Wordcraft-80

Commodore PET.
$400.
Commodore/MOS Technology
950 Rittenhouse Road
Norristown, PA 19401

I wrote this publisher but got no answer.

Word IV

TRS-80
$50
Micro Architect
96 Dothan Street
Arlington, VA 02174

Word Handler II

Apple II.
$250.
Silcon Valley Systems
1625 El Camino Real, #4
Belmont, CA 94002

Instead of providing useful information on their handout, SVS makes statements like "the *only* word processor in the world [where else?] for the Apple that gives you full line capability on the screen, no boards necessary" — which isn't true.

Word Juggler

Apple III.
$300
Quark Engineering
Suite 1102
1433 Williams
Denver, CO 80218

Quark Engineering responded promptly and fully to my request for information but indicated that Word Juggler was to be replaced with a "much more comprehensive" program shortly after my deadline for finishing this book. For that reason, and because of time restraints, I didn't give this incarnation of Word Juggler a full evaluation. But Dan Donelly did read through the manual, and so I can tell you something about the program.

Word Juggler takes advantage of the fact that it only runs on one kind of machine and provides you with a template that fits over the Apple III's keyboard; this is a very efficient way to remind you what the various commands are. The program has many basic editing and formatting features: block moves, search and replace, boldface, overstriking, subscripts and superscripts, delete word, delete to end of line, delete to end of paragraph, etc. It's also missing some, like continuous underlining.

Word Juggler could protect your text better — attempting to access a non-existent drive (which you could easily do if, for example, you accidentally hit V instead of B) "locks you up beyond all hope of salvation." At least Quark warns you about it. Error messages are also listed.

The manual is sometimes confusing to a beginning user. The training section is in the form of lessons, which can be annoying if you want to move ahead faster than the lessons do. The reference section, which lists some terms and functions in no apparent order, could be more complete. The index is clear but somewhat skimpy.

Word Juggler's promotional flyer lists 67 commands. The new version (available as an upgrade to current Word Juggler users at less than the full price) will incorporate merge printing and a spelling checker.

Word/Magic II

TRS-80 Model II with 64K.
$200.
Data Strategies
Box 28726
San Diego, CA 92128

This program is written in BASIC, so it can be modified by the user. In addition to automatic headers and footers and automatic page numbering, Word/Magic II can generate a table of contents and do merge printing.

Word/125

HP-125.
Hewlett-Packard
19410 Homestead Road
Cupertino, CA 94014

This is a version of Spellbinder published by Hewlett-Packard especially for their HP-125 system. Since HP didn't answer my request for information about this program or about their hardware, see **Spellbinder** for more information.

WordPro 4-Plus

Commodore CBM 8032.
$450.
Professional Software
166 Crescent Road
Needham, MA 02194

Also available are WordPro 1 (for the PET), WordPro 2-Plus (for a 16K or 32K CBM), and Word Pro 3-Plus (for the 32K CBM).

This publisher sent me their manual and a bunch of other stuff, but unfortunately it arrived too late for me to be able to do a full evaluation. From glancing at the documentation, it seems that WordPro 4-Plus has many of the features listed on my 100-point scale. The manual itself is clear and readable, although it suffers from long, unindented paragraphs. Unfortunately, its index is nowhere near detailed enough — it's shorter than the table of contents.

The manual is supplemented by the best reference card I've ever seen. It sticks to the top of your keyboard and flips to eight different pages, all labelled and numbered with each label visible. (All it needs is a marker at the center so you can get back there easily.) There's also a set of stickers that go on the front of the keys, as added reminders.

WordPro 4-Plus is available from about 500 Commodore dealers across the country.

Wordsmith

CP/M.
$400.
Scion
8455-D Tyco Road
Vienna, VA 22180

I wrote this publisher but got no answer.

WordStar Version 3.0

CP/M, including Apple II with SoftCard and IBM Personal Computer.
$500 ($375 for Apple version).
MicroPro International
33 San Pablo Drive
San Rafael, CA 94901
(plus more than 1200 dealers word-wide)

Related programs available from same publisher:
MailMerge (merge-print program) — $150.
SpellStar (spelling checker) — $250.
Wordmaster (text editor for programmers) — $150.
DataStar (data entry and retrieval program) — $350.
SuperSort (sort program) — $250.
CalcStar (MicroPro's imitation of VisiCalc) — $300.
InfoStar (report generator) — price to be determined.

I think of WordStar as the Cadillac of word-processing programs — big, solid, with just about every feature you could dream up, from Magic Fingers in the driver's seat to automatic climate control in the trunk. Or maybe it's the Winnebago of word-processing systems, with a waterbed, a bar, and a color TV. In either case, it shares one not-so-great quality with those two vehicles — it's clumsy and hard to maneuver.

There's a wonderful programming term — **kluge.** To kluge a problem is to patch it up locally rather than going back, finding the root of the problem, and correcting it in a way that makes the whole design clean and elegant.

Some programs end up being nothing but one giant kluge — thousands of Rube Goldberg straps and ropes holding things together without any overall unifying concept (or even a dozen). In my opinion, WordStar is such a program. I guess that whenever a user requested a feature and MicroPro thought it made sense to have it, they just slapped it on somewhere. This makes for a lot of features — and a lot of confusion.

As a result, using WordStar is sort of like going on a backpacking trip with someone who brings along 200 pounds of equipment because ''you never know when you might need this . . . or this . . . or this . . . or this . . . .''

But enough of my subjective blathering. WordStar is the most popular word-processing program ever published, and that's because it can do so many different things. Its fans figure that they can eventually learn to use any word-processing program, no matter how complex, and they're willing to invest the time and effort required to learn WordStar in order to have the capabilities they want later on.

On the whole, WordStar works well. In fact, it's one of the most thoroughly debugged programs you can buy.

Here are some detailed comments on WordStar and explanations of its scores on my 100-point evaluation scale.

Safety and error handling

There are at least six ways WordStar can lose text:
1) A disk-full error can occur for many reasons, the simplest of which is trying to save a file there isn't room for on the disk. Disk-full errors don't occur very frequently and normally they aren't hard to recover from, but they can be if the error is severe enough.
2) You can delete a block of text up to the size of the entire file (with ^KY) without being asked, ''Are you sure you want to do that?'' It's true that you can protect a block by hiding the block markers with ^KH, but this is a clumsy procedure and involves losing track of the actual boundaries of the block.
3) Moving backwards in a long file can give you a disk-full error (see #1 above).

4) Changing disks anywhere but at the no-file menu can result in the destruction of existing files.
5) You can lose keystrokes typed after a ''disk wait'' message comes on the screen.
6) If you try to save more files than the number allowed (usually 64), you'll get a directory-full error, which is fatal. Fortunately, you usually run out of space before you run out of directory names.

A program with six ways to lose text would normally be penalized severely, but I know many experienced users of WordStar who say that they have never had a problem with any of them. (In fact, none of the WordStar users I've interviewed has complained about losing text.) I had a lot of problems with severe disk-full errors I couldn't recover from using an earlier version of WordStar on an Apple, but I'm told that's been fixed.

Even if experienced users can steer clear of all six ways to lost text, they still represent far too many pitfalls for the beginning user. I give WordStar two points on ''how hard is it to lose text?'' (and consider that generous).

All these errors are well documented, once you find the place they're discussed. But since the warnings tend to get lost in the labyrinth of WordStar manuals, and since there's no index to help you find them, I subtract another half a point here.

WordStar gets full credit for all of the other error-handling items, making a total of seven and a half points.

Documentation

An earlier version of the WordStar manual was the first microcomputer word-processing documentation I ever read. (This was back a couple of years ago when I knew nothing about the field.) Masochistically I spent a weekend ploughing through all 200 disorganized, poorly written pages of it, and, when I had finished, I vowed I would never use WordStar if I could help it.

WordStar's documentation has improved considerably since then; now, for example, there's even a training manual. But it's still too long, too repetitive, and too stuffy.

The training manual is the better of the two, but still not terrific. It's pretty well organized but loses half a point for not being presented in a more straightforward way, instead of walking you through one tedious exercise after another. The manual loses one point for readability — it's a little stiff in places, and the practice of numbering each step is distracting and annoying. It gets full credit for completeness.

The reference manual is very complete in the sense that every topic's in it. But sometimes parts of explanations are missing, and not all the questions that are likely to come up in a user's mind get answered. I take off half a point here.

The Version 3.0 reference manual is much better organized than earlier ones, but it still repeats lots of information. It tends to give you an overview of a topic, then a more detailed explanation of it later on, and sometimes even goes over the same points in a third place; maybe ten percent of the information presented on each successive level is new and the rest is simply repeated. It's as if you're reading an outline rather than a reference book. Minus one point.

The writing in the reference manual varies in quality; at some points, it's even quite good. But on the average, it's mediocre. Taken as a whole, the reference manual can't be given more than one point out of two for comprehensibility.

Amazingly, despite the great size and number of WordStar manuals, only the installation manual has an index. Although the reference card refers you to sections of the reference manual, it's not in alphabetical order and only lists commands. The various tables of contents, although extensive, are also not in alphabetical order and only list general topics. I give a quarter point total for both these pseudo-indexes; a real index is badly needed.

The manuals are neither typeset nor proportionally spaced, the printing is splotchy, and the paragraphs aren't indented. There are a lot of subheads and charts, but the overall effect is intimidating and discouraging. Half a point for layout and design.

WordStar's reference card, key top stickers, help menus, and ^J on-screen explanations gain it full credit for special kinds of documentation, making a total of 11¾ for this category.

Ease of use

WordStar swaps its workfile on and off disk. Its performance on the 23-command sequence was better than average.

It doesn't take any extra keystrokes to open a WordStar file, because instead of typing >ws RETURN, you type >ws {FILENAME} RETURN (the filename is free this first time). ^OC centers a line, and ^PB ^PS at the beginning and end of it will underline and boldface it. This gives 12½ keystrokes for the first four items. RETURN skips lines and ends paragraphs and TAB indents five spaces, so items 5–9 take another five strokes.

To force a page break, you need .PA on a line of its own: .PA RETURN–four strokes. Margins require 15 keystrokes: ^OL {NUMBER} RETURN, ^OR {NUMBER} RETURN, .MT {NUMBER} RETURN, and .MB {NUMBER} RETURN (the numbers don't count). Doublespacing takes three and a half strokes — ^OS RETURN. Saving the file takes two and a half — ^KD.

Printing the file takes four and a half keystrokes: P ^R RETURN ESC. P stops the printout, and D ^R RETURN puts you back in the text — another three and a half strokes. (^R recalls the name of the last file edited, which saves many keystrokes.)

^T deletes a word, and ^Y a line (three strokes). Saving the new version takes six and a half more — ^QR ^B ^KD, and to begin printing it out again takes another four and a half — P ^R RETURN ESC. (Here ^R recalls the name of the last file printed.)

That makes an impressive total of just 64½ keystrokes, for four points.

The reference card, key tops, cursor diamond, menus, and limited mnemonics all help the WordStar user remember commands, but in actual practice, there is such a bewildering number of (mostly two-character) commands that it takes a long time to learn even the ones you use most often. What WordStar lacks is a logical command structure, and that's a hard thing to make up for. I give WordStar two points out of three on this item.

WordStar tells you what page of a file you're editing but not what percentage of it is behind you. You can find out its size (by moving to the end and changing the status line to show total number of characters), but it takes more than three keystrokes. So WordStar gets one point out of a possible one and a half.

Although the total size of WordStar is 78K (WS.COM — 16K, WSMSGS.OVR — 28K, WSOVLY1.OVR — 34K), it only occupies 25K or so of RAM at any one time. So I give it half a point. All three files must be on the disk for the program to work. WordStar is constantly going to the disk to access its overlay files, and that's one of the reasons it's such a slow program to use.

You can't rename the workfile, but you can rename and delete other files while editing it. The directory doesn't give you the size of files, nor can you ask for just part of it.

WordStar gets a total of 13 points for ease of use.

Editing power

WordStar's reference card lists "only" 157 commands (not counting those for MailMerge and SpellStar). But this doesn't include: answers to option questions when you're printing; any of the commands to call up various on-screen explanations (it just lists ^J, not the second letters); the numbers for the various help levels (i.e., ^JH1, ^JH2, etc.); the answers to choices given by various command displays (e.g., LA and LB are separate commands); etc. etc. etc. WordStar clearly has well over 200 commands, if you count every option it offers you.

WordStar has one-stroke (or one-control-character) commands for the following functions: forward one word (^F), back one word (^A), delete one word (^T), delete one line (^Y), and switch between insert and writeover mode (^V). These gain it three points. It has two-stroke commands for end of line (^QD), beginning of line (^QS), top of screen (^QE), bottom of screen (^QX), beginning of file (^QR), and end of file (^QC). At half credit, these earn it another point and a half, for a total of four and a half points for ease and power of basic commands.

WordStar uses scrolling, rather than calling up pages by number, to travel long distances through the text. The speed is variable if you use ^QQ. It can do all the block and global operations I look for, except for storing stock phrases in memory and substitutions that affect more than one file. It has all kinds of other global capabilities than earn it the last quarter point.

There's a command to move the cursor to where it was before the last command was executed — and it's needed, because whenever you save the file the cursor is moved to the beginning of it. You can edit one file while printing another, but things are slowed down (how much depends on the hardware).

WordStar has lots of other editing features: ten numbered place markers, the ability to run another program without having to exit WordStar, commands to move up and down a screenful, a one-stroke command to make the same global search or replacement again, etc. It gets the full point and a half for that item, which makes an impressive total of 22 points for editing power.

Formatting power

WordStar gets all the points for margins, spacing, tabs, and indents. It can also outdent (with ^OG). It gets all the points for automatic page numbering, headers, and footers. Horizontal scrolling, no-fill mode, and no (practical) limit on line length make it a good program to use with tables and especially wide text. WordStar can boldface, overstrike, underline continuously, and center lines automatically. It also features subscripts and superscripts.

So far we're batting a thousand; eleven points and not a feature it doesn't have. But all good things must end. Like most word-processing programs, WordStar can't produce automatic two-column printouts. Nor will it let you link files or print out multiple copies of the same file, unless you have MailMerge. (If you get WordStar, I definitely recommend getting MailMerge to go with it.)

You have a choice of single-page or continuous printout; you can embed a stop-and-wait command, and the print options let you specify the page number your printout begins and ends at. (This means you can't begin in the middle of a page, but how often do you want to do that?) You can justify the right margin, but there's no proportional spacing. WordStar shows line breaks, page breaks, and centering on the screen, and its print-to-disk feature earns it the extra half point.

WordStar has an automatic hyphenation feature that offers you lots of choices (including turning it off). In normal operation it finds words that should be hyphenated and guesses where the best place to put the hyphen is. You can OK its decision or move the hyphen elsewhere.

The normal on-screen formatting features are provided, plus the ability to display a full page (on a screen that's capable of it). WordStar can also show right justification thanks to the ^OD command, which suppresses the display of control characters. So the program gets four points for on-screen formatting.

WordStar has all the other features listed except instant print. In addition, it lets you release the margins (just like on a typewriter). You can embed commands to change the character spacing (from pica to elite, for example) or the ribbon color (from black to red, for example). There's a single command to overprint a whole line and also to dash out any amount of text with hyphens. There are even four printer commands you can assign functions to yourself.

All this earns WordStar the full point and a half for other formatting features and gives it an impressive total of 22 for formatting power.

Publisher support

I've had some trouble getting information out of MicroPro, and so have some other people I know. But none of us are dealers and, as Jennifer Rowe, the head of MicroPro's customer support department, points out, dealers are the people end users should go to with their questions. For one thing that's what the dealer's markup is for, and, for another, dealers need to learn the answers to the questions themselves, for the next user who asks them.

''Customer'' support at MicroPro refers to their own direct customers — i.e., dealers — and Jennifer assures me that dealers get great service on their questions. I believe it, too. When I finally got to talk to Jennifer herself — I happened to call on a day when no one else was in — I was impressed with how much she knew about WordStar. I'd be impressed by anyone who knew that much about *anything*.

In addition to supporting their dealers, MicroPro has continually improved their product and come out with other programs to complement it. So I give WordStar a full four points for support, in spite of my own bad experiences on the phone with the MicroPro bureaucracy. This gives WordStar a total of 80 points overall.

Word III

Apple III with SOS and at least 96K of RAM.
$200.
System Decisions Group
149 Rowayton Avenue
Rowayton, CT 06853

InfoWorld reviewed this program and didn't like it much — good for documentation, only fair for performance and ease of use, and poor for error handling (confusing error messages, easy loss of text, frequent crashes). Personally, I don't want anything to do with a program that's even a little bit unsafe, regardless of what other virtues it might have.

Word Worker

Apple II, PET, TRS-80, IBM PC (disks and cassettes available); most other machines (if you type in the listing yourself from the book).
$30 (disk or cassette); $28 (hardbound book); $20 (paperbound book).
Design Enterprises of San Francisco
Box 14695
San Francisco, CA 94114

This program is written in BASIC and will therefore run on virtually any machine. The publisher will provide disks and cassettes for the most common machines; if you have a different one, you can type the program into it from the listing in the book. Word Worker is designed to be easily and extensively modified by the user; the book explains how to do that. There's also an appendix which gives you the conversion codes for the most common typesetting machines so you can adapt the program to interface with them.

This is a line-oriented editor, which means that you see only one line of text on the screen at a time; you can't move the cursor around the screen. This is, of course, a major drawback; what you get to compensate for it is a very powerful program (which uses ten overlays to give you graphics, charts, automatic suppression of widows and orphans, proportional spacing, and two-way communications capabilities) at a very low price.

The program is very user-friendly and has been tested for several years; more than one book has been written *and typeset* using it.

Wp

Alpha Micro
Bob Toxen Computer Systems
2319 De La Cruz
Santa Clara, CA 95050

I wrote for information on this program but got no response.

WpDaisy

CP/M and I/OS (InfoSoft Operating System).
$500–600 (with I/OS).
InfoSoft
25 Sylvan Road South
Westport, CT 06880

WpDaisy bills itself as "the WORD PROCESSOR designed with YOUR secretary in mind." Even aside from the question of how InfoSoft got to know YOUR secretary well enough to design a program for her (or him), this does seem to leave those of us who want to use the word processor *ourselves* out in the cold.

Although InfoSoft sent me a copy of their manual and got it to me on time, they omitted other information I asked for, like the names of satisfied users or even the price of the program (I had to get it from a newspaper article). Nevertheless, I had Dan Donelly look through the manual, and he came to the following conclusions:

WpDaisy can do many things, but almost anything it does takes a lot of keystrokes. The manual is physically hard to read; the bottom right corner is missing from many letters and all the text is too faint. Unindented paragraphs and frequent lists don't help things.

The writing itself is pretty clear, and for training a new user the manual is not bad. But it's virtually useless as a reference. For one thing, there's no index (although the table of contents is extensive). For another, the sections that are supposed to cover the material in greater detail typically add little, or nothing, to what has already been said, and occasionally even omit information included the first time around. There is, however, a decent reference card, which lists 127 commands.

Most of the commands are fairly involved. For example, to move forward one word, you hit ESC, shift W, and RETURN (which is bound to be harder than just moving over character by character).

WpDaisy does block moves; in fact, there are 26 separate buffers to store text in. The global editor allows you to use wildcards. WpDaisy also has most of the formatting features on my list.

WPS-78

Dedicated word processor.
Digital Equipment Corporation
Merrimack, NH 03054
(sales offices in most cities)

I wrote DEC asking for detailed information on their word processors, but they just sent me brochures.

WP-730.4

TRS-80.
$35 (cassette).
GB Associates
Box 3322
Granada Hills, CA 91344

WP 6502

Ohio Scientific.
$100–250, depending on the version; $50 on cassette.
Dwo Quong Fok Lok Sow
23 East 20th Street
New York, NY 10003

WRITE, Version 1.4 (pre-release)

CP/M.
$400.
Ashton-Tate
9929 West Jefferson Boulevard
Culver City, CA 90230

I've used this program for well over a year and, despite the fact that it was still in the development and debugging stage (I was beta-testing it, in effect), I found it to be extremely well thought out, easy to use, and powerful. There aren't too many word-processing programs you can write four books on while they're being developed, or that are fully functioning — better than most of the competition, in fact — two years before they're released.

The version of WRITE that is finally released (2.0) will be a much more powerful program than version 1.4, which I review here. Still, 1.4 did pretty well for itself.

Tony Pietsch, WRITE's author, impresses me as being very dedicated to thinking about what users need and want and also very good at figuring out ways to meet those needs. He's particularly sensitive to the issues of safety and ease of use.

Safety and error handling

If you try to delete a file, WRITE asks you if you're sure you want to do that. If you try to delete a block of text, WRITE asks you if you're sure you want to do that. In fact, if you do anything that would destroy more than a line of text, WRITE asks you if you're sure you want to do that.

If you try to save a file to a disk there's no more room in, WRITE tells you there's no more room and puts you right back where you were with nothing changed. As you approach the maximum file size, the screen blanks except for the words "WARNING! APPROACHING INSUFFICIENT SPACE." But there's nothing to fear, because if you keep going right up to the limit (as I did, to test it), WRITE stops you from continuing. Each keystroke blanks the screen, flashes the message "INSUFFICIENT SPACE," and puts you back in the text with your file intact.

About the only way you can provoke a fatal error is by trying to save more files than are allowed on the disk, and even then, WRITE usually protects you from it. (This kind of "directory error" is very hard to prevent totally in a CP/M program because CP/M has no way of counting the number of files on a disk.)

But even if you do get a fatal error, you *still* don't lose text. You just call up a program called SAVETXT; it finds any text that's in memory and saves it (when a program crashes, it doesn't actually erase the text; it just makes it hard to find again). Then you re-enter WRITE, load the file named SAVE.TXT, and you're in business again.

I could go on with examples all day, but the point is simple: If you can outsmart WRITE's error handling capabilities, you're smarter than I am.

WRITE's errors are fully documented in both the reference and training manuals, and the error messages are clear. All saves are fully verified character for character, and backup copies are automatic. CP/M freaks out when you switch disks on it, but WRITE couldn't care less. You can save to either disk you have in, or to any other one you put in. You don't even have to notify WRITE that you've changed disks.

There are all kinds of other safety features WRITE has that I don't have listed on my checklist (like the ability to keep reading or writing a file that has garbage in it, so you can salvage the part of the file that isn't garbage). WRITE gets a perfect ten for safety and error handling (and probably deserves a fifteen).

Documentation

I wrote the first version of the WRITE training manual, and I put a *lot* of time and effort into making it the way I wished other training manuals had been. I spent more time revising and reorganizing it than most companies spend writing theirs. If it doesn't deserve the full seven points, I don't know what does.

I wrote parts of the reference manual too, but mostly it's the work of Tony Pietsch. His writing can be a little stuffy, but it's always clear and *very* thorough. The reference manual is well organized and complete. It also gets the full seven points.

The manuals hadn't been published in their final form at the point when this was written, so I had to assume that they would neither be typeset nor proportionally spaced. The layout of both is intelligent (half point); I assumed that the design would be average (quarter point). Since Tony is writing an integral indexer for WRITE, and since that program will be used to make the indexes for the manuals, I assume that they will be fairly good (three quarters of a point).

Ashton-Tate may come up with some special kinds of documentation other than the manuals, but at this point there aren't any. So WRITE gets 15½ points for documentation and might earn more by the time the program is released.

Ease of use

WRITE keeps the workfile completely in memory. It does very well on the 23-command sequence.

Opening a file takes three and a half keystrokes (^K O {FILENAME} RETURN). .ce (RETURN) on the line before the title centers it (four strokes). A vertical line and an underline at the beginning of the title boldface and underline it (two strokes), and they're turned off automatically by the line break at the end. This is a great feature that not only saves a few keystrokes but also prevents pages and pages of printout from being boldfaced or underlined when you accidentally forget to turn one of those features off.

The LINE FEED key skips lines and ends paragraphs, and TAB indents five spaces, so items 5–9 take five strokes. ^L forces a page break (1½). The margins and line spacing changes take 13½ strokes — ^P TM {NUMBER} BM {NUMBER} LM {NUMBER} RM {NUMBER} VS {NUMBER} RETURN (the numbers themselves don't count, of course) — and saving the file takes another three and a half — ^K S RETURN.

^P PC RETURN prints out the file and ESC (the escape key — one stroke) will stop it and return you to the the text (five and a half strokes). ^T kills a word and ^Y a line (three strokes). ^B ^K S RETURN saves the new version (the backup is automatic) and ^P PC RETURN restarts the printout. These last nine and a half strokes make a total of 51, for five points on this item.

WRITE has a very logical command structure and a series of very clear and informative menus. The basic cursor movement keys are in a diamond and mnemonics are used in a limited way. About the only things WRITE is lacking are key tops or dedicated keys, so it gets two and a half points.

WRITE uses the ESC key in a helpful way. It serves as a "panic button," stopping virtually any command that's executing and returning you to the text. When you're already in the text, it takes you to the main menu and back again. So if you forgot a command, you just hit ESC, find it on the menu, and hit ESC again. The cursor stays in place. (Actually, the main menu is a series of three menus that you move between with the spacebar. So, at most, you have to hit ESC, SPACEBAR, SPACEBAR to find the command you're looking for.)

Keeping the main menu off the screen while you're editing gives you more room for your text and allows the writing on the screen to be larger. Yet ESC makes the menu quite accessible. (This is all by way of saying that WRITE gets the half point for keeping the menu off the screen.)

There's no way to know what page you're on or how much of the file you're through. ^K shows you the size of your file, and ESC puts you back in the text (two and a half strokes).

One of the most amazing things about WRITE is the small size of the program, given all the things it can do. In this version (1.4), everything — editor, formatter, an extensive global editor, and many internal disk operations — takes up only 18K. This means I can put WRITE along with the text on every disk; I don't have to load it in with a program disk and then replace the program disk with a text disk if I want to be able to save to either disk. Another nice thing about WRITE's small size is that it leaves me a workspace of 37K to put text in.

The directory gives you the size of each file in K, and you can ask to see different parts of it. You can also see the directory of the other disk and still stay logged on to the one you're on. The type-ahead buffer is completely adequate. This version of the program runs only on memory-mapped systems, but the next version will also run on terminals.

WRITE gets an outstanding total of 16¾ for ease of use.

Editing power

WRITE offers a total of 139 commands and choices, which earns it three points. It performs all the basic commands with one control character, except for two:

RETURN takes you to the beginning of the line, or to the end of the line if you're already at the beginning of the line — so you normally have to hit RETURN twice to get to the end of the line (the LINE FEED key does what the carriage return does on a typewriter, i.e., moves you to the beginning of the *next* line).

^Q takes you to the top of the screen. If you're already there, it takes you to the bottom of the screen, so normally you have to hit it twice to get to the bottom of the screen.

So WRITE gets five and a half points for this item.

WRITE uses scrolling to travel long distances through the text. It give you ten different speeds to choose from and also lets you scroll line by line.

WRITE can do all of the block operations except move a block (you have to copy it and then delete it). It can do all of the global operations except search for whole words only and store stock phrases in memory. And it can do a whole lot more — WRITE's global editor has some unusual features:

In addition to having all your substitutions made at once or approving each one, you can see them as they're made without having to approve them, choose how long WRITE lingers at each substitution, and change that rate while the process is going on. You can use three different kinds of wildcards in your search string, make bulk insertions, or put strings of commands in repeating loops. You can combine commands into chains up to 128 characters.

The second level of WRITE's global editor is so powerful it virtually amounts to a programming language. It not only earns WRITE the extra quarter point for special global capabilities, but also contributes under special editing features. With the addition of keeping the cursor in place during a save and multiple user directories under CP/M 2.2, WRITE gets a total of one point on that item, which makes for 19 points total.

Formatting power

WRITE doesn't have decimal tabs or horizontal scrolling. It can't overstrike or produce two-column printouts automatically. It can only link files by embedding a link line at the end of each file, not by specifying their names when the print command is given. It doesn't have proportional spacing, on-screen formatting, no-break spaces, or automatic hyphenation, but it does let you insert conditional hyphens yourself.

Everything else listed under this category, WRITE can do, as well as a few things that aren't listed. For example, when it's justifying the right margin, WRITE will not only space lines out, but also compact them slightly. These compacted lines look good and cut down on the number of overly spaced-out ones.

WRITE can display a line at the bottom of the screen to show you where your tabs are. You can also vary the right margin of the screen display. These three abilities earn WRITE the extra point and a half for special formatting features.

In the near future, WRITE will incorporate an overlay to let you do on-screen formatting, will hook up with a spelling checker, and will feature an extremely powerful and useful automatic hyphenation program. For the time being, however, WRITE gets a total of 17½ points for formatting power.

Publisher support

Tony Pietsch has always been very responsive to my questions and problems, and improving the product is almost an obsession with him. And Ashton-Tate has a good reputation for the support they've provided users of another program they publish, dBASE II. But I met someone who really got the run-around from them on some problems he had with dBASE II. Although this is only one person, I have to take half a point away from WRITE in this category.

This gives WRITE an impressive overall score of 82¼.

Writemaster Version X.YY

Cromemco
280 Bernardo Avenue
Mountain View, CA 94043

This is Cromemco's own word-processing program for the microcomputers they manufacture. It can generate an index, merge print, check spelling, and scroll *or* move to a specified page, as well as perform more common functions like block moves, search and replace, right justification, automatic page numbering, etc. It also has on-screen formatting and extensive help menus.

Cromemco responded to my letter too late for me to give Writemaster a full evaluation, but I was able to look through the manual they sent. It has a pretty good index (although there are terms missing from it).

Despite unindented paragraphs and excessive use of numbered lists, the manual is reasonably well organized and readable. Unfortunately, it tends to walk you through lessons rather than just tell you how things are done.

There's a quick reference section before each chapter which summarizes the commands to be covered. This is quite useful, but a separate reference card is also needed.

My general impression of Writemaster is that it's a professionally designed word-processing program with a lot of features. But there's room for improvement. For example, here's how you could delete a whole file with a one-keystroke mistake:

To pull a word out of the index, you type ESC di RETURN. To delete a block of text, you type ESC ds RETURN. To delete underlining, you type ESC du RETURN. But let's say you get mixed up and instead you hit ESC db RETURN, or ESC dc RETURN. Those commands delete all of the file from the cursor to the end, or from the beginning to the cursor, respectively. Depending on where the cursor is, this could amount to a lot of text. Both these commands should generate a safety ("Are you sure?") question. (There is a way to recover lost text, but only if you do it immediately.)

Write-On

Apple II and III, IBM Personal Computer.
$130.
Datamost
9748 Cozycroft Avenue
Chatsworth, CA 91311

Writer's Companion

CP/M, CP/M-86, TRS-80, IBM Personal Computer.
$130–180, depending on the version.
Aspen Software
Box 339-W
Tijeras, NM 87059

This company also makes a spelling checker called Proofreader ($60–130) and a program that not only catches things like repeated words (''the the''), but even tries to help correct poor style! (by looking for 500 commonly-misused phrases writing manuals warn against). It's called Grammatik and costs $60–150.

Zardax

Apple II.
$300.
Action-Research Northwest
11442 Marine View Drive S. W.
Seattle, WA 98146

This program, from Computer Solutions of Australia, lets you insert stock phrases with a coded command and has an integrated merge-print capability. *InfoWorld* gave it an excellent in all categories except error handling, where it was rated good. The program is not copyable; you get two disks and additional ones cost $20 each.

7

Other Kinds of Programs

For the first nine months I owned my computer, I used it exclusively as a word processor. Then I needed to do a mailing list. Thanks to having a choice of several programs, I was able to find an adequate one at a good price, and I typed in the information for a thousand labels in about half the time it would have taken me to do it on a typewriter (because the program prompted me for each item and told me when I made a wrong entry, like a four-number zip code, and because it's much easier to correct mistakes on a computer than on a typewriter).

Then I used the program to sort the labels, so I could eliminate duplicates and quickly check whether I had forgotten anybody. Doing that took a tenth the time it would without a computer. (Printing out the labels took virtually no time or effort at all, of course.)

Now I have all those names stored on disk, so I can produce another thousand labels (or just those for specific zip codes, or for journalists, or for childhood friends) in a hundredth the time it would otherwise take.

The point — which I've made several times before — is simply this: since a word processor is a computer, it makes sense to use it as one. How well you can do that depends on what other programs run on it. Some of these programs — games, data base managers, programming languages, spreadsheets and other forecasting tools, tax programs, accounting programs, mailing list managers, and sort programs — are beyond the scope of this book and I won't discuss them, except to say that if your word processor's operating system supports a wide variety of software, they'll be available to you, and if it doesn't, they won't.

There are other programs, however, that relate more closely to word processing, and these fall into three main categories: spelling checkers, which proof text to catch spelling errors and typos; merge-print programs, which let you produce customized computer letters; and indexing programs, which automatically generate an index and table of contents. There's a fourth kind of program which provides a series of commands that are easier to understand than the ones offered by your operating system (typically, CP/M); I call this a substitute menu program.

I'll describe each of these four types of software below, as well as a couple of other more minor categories. Be aware that I'm describing model programs. Actual programs may do more than what I describe or — more likely — less; they may be easier to use or — more likely — harder. I'm only trying to give you a basic idea of the job each kind of program is designed to do.

Spelling checkers (also called **proofing programs**) go through a file and compare every word in it to a list, which is called their **dictionary**. If a word in the file can't be matched up with an identical word in the dictionary, it gets flagged and presented to you for your consideration. Then you can:

1) Add the word to the spelling checker's dictionary, so that it can be matched up (and therefore ignored) the next time it comes up. You want to do this for words you use fairly frequently.
2) Correct the word if it's misspelled or a typo.
3) Skip over the word, neither changing it nor adding it to the dictionary. You do this with infrequently used words you don't want to clog up your dictionary with — since there's a limit to how big the dictionary can be (and since the larger it is, the longer it takes the program to check a file).

There are lots of fine spelling correction programs available; for example, there are at least five that run under CP/M — **The Word**, from Oasis Systems of San Diego; **Spellguard**, from Innovative Software of Menlo Park, California; **Wordsearch**, from Keybits Inc. of Miami; **Microspell**, from Lifeboat Associates of New York City; and **Microproof**, from Cornucopia Software of Walnut Creek, California.

In addition, some word-processing programs — like Select — come with a built-in spelling checker, and others — like Magic Wand and WordStar — offer separate, but integrated, proofing programs.

A similar sort of program — and a rare one — is an **automatic hyphenator**. Many word processing programs are able to go through a file and find words that need hyphenating (because if they get moved down to the next line during printout, there'll be a big gap at the end of the line they're on now). Some programs will even guess where the hyphen should go. But I'm talking about something a lot more foolproof — a **hyphenation dictionary**.

This is a large list — like a spelling checker's dictionary — composed entirely of words more than nine or ten letters long. Each word on the list has **conditional hyphens** inserted between each syllable. (A conditional hyphen is one that breaks the word it's in — and becomes visible — only when it falls at the end of a line; when it ends up anywhere else in the text, it leaves the word in one piece and stays invisible.)

An automatic hyphenator goes through a file and, when it finds any word that's on the list, puts conditional hyphens in it. Thus, when the file is printed out, every long word in it is automatically hyphenated whenever it needs to be.

There is also at least one **thesaurus program** (from Refware, of Chappaqua, New York; it runs on TRS-80s). You type in a word, and it gives you from nine to 45 synonyms for it.

Merge-print programs (sometimes called **mail-merge programs, form-letter generators,** or **repetitive-document generators**) save you the effort of retyping, over and over and over again, hunks of text that get repeated in many similar (but not identical) documents. The most common uses of a merge-print program are:

- Personalized form letters (you've seen them: ''so, MRS. ARTHUR NAIMAN of OAKLAND, CALIFORNIA, you may have won $100,000,000.00!!!, tax-free!, every month for the rest of your life'').
- Grant proposals with lots of boilerplate.
- Business letters with standard paragraphs.
- Legal documents, like contracts, which also have standard paragraphs or many places where a name has to be inserted.

Merge-print programs work like this: you type in the text that doesn't vary from one letter (or whatever) to the next. Wherever you have a name, or a paragraph, or anything that varies with each letter, you type in a **variable name**. You have to **flag** the variable name somehow (so the program will know that it's come across a variable and not just another piece of text); let's say you put a backslash (\) on either side of it.

(Since a backslash never occurs in normal text, you can use it to tell the computer that something special is up. Some other symbols useful for that purpose are the vertical bar (|), the caret (ˆ), a tilde (˜) over a blank space, and one or more periods (..) at the beginning of a line. You can also double any character that is never doubled — e.g., @@, %%, &&, or you can combine them — @%, &@, %@, etc.)

When the computer sees a word between backslashes (if that's the variable flag), it will do one of two things: ask you to provide the input; or look to some other file, like a mailing list, for it. So a personalized form letter might look something like this:

August 27, 1982

\M\ \first name\ \last name\
address\

Dear \M\ \last name\ ,

Your bill of \date\ in the amount of \amount\ is \ask me\ over due. \ask me\

\ask me\

Yours truly,

Larson E. Whipsnade

The merge-print program (usually in collaboration with a word-processing program) starts typing the letter out. When it gets to \M\, it goes to a mailing list you've previously specified (in response to a question from the program). It looks at the first entry, sees if the first line starts "Mr." or "Ms.," and inserts whichever it is into the letter.

When it gets to \ first name\, it looks at the mailing list entry again and types the first name. Then it does the same for the last name and the (two- or three-line) address. At "Dear \M\ \last name\", it again types Mr. or Ms., followed by the last name (leaving out the first name because you haven't asked for it).

At \date\, it looks at *another* list (because you previously told it that \date\ would be on the accounts receivable list and not on the mailing list), finds the entry corresponding to the name it's already typed, and inserts the date of the original invoice. It also uses the accounts receivable list to get the information for \amount\.

At the first \ask me\, the program stops and waits for you to think about this account, perhaps look at a record of its bill-paying history, and insert some word or phrase — "somewhat," "long," "too long," "incredibly" — whatever you feel is appropriate.

At the next \ask me\, the program stops so you can choose from a selection of standard paragraphs with varying tones — diffident, demanding, exasperated, threatening. You pick paragraph C — exasperated. You don't have to type in the paragraph — just the letter that tells the program which paragraph you want.

At the next \ ask me \ , you pick from a second series of paragraphs:

P) Please give this matter your immediate attention. . .

Q) We don't know what to do about this matter. . .

R) If we don't receive your check within ten days. . .

S) My cousin is in the Mafia. . .

As soon as you give the program the code for the paragraph you want, it types it in, finishes the letter, maybe even prints out an envelope, and goes on to repeat the process for the second name on the mailing list.

(This is pretty much an idealized merge-print program; don't expect to be able to buy one quite like it down here in the real world.)

Since merge-print programs involve printing out a file, they tend to be tightly integrated with particular word-processing programs — the way MailMerge is with WordStar. Many — maybe even most — word-processing programs offer such integral merge-prints programs, and there are also generic ones that will work with any word processor.

The third sort of program is an **indexer** (or **indexing program**). It works like this:

As you write your document, you mark words you want to appear in the index with a symbol — let's use an asterisk and an each sign: *@. So if I wanted the word *@indexer*@ indexed, I would mark it just as I have in this sentence. The *@'s are ignored when the text is being printed out — both the *@ marks and the spaces they occupy are deleted.

When you run the file through the indexer, it pulls out all the words surrounded by *@'s, sorts them — along with the page each one is on — into alphabetical order, and prints out an index.

If the page on which a word appears changes — due to reformatting, adding or deleting text, or whatever — the page number in the index automatically changes too.

Indexers can also generate tables of contents. And they also can give you **hierarchical entries:**

War criminals, 5, 12,

   Living, 19, 41

      Kissinger, Henry, 41

To facilitate this, most indexers require that you type the index (or table of contents) entry on a separate line. Let's say a program uses the symbol .! to begin lines that contain items for the index and the symbol .ˆ for lines with items for the table of contents. At the start of this chapter, I would have inserted a line that read:

.^OTHER KINDS OF PROGRAMS

Three paragraphs back, I would have inserted two lines that read:

.^   Indexers

.!Indexers

I indented ''Indexers'' on the .^ line so it would show up that way in the table of contents:

For an index, you have to specify each level of the entry each time, because index entries don't go in order by page number the way a table of contents does. Thus you need some sort of symbol to separate the levels:

.!War criminals\Living\Kissinger, Henry

One indexing program that I know of is **Documate/Plus**, published by Orthocode, of Albany, California. There are doubtless others.

Since a certain popular operating system is about as easy to learn as medieval Japanese (I'm not going to tell you which one, but its initials are CP/M), several **substitute menu programs** have sprung up to make it more ''user-friendly.'' These programs give you replacement commands for every function CP/M performs (some word-processing programs have that feature already built in).

Charles Merritt Software of Fayetteville, Arkansas, publishes a couple of substitute menu programs, one called **Magic Menu** (which works with Magic Wand) and another called **Spell Menu** (which works with Spellbinder). Here's an example of how they operate:

To copy a file from one disk to the other under CP/M, you call up a program called PIP. (Why ''pip'' instead of ''copy'' or even ''cp,'' you ask? Don't ask.) Next you list the name of the drive you want the new copy of the file on, and a new name for the file (if you want to change it). *Then* you list the name of the drive you're copying from and the name of the file being copied. So the command looks like this:

pip a:newcopy = b:origfile

The problem with this is that it reverses normal English word order, which would be: ''Copy origfile from disk b onto disk a and call it newcopy.'' An even more basic problem is that it reverses simple logic, since it's not possible to think of where to put something, or what new name to give it, without first thinking of it.

Under Magic Menu, however, things make a whole lot more sense. There's a line on the main menu that reads:

C.....COPY A FILE.

You hit C, and the screen reads:

NOW WORKING ON.....*COPY*

ENTER THE NAME OF THE FILE TO BE COPIED...........

You do that, and it says:

ON WHAT DISK IS THIS FILE? (A-B)..................

Next comes:

IF YOU WISH TO CALL THE COPY BY ANOTHER NAME,

ENTER THE NAME. OTHERWISE JUST PUSH ''RETURN''......

Followed by:

ON WHAT DISK DO YOU WANT TO PUT THE COPY? (A-B)...

Answer that and the command executes, and you're returned to the main menu.

Another substitute menu program is **Supervyz**, published by Epic Software of San Diego. According to the publisher, Supervyz is compatible with over 2000 programs and 300 computers.

The tradeoff with substitute menu programs, of course, is that they take up additional RAM space — sometimes more than the whole operating system does.

Although I can't get into evaluating specific indexers, spelling checkers, and merge-print programs in this book, the general principles and strategies I use to evaluate word-processing programs are applicable to a whole range of software and hardware products.

There are catalogs of software for most of the popular machines and operating systems, and I've listed some of them in Appendix A.

8

Screens, Keyboards, And Video Terminals

You can buy a screen and keyboard separately and hook them up, or you can buy them together, as part of a **terminal**. All of what follows will apply to both approaches (except, of course, when I refer to one or the other specifically). When I say "terminal," I usually mean to include a screen and keyboard bought separately.

Some computer terminals have no screens. What you type on the keyboard, and what the computer answers, are both printed on paper. These **printer terminals** look like typewriters or KSR printers (and, of course, that's just what they are — with a few brains added). The most famous printer terminal is the **Teletype**, which (as its name implies) was originally built and designed for transmitting data over long distances and was adapted to communicating with computers only as an afterthought.

Many such **printer terminals** are still in use, but they're next to useless for word-processing applications. When I use the word "terminal" in this book, I mean a keyboard and a *screen* — a **video display terminal**.

HEALTH QUESTIONS

There's been some concern about the safety of sitting in front of a VDT all day long. Even if it's not harmful, it's certainly not a *natural* thing to do. So three unions asked the National Institute of Occupational Safety and Health (**NIOSH** — pronounced NEI-ahsh) to make a study of VDTs and decide if they're unsafe.

This 77-page study, *Potential Health Hazards of Video Display Terminals*, is available free from the U.S. Health Department's publication office in Cincinnati (OH 45226). You can also order it by calling (513) 684-4287. For the lazy among you, I'll summarize the findings here (less completely, but infinitely more readably):

First NIOSH asked VDT operators and other workers at three work sites in Northern California a very comprehensive series of questions: Did they have any one of 59 health complaints? Did they have any of them frequently? Had a doctor diagnosed any of 23 disease states in the last five years?

In addition, both groups of workers were tested to determine if they felt anxious, depressed, angry, tired, energetic, or confused.

NIOSH didn't consider a problem significant unless at least 20 percent more VDT operators than non-VDT operators (or vice versa) reported it. So when I say "more" below, I mean "at least 20 percent more." (The results of the surveys were presented work site by work site, but I'll combine the findings here.)

VDT operators at one or more work sites reported more (or more frequent occurences) of the following:

- Emotional problems.
- Gastrointestinal problems.
- Stiff arms and legs, swollen muscles, and pains in the wrists, back, neck and shoulders.
- Cramps in the hands and fingers.
- Loss of strength in the arms or hands.
- Painful joints.
- Eye strain and other eye problems, like sore, itching or burning eyes or loss of the ability to see colors.
- Anxiety, irritability, and "shaking inside."
- Depression.
- Anger.
- Fatigue and periodic exhaustion.
- Confusion.
- Skin problems.
- Headaches.

Workers who didn't operate VDTs reported many fewer problems. The only complaints they had more of than VDT operators were back pain, fever, arthritis, and rheumatism.

This data should be taken with a grain of salt, since, at the time the surveys were made, "very difficult labor negotiations were underway and health and safety issues relating to VDTs were a component of that bargaining." At one site, a letter was sent to all VDT operators by the union steward on the day before the NIOSH survey. It urged the workers to participate and added that a prior NIOSH evaluation had "indicated the likelihood of visual problems for VDT operators."

But the list of problems reported by VDT operators is still impressive, and there are also many other indications of VDT hazards than just this NIOSH study. For example, two copy editors for the *New York Times* — aged 29 and 35 — developed cataracts, a potentially blinding eye disease usually found only in people over 65. Their union, the Newspaper Guild, claimed that VDTs were the cause. Although arbitrators decided that this was not the case, the Newspaper Guild subsequently discovered eight more young

VDT operators with cataracts.

There also is some evidence — discussed in a paper given before the National Academy of Sciences symposium on VDTs and vision, by the Norwegian W.C. Olsen — that VDTs cause facial rashes.

The NIOSH report lists several other studies in its references section. They show quite convincingly that some sort of strain on the eyes results from working at VDTs. Exactly what causes it is unclear. Whether *all* VDTs cause it is also unclear. There is also less conclusive evidence of psychological stress.

Some of this information is summarized in a 50-page report published by Working Women, a national association of office workers. It's called *Warning: Health Hazards for Office Workers* and covers many other areas aside from VDTs. You can get it by sending $4.80 to 1224 Huron Road, Cleveland, OH 44115.

The most common complaint of VDT operators concern the eyes — eyestrain, soreness, itching, or burning. One possible reason is that our eyes are designed to see things at a great variety of distances and to keep changing their focus frequently. Everything on a screen is, of course, just one set distance away, and thus working at a VDT deprives our eyes of necessary exercise.

Getting up frequently and looking at objects that are closer and farther away than the screen is one way to deal with the problem. Another is to have your eyes examined frequently. As NIOSH puts it, "Given the mounting anecdotal evidence of ophthalmologic complaints associated with VDT use and the paucity of research pertaining to the incidence, etiology, or pathophysiology of these events,. . . at the very least VDT workers should have a comprehensive pre-placement vision examination."

Let me translate that into English for those of you who don't read bureaucratese: "VDTs seem to bother some people's eyes. Nobody knows how or why. So you should get your eyes checked before you take a job working on a VDT, and probably later on, too."

NIOSH recommends optometric testing that meets the American Optometric Association's minimum standards, or those of Hirschfelder of the National Society for the Prevention of Blindness. If you have any problems with your eyes after you begin working at a VDT, you should have them rechecked. It also makes sense to have a general eye exam repeated periodically, but nobody knows just how often.

NIOSH is continuing research in this area so it can get some more conclusive answers to these questions (assuming it survives Reaganomics, of course). I don't know about you, but I consider the government's attempts to prevent me from going blind an unnecessary intrusion into my private life.

In addition to asking workers questions, NIOSH made several kinds of concrete physical measurements.

The first area they looked at was radiation. They tested for X-rays, emissions in the radio frequencies, and ultraviolet light (just above the visible spectrum). In no case were any X-rays or radio frequencies detectable. The near ultraviolet ranged from .0001 (one ten-thousandth) to .00065 (six and a half ten-thousandths) of the allowable amount. In other words — on those terminals, at those work sites — there was absolutely no radiation hazard.

COMFORT

Next NIOSH measured elements of the work station design — how high off the ground were the keyboards, what kind of angle was the screen at, and so on. I can testify from personal experience that both of these factors can make an enormous difference, so I'll throw my own comments in as I discuss each subject.

NIOSH recommends a height of 29–31 inches from the floor to the home row of the keyboard (asdfghjkl — boy, that was easy to type!). I think this is too high. The home row on my keyboard is 27 inches off the floor; that seems ideal for me and I'm five ten. Many people with separate keyboards put them on their laps to type. I find that uncomfortable for extensive touch typing, but only because the keyboard shifts around, not because it's too low.

Keyboards are almost always placed too high for comfort (typically on top of a standard 30-inch desk or table). Thirty inches may be a good height for writing or eating, but it's too high for typing.

Of the 53 work stations studied by NIOSH, none had a keyboard as low as mine; 51 percent had keyboards over NIOSH's 31-inch maximum; only six percent had keyboards under 29½ inches. This is because the guy who decides on office furniture wouldn't be caught dead at a keyboard and thus knows nothing about typing comfort. He's always pictured leaning officiously over the typist's shoulder and checking her work as it comes off the machine.

Of course the right keyboard height also depends on the height of the chair, but here again, lower is better. To minimize low back pain, a chair should put your knees on the same level with your hips — that is, your thighs should be parallel to the floor. Some people even say your knees should be higher. (This applies only to conventional chairs, of course, not the new Norwegian ones you kneel on.)

Once you have a chair of the right height, place the keyboard so that your forearms are also parallel to the floor, or slanting downwards slightly. The thing to avoid is having to reach up to the keyboard — *your wrists should never be higher than your elbows*.

NIOSH also recommends that the screen be about 17–20 inches away. I think this depends entirely on the size of the letters on it. Mine are one-quarter inch high (the caps), and my screen is quite comfortable at 22 inches. In any case, the screen shouldn't be too close.

More crucial is the angle at which you look at the screen. NIOSH recommends that the top edge of the screen be no higher than eye level and the bottom edge no lower than 40 degrees below eye level. The distance from the home row of my keyboard to the bottom line of text on my screen is usually about 11 inches (I vary the height). In addition to putting the screen at the right level, this leaves plenty of room for me to put newspaper clippings, binders, and books between the keyboard and the screen so I can refer to them when I type.

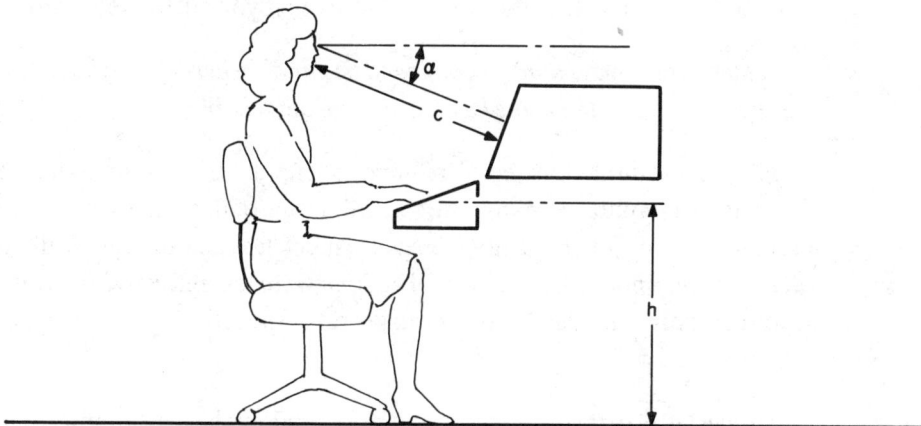

α = VIEWING ANGLE, FROM HORIZONTAL
c = VIEWING DISTANCE
h = HEIGHT OF KEYBOARD HOME ROW

Critical workstation variables.

To sum up, a comfortable VDT work station will have a *lower chair*, a *lower keyboard*, and a *higher, more distant screen* than is usual.

There's no way to build a work station that will make everyone comfortable. The solution is to make work stations that are totally adjustable, so the people who work at it can adjust it to *their* tastes. NIOSH agrees. Among the things they (and I) believe should be independently adjustable are:
- The height of the chair seat.
- The height of the chair back.

- How hard the chair back pushes against your back.
- How curved it is where it hits the small of your back.
- The tilt of the screen (up and down).
- The angle of the screen (side to side).
- The brightness and contrast of the screen.
- The height of the screen.
- Its distance from you.
- The height of the keyboard.
- The angle of the keyboard.

Now this may sound like a lot to ask, but it's really quite easy — *if* you have a separate screen and keyboard. If they're part of one package — as most VDT's are — there's no way you're going to be comfortable at one. You'll be forced to look down at the screen and, unless you *really* want to look down at it, you'll have to put the keyboard too high. The screen will be too close to you, even if you put the keyboard too far away.

For these reasons, *I don't recommend terminals where the keyboard and screen are integrated into one unit and the keyboard is not detachable*.

Tiltable and turnable screens are important for another reason — they help you control glare. The phrase ''non-glare screen'' is one of the greatest misnomers around. Most of them barely even cut down on glare, much less eliminate it. Well, all right . . . *on the average*, a non-glare screen will be *somewhat* less reflective than other screens. But you certainly can't depend on one to get rid of the reflections of fluorescent light fixtures or windows.

The best way to deal with the problem of windows is to position terminals on the same wall as the windows. If this isn't possible, put the terminals on side walls with partitions shading them. It also helps to have heavy drapes. **Screen hoods** can be used to shade the screen. If light from a window hits a terminal screen directly, nothing will suppress the reflection.

Fluorescent fixtures in the ceiling are an even worse problem, because there are usually more of them than windows and thus they're harder to get away from. The solution is simple, however: turn them off. Fluorescent lights are incredibly unhealthy and they always light the room too brightly. With all the pompous posturing about reducing this country's dependence on foreign oil, you have only to look at a bunch of office buildings around 8:00 PM to understand what waste really means.

So — the simplest solution is just to take the bulbs out of any fluorescent fixtures that reflect in your screen. There will be plenty of light without them. Even your boss may be able to understand that this will S*A*V*E* M*O*N*E*Y as well as make you happy.

Recessing fluorescent fixtures helps a little (if they're not already recessed), as does putting baffles on them (if they don't already have baffles). And there are special covers which direct the light downward rather than sideways. But there's nothing half as effective as just eliminating the bulbs.

Whatever causes VDT problems, it obviously isn't going to help things to slave away at one for hours with a break. NIOSH recommends a 15-minute break every two hours if the VDT work is moderately demanding, or a 15-minute break every hour if the work is very demanding or very repetitive. You can still work during these breaks, just not at the VDT.

CAPABILITIES

Many of the features you want in a terminal (or video board) can be produced by the computer it's hooked up to or by the software the computer runs. Some others are necessarily dependent on the terminal. In any case, it shouldn't make much difference to you where or how a feature is implemented. So I just give a list of what to look for.

(Since some people will skip right to this list without reading the first part of the chapter, I've repeated — briefly — some of the advice I gave there.)

1) First you need to decide if you want to run in **terminal mode** or **memory-mapped**. The distinction is discussed in the Ease of Use section of Chapter 5, but the basic difference is that memory-mapping gives you quicker screen response, and terminal mode takes some of the load off your computer and its software by providing various capabilities on its own. For example, a **smart terminal** can provide its own editing commands, graphic capabilities, or alternate character sets like foreign alphabets and scientific symbols.

The **video board** which controls memory-mapped video usually takes up 2–3K of RAM, which you might want for some other purpose. On the other hand, it's generally easier to pop in a new video board or put a new chip on it than it is to modify a terminal.

2) Look for a **separate** (or separable) **keyboard**. If you want to run memory-mapped, you can get a keyboard from one manufacturer, a **monitor** (a CRT screen just by itself) from another, and a **video board** (which does the thinking for the monitor) from a third. If you want to run in terminal mode, make sure the terminal has a **detachable keyboard**.

3) The screen should be both **tiltable** and **turnable**, its height should be adjustable, and it should have conveniently located brightness and contrast controls.

4) Needless to say, you want a terminal that will produce lowercase as well as capital letters. I only mention this because some systems don't give you lowercase and

are therefore virtually useless for word-processing applications.

5) You spend most of your time looking at your terminal. Do yourself a favor — don't buy an ugly one. You can probably get the same features in other models that have given some consideration to how they look. (If not, of course, go for the features.)

THE SCREEN

6) First of all, you want **full screen editing** with a **controllable cursor**.

7) The screen should measure at least nine inches diagonally (or the equivalent) and should be capable of displaying at least twelve lines of text.

8) Each line should be at least 64 characters wide, and ideally 80. More than that is fine, but the capital letters should be at least 1/8 inch tall (mine are 1/4 inch and they're very easy to read). There are screens that show up to 132 characters on a line so you can display an entire spreadsheet or ledger, but they're expensive.

What's nice about 80 columns is that it can show the line breaks on an 8-1/2 x 11" page (actually, about 75 columns would be adequate), but that's not where the 80-column format comes from. It comes from the fact that there are 80 columns on a punched card.

9) **Horizontal scrolling** can be offered by your terminal as well as by your software. Another hot feature is **zoom video**, which enlarges the portion of the screen around the cursor. Personally, I think the characters on the screen should always be large enough so that this isn't necessary.

10) You want characters that are fully defined as well as large. This is a function of the dot matrix or grid used. Five by seven (35 dots) is the minimum grid size and produces characters that are barely recognizable. Nine by sixteen (144 dots) is about the most you'll ever find. I think a matrix of at least 80 — and ideally more than 100 — dots is desirable, especially if you like fine touches like serifs on your lowercase t's and i's.

In any case, you definitely want **true descenders**. That is, the tails on small p's, q's, g's, y's, and j's should actually descend below the line. Some screens (and printers) with inadequate grids squeeze them in above the line, which makes these letters strange-looking and ugly.

11) In most microcomputers, the printer is capable of finer work than the screen. This means it can produce things the screen can't display. **High-resolution** screens (i.e., ones with more dots per square inch) solve this problem. If they're the 66-line screens that are taller than they're wide, they can also show a whole page of text. They're great — the only question is whether you can afford one.

12) Don't try to use a TV screen as a monitor. One reason is the **phosphor** (the coating on the inside of the tube that emits light when the cathode ray hits it). The **high-persistence** phosphor on computer monitors and terminals holds an image — glows — longer than the phosphor on TV screens. (This kind of phosphor costs more, and that's the main reason monitors cost more than TV screens.) Because its phosphor won't hold an image long enough, a TV screen adapted to be a computer monitor will appear to flicker more. (The **refresh rate** — how often the image on the screen is rewritten — also affects flicker.)

TVs display less information (fewer lines of fewer characters) than monitors — both because they have to scan more often to keep their phosphor activated and for other reasons. They can be forced to display the same amount of information, but the clarity of the characters suffers.

Some inexpensive monitors (like the TRS-80 Model I monitor or the Leedex Video 100) are nothing more than a TV screen without a tuner and a speaker. They also have these problems.

13) Although there's a lot of talk about how **green phosphor** is more restful to the eyes than the normal white, some people say that looking at green all the time deprives your eyes of the color stimulation they need (white, of course, includes all colors). But then other people say that all you have to do is put something red on top of the CRT and the problem is solved. In Europe, orange letters on a brown background are popular. You should just follow your inclinations on this question. I don't know what color is best, and I don't think anybody else does either.

One interesting fact: green phosphor happens to hold an image longer than white phosphor. Maybe this, rather than the color, has something to do with its popularity.

14) Whatever color you decide on for a screen, stick with black and white. (Huh?) Color screens — that is, screens that display full color images — are almost certain to cost more than they're worth for word-processing applications. Since it takes (at least) three times as much information to produce a color image as a light and dark one, a color screen will always cost more for a given amount of resolution (or, alternatively, have a coarser image for a given price).

Using a color TV as a monitor for a word processor is an even bigger mistake. The image will be full of color shadows and moiré patterns that will drive you nuts.

15) Some terminals offer **smooth scrolling**. This is a nice feature, although hardly a vital one. It works like this:

In normal scrolling, the text moves a line at a time; it jumps from one line to the next. In smooth scrolling, each line of text moves one row of dots at a time; thus it appears to slide smoothly up and down the screen, which makes it much easier to read.

16) Some terminals let you display text in **reverse video** (dark letters on a light background, instead of light letters on a dark background, or at one or more levels of **reduced intensity** (i.e., dimmer). Both of these are useful for **highlighting** text.

Some systems — like the Xerox Star and the CPT 8100 — normally operate in reverse video. I haven't seen any studies on this, but to my mind, it's a really good idea for at least two reasons: a light background picks up less glare, and after a lifetime of looking at black ink on white paper, looking at dark letters on a light screen is obviously going to take less adjustment and cause less trauma than learning to look at light letters on a dark screen.

(I've recently switched over to dark letters on a light screen and I *much* prefer it.)

17) Other fancy features you can get include the ability to hide characters, underlining, double underlining, blinking characters, and an adjustable blink rate.

Some terminals can display the effect of control characters sent to them by the computer, rather than just show the control characters and wait for printout to do what they say. This, of course, is exactly what dedicated word processors with virtual representation do.

18) A **split screen** lets you look at two pieces of text at the same time. This capability can be implemented by a terminal as well as by software. Either way, it's a very useful feature.

19) Throughout this book I've railed against **flashing cursors**. The justification for them is that they're easier to find on the screen. But I've never lost track of my non-blinking cursor, and it seems to me that if you can't find a plain block of light on a screen, you need medical care, not a blinking cursor.

But, in fairness, I have had people who appear to be sane tell me that they actually *prefer* a flashing cursor. And certainly it's true that — depending on the blink rate — some flashing cursors are less obnoxious than others.

So all I recommend is that, if you're going to buy a terminal or system with a blinking cursor, spend some time working at it first. Make *sure* it isn't going to bother you.

THE KEYBOARD

20) The primary thing to look for is a comfortable feel. Spend however long it takes to make sure you like the keyboard. A computer keyboard should let you type faster than an electric typewriter, and with less effort. The key action on even an average microcomputer keyboard is better than on an IBM Selectric. So be fussy.

21) Some keyboard manufacturers will make a big deal out of the fact that their layout is similar (or identical) to that of an electric typewriter. Although it does help at first not to have to relearn the location of certain keys (like ' and : and''), it doesn't actually take very long to switch over. So in the long run, this feature doesn't make much of a difference.

22) The control key should be located in some reasonable place where you can get to it easily.

23) There should be no **dangerous key** — one that can result in the loss of text all by itself — anywhere on a keyboard, and *certainly* not in a place where it's likely to be hit accidentally. Apple II's are famous (or infamous) for their reset buttons, which make it way too easy to lose your entire workfile.

Reset buttons — which put a machine back to where it was when you turned it on, with the programs or text files you loaded into it erased — either should be located on the computer box itself, some distance from the keyboard, or — if the keyboard and computer are one unit — should require at least two, and ideally three, keystrokes to be activated.

24) **Auto-repeat** means that if you hold a key down, it repeats rapidly and automatically (after an initial pause). These are very good features. Some keyboards have an **auto-repeat key**. If you hold it and another key down, the other key will repeat automatically.

25) One of the most useful things you can have on a keyboard are **cursor arrows** — keys that move the cursor in various directions. These should definitely be arranged in a diamond and should auto-repeat. Cursor arrows save a *lot* of time.

26) **Function keys** are great to have. I talked about them in Chapter 2, but I'll give you a brief review. There are two kinds: **dedicated** and **programmable** (also called **soft**) **keys**. Dedicated keys have the function they perform written right on them, which makes it easy to remember what they do. Soft keys are good because you can change what they do for different pieces of software. You also need fewer of them, since a program can reassign them to different functions at different points in time.

Hewlett-Packard, IBM, and Corvus have the ultimate in soft keys. They sit right below the screen and the software labels each one for you. This saves having to say to yourself, ''OK, f5 is the key that does what I want. Now where is f5 again?''

Screen-labeled soft keys on a Corvus Concept.

27) If you deal with numbers a lot, you'll find a **numeric key pad** — ten keys laid out in a box — a convenience. But it really isn't necessary for normal word processing.

28) As I mentioned in Chapter 3, the arrangement of the keys on a standard keyboard (called **QWERTY** after the first six letters on the second row) was originally designed to be clumsy. The original (alphabetical) layout worked too well and jammed the keys of the first, primitive machines.

Rather than make the typewriter mechanism more efficient, the inventors took the easy way out and made the keyboard less efficient. They came up with a layout that makes it almost impossible to hit keys in rapid succession. This was QWERTY. About the only thing QWERTY is good for is typing the word "typewriter" without taking your fingers off the second row.

In 1932, after studying letter frequencies and sequences and observing the movements of typists fingers for several years, Dr. August Dvorak of the University of Washington came out with his Simplified Keyboard (now always called the **Dvorak keyboard**). Typists using the Dvorak keyboard set 26 international records, and when Dr. Dvorak trained Navy reservists to use it during the Second World War, their speed increased 74 percent.

CONVENTIONAL KEYBOARD

| 2 | 3 | 4 | 5 | 6 | 7 | 8 | 9 | 0 | *
— | '
/ |

| Q | W | E | R | T | Y | U | I | O | P | 1/4
1/2 | —— 52% |

| A | S | D | F | G | H | J | K | L | :
; | ¢
@ | —— 32% |

| SHIFT | Z | X | C | V | B | N | M | ,
, | .
. | ?
/ | SHIFT | —— 16% |

SPACE BAR

DVORAK SIMPLIFIED KEYBOARD

| 7 | 5 | 3 | 1 | 9 | 0 | 2 | 4 | 6 | 8 | +
= |

| :
? | ,
, | .
. | P | Y | F | G | C | R | L | &
/ | —— 22% |

| A | O | E | U | I | D | H | T | N | S | —
- | —— 70% |

| SHIFT | ;
, | Q | J | K | X | B | M | W | V | Z | SHIFT | —— 8% |

SPACE BAR

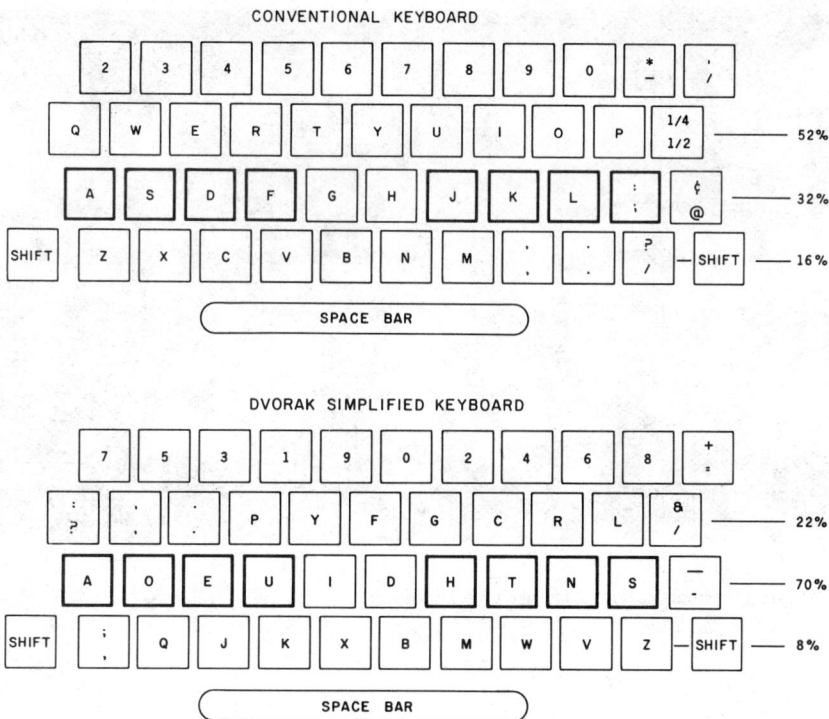

The placement of keys on a Dvorak keyboard.

Smith-Corona and IBM have both offered the Dvorak keyboards as an option on their machines for several years. Unfortunately, they haven't gotten many orders for them, because:

- People who have invested considerable time and effort in learning how to touch type on QWERTY keyboards don't want to have to go through it all again.
- People who are learning to touch type want to be able to use the greatest number of machines, and almost all machines have QWERTY keyboards.
- Office managers and purchasing agents want machines that the greatest number of typists can operate, and most typists already know QUERTY.

So, by the sheer weight of momentum, clumsy QWERTY is still with us today, and probably will be forever, unless there's some sort of coordinated mass conversion to a better keyboard.

One new keyboard that may eliminate that necessity is the **PCD-Maltron**, invented by Lillian Malt of Great Britain (and distributed in the United States by Applied Learning

A Maltron keyboard adapted for use with WordStar.

Corporation of King of Prussia, Pennsylvania). It uses an improved version of Dvorak's key arrangement and has a radical new shape designed to cut fatigue and increase speed.

Because the length and strength of our fingers vary, the Maltron's keys are set at different heights and curved to fit the hand. They're separated into two groups, one for each hand, to relieve the shoulder strain caused by placing your hands next to each other (as on a conventional keyboard). The thumbs, traditionally underutilized, are given up to eight keys each.

In an analysis of a million English words, the Maltron keyboard required a typist to use the same finger twice in a row only eleven percent as often as a QWERTY keyboard did, and it required the fingers to leave the home row only once for every 256 times a QWERTY keyboard did.

But probably the best thing about Maltron keyboards is that you don't have to unlearn QWERTY to learn to use them. Because of their unusual shape, typing on them gets filed away in a separate part of the brain from typing on a standard keyboard. When you feel a standard keyboard under your fingers, you type QWERTY. When you feel a Maltron keyboard under your fingers, you type Maltron — automatically and unconsciously. In fact, some typists who've learned Maltron say their QWERTY speeds have actually increased.

The worst thing about Maltron keyboards is what they cost — from $600 to $1200, depending on the number of keys you want.

29) The Xerox 8010 Star features a **mouse**. This is a small device with wheels on the bottom and a button or two on the top. (It's called a mouse because it's small and grey, and the wire coming out of it looks like a tail.)

You roll the mouse around on the table next to your keyboard, and the cursor imitates its motion on the screen. People who have used the mouse say it gets so you feel you're moving the cursor with your hand; you forget there's an intervening device.

One clear disadvantage of the mouse: you have to move your hand from the keyboard (and thus lose the home row) every time you want to use it.

30) Some HP terminals have a device that works in much the same way as a mouse. It's a circle mounted in the keyboard, and it's called a **rotary control knob.** You move the cursor by turning it.

Xerox has a similar device, called a **CAT** (I don't know what the letters stand for, and neither did the Xerox PR manager I asked about it). The CAT is also circular, but you control cursor movement by placing your fingers at various points around its perimeter, rather than by turning it.

31) You can do a lot of damage to a keyboard by spilling liquid on it. Some keyboards are designed to resist spills and that's a nice feature, if you're a clumsy oaf like me.

32) As I type this, I have to clobber the letter p, the numbers 9 and 0, and sometimes the letter e, to get them to register. This is because the little contacts (called **switches**) under the keys on my antique keyboard are bent out of shape (and also, of course, because I can't afford a new keyboard).

When I can afford one, I'm going to get one with **Hall-effect key switches.** They work by passing a plunger through a magnetic field, which trips the switch. There is no contact at all between the key you push down and the wire that sends the signal out of your keyboard (thus these are also called **contactless key switches**).

The advantage of Hall-effect key switches is obvious: if things don't touch each other, they can't wear out.

THE FUTURE

The cathode ray tube (CRT) was invented more than a century ago by William Crookes, in the processes of research that led eventually to the discovery of the electron. Little did this humble British researcher dream that his inquiry into trivial matters like the basic nature of reality would one day make it possible for millions of people all over the world to watch reruns of Charlie's Angels.

Despite its great age, the CRT still completely dominates the field of computer displays, but its competition keeps getting fiercer.

One problem with CRTs is their fragility. Another is the fact that the higher and wider a picture tube is, the deeper it has to be. CRTs also contain high voltage, consume large amounts of energy, weigh a lot, and put out large amounts of heat. The new **flat panel** displays solve all these problems.

There are many different technologies involved in flat panel displays, but they can be divided into two basic categories — luminescent and nonemitter. The most common **luminescent** displays are those small, red **LED**'s (light-emitting diodes) you used to find on digital watches and calculators. Another example is the **gas plasma** display often used on thin-window word processors.

Luminescent displays share the problem of washing out in bright light. That's why they've been replaced on watches and calculators by **nonemitter** displays like **LCD**s (liquid-crystal displays). It's possible (although somewhat difficult and expensive) to build a TV or computer display screen using LCDs. A few such have already been introduced, and as time goes on, they will get cheaper and have higher resolution.

Why, then, if flat panel displays are so wonderful, does everybody continue to use CRTs? Because they are still far and away the cheapest way to display large quantities of information. Since CRT technology is progressing just as fast as flat panel technology, we may be using CRTs for computer displays for quite a long time to come.

Ultimately, of course, neither CRTs nor flat panels will be the victors; **holograms** will. Imagine your text dancing in space, and imagine the sort of writing that will emerge when that's how people read books. A whole new dimension to work with — James Joyce would have loved it.

CHECKLIST FOR SCREENS, KEYBOARDS, AND VIDEO TERMINALS

SCREEN:

Basics:

Size: ____" diagonal (or ____" horiz. by ____" vert.).

Displays ____ lines of ____ characters each.

Size of capital letters: ____" (or ____ mm).
Character matrix: ____ x ____
   True descenders?
   Serifs on small t's and i's?
Color of text: _____   Color of background: _____
Cursor:
   Shape: block / underline / triangle / _____
   Blinks?
   Bearable?
   Can be turned off?
CRT / flat panel (luminescent / nonemitter)

Comfort:
   Tiltable?
   Turnable?
   Brightness control?
     Easily accessible?
   Contrast control?
     Easily accessible?
   Ugly / pleasant to look at?

Special features:
   Horizontal scrolling?
   Smooth scrolling?
   Zoom video?
   Reverse video?
   Reduced intensity:
     How many levels: _____
   Displays:
     underlining?
     double underlining?
     boldface?
   Hides characters?
   Blinking characters?
     Adjustable blink rates? How many: _____
   Split screen?
     How many windows possible?
   Displays more than one full page?

KEYBOARD:

Comfortable feel?
Comfortable layout?
Control key in convenient location?

Any dangerous keys?

Auto-repeat?

   Separate key?

Cursor arrows?

   In diamond?

Function keys?

   Dedicated?   How many: _____

   Assignable? How many: _____

QWERTY / Dvorak / Maltron ? _____

Special Features:

   Mouse?

   Rotary control knob?

   Other similar device? _____

   Spill protection?

   Hall-effect (contactless) key switches?

9

Printers

A printer can spit out pages of text at an impressive rate; it can produce beautiful, crisp printouts; and it can cost less than a good portable typewriter. What no printer can do is all three of those things. The better it is at one, the worse it will tend to be at one — and usually both — of the others. So you have to choose.

For most word-processing applications, the quality of the printout is more important than speed and worth spending some money on. (After all, if you can't send out a decent looking letter or submit a manuscript an editor is willing to read, what do you need a word processor for in the first place?)

The neatest, most professional printouts are produced by —

FORMED-CHARACTER PRINTERS

These work by pressing a fully formed image of each character through a ribbon and onto the paper. This is just what typewriters do, but instead of using rods with letters on the end of them (or a ball with letters all around it), formed character printers use **daisy wheels** or **thimbles** (referred to generically as **print elements**).

A daisy wheel and a type ball.

A close-up of characters on the spokes of a daisy wheel.

As the print element spins around, the printer keeps track of which character is in front of the ribbon slot at each moment. When the character to be printed is there, a small hammer very quickly darts out and pushes it against the ribbon and paper. Since the print element spins at a very high speed — and since if the hammer were off by the slightest fraction of a second every character printed would be wrong — this represents an exquisite masterpiece of timing.

Print elements come in various typefaces and with different symbols on them, including foreign alphabets. They're made of plastic, except for some daisy wheels that are made of metal. Metal daisy wheels produce a sharper image for a longer time, but I think you have to be pretty fussy not be be satisfied with the plastic ones. The metal daisy wheels also limit the maximum speed of the printer. Another reason for preferring plastic is that metal daisy wheels are brittle and prone to break. They cost about $50 to replace, whereas plastic daisy wheels cost $7–10.

Printouts from formed character printers are at least equal in quality to those from electric typewriters. And printers can do several things electric typewriters can't — if they're capable of **incremental spacing** (or **microspacing**). This means they can move as little as a 1/48 inch vertically and a 1/60 or 1/120 inch horizontally.

Like a typesetting machine, a printer with microspacing lets you do proportional spacing. The fine horizontal movement can also be used to create **boldfacing** (by printing the text to be boldfaced, going back to the start of it, moving the print element 1/120 inch to the right, and printing it again. This is also called **shadow printing.**)

The speed of printers is measured in characters per second (**cps**). Appendix B includes a table that converts cps into official, five-character words per minute (**owpm** in this book, but just plain **wpm** in ads); real, six-character words per minute (**rwpm**); and

Like a typesetting machine, a printer with microspacing lets you do proportional spacing. The fine horizontal movement can also be used to create **boldfacing** (by printing the text to be boldfaced, going back to the start of it, moving the print element 1/120th of an inch to the right, and printing it again. This is also called **shadow printing.**)

Normal and boldface formed-character printing.

standard, double-spaced pages per hour (**pph**).

Some manufacturers give their printers' speeds in lines per minute (**lpm**). This is confusing, since lpm obviously varies with the number of characters in each line. At best — if you know the line length — an lpm figure involves a bothersome calculation. At worst — if you don't know the line length — it's completely meaningless.

I'll get into a lengthy discussion of how fast various kinds of printers are in a little while; for the moment, suffice it to say that virtually all printers are much faster than typewriters. An IBM Selectric running at top speed will do fifteen characters per second, which is equivalent to 180 official words per minute. But even a slow formed-character printer produces 25 cps (300 owpm). A relatively fast formed-character printer does 55 cps (660 owpm), and there's even one that runs at 80 cps (960 owpm).

In spite of their speed, formed-character printers are also more reliable than typewriters because they have many fewer moving parts. Sometimes electric typewriters are adapted (or retrofitted) to work as computer printers, but they're notoriously unreliable. A typewriter's complicated mechanism just isn't designed to take the kind of constant beating computers dish out.

Still — if you can't afford a real formed-character printer but must have letter-quality text, an adapted electric typewriter may be the only alternative.

There's another major category of printers that tend to be faster and cheaper than formed-character printers but can't produce letter-quality printouts (although some come pretty close). Read on.

DOT-MATRIX PRINTERS

Dot-matrix printers form characters the same way a CRT does — by making them up out of dots. The matrix is the total number of dots possible for one character. Thus a 5×7 matrix would allow for five dots across and seven dots down (35 dots total); a 7×9

```
The  quick  brown  fox  jumped  over  the  lazy  old  dog's
            9  x  24  dot-matrix  printer
```

```
The  quick  brown  fox  jumped  over  the  lazy  old  dog's
            7  x  9  dot-matrix  printer
```

```
The  quick  brown  fox  jumped  over  the  lazy  old  dog's
            multipass  dot-matrix  printer
```

Samples from different dot-matrix printers.

matrix, seven across and nine down (63 dots total); and so on. The more dots in the matrix, the more finely defined each character will be. This is called a **dense** matrix and produces **high-resolution** printouts.

For word-processing applications, a minimum of at least 80 dots in a matrix is necessary to produce copy you expect anyone else to read. More than 100 dots produce what I consider **near-letter-quality** printouts. But at this point in time, no dot-matrix copy, regardless of how dense the matrix, is acceptable for business correspondence or for submissions to editors (except in certain fields like science fiction and, of course, computers).

The matrix can be put on the paper a number of different ways. Impact is the most common. **Impact printers** have a series of small needles, one for each dot in the matrix. When these are activated by magnets, they push through a ribbon onto the paper (just as on a formed-character printer). The needles can do their work more quickly than the hammer on a formed-character printer for two reasons:

1) Since each needle is much smaller than the hammer, it has less inertia and can thus move much faster.
2) All characters are formed by the same set of needles, so there's no time spent waiting for the right character to come around on the print element.

Two other kinds of dot-matrix printers are **thermal printers** that burn the dots into specially treated paper and **electrosensitive printers** that use electricity (instead of heat) to zap the characters into another kind of specially treated paper coated with aluminum. Both are **nonimpact printers** and therefore quieter than either formed-character or impact dot-matrix printers.

Some dot-matrix printers produce much better looking copy by moving the print head over and reprinting the text a second (or third) time, so the spaces between the dots get filled in. These are called **multipass printers.**

In some ways, the output of multipass printers is inferior to that of formed-character printers. If you look closely at the characters, you can see the dots. In other ways, however, the output is superior. Most multipass printers let you select different sizes of type and different typefaces or **fonts** (like italics) without changing print elements. The only other way to get this capability is with a typesetting machine.

Malibu Dual-Mode 200 Character Sets

Titan 10 LQ prints 10 characters per inch at 42 cps to provide letter perfect output for business correspondence.

Standard 10 DQ prints at 165 cps and is ideal for data processing requirements and draft printing.

Titan 12 LQ prints 12 characters per inch at 50 cps and is ideal for business correspondence.

Gothic 12 LQ prints at 50 cps and provides crisp, highly readable characters for reports and technical manuals.

Italics 12 LQ prints at 50 cps and is perfect for emphasizing text or use as a script-like font.

Standard 12 DQ prints at 200 cps and is ideal for data processing requirements and draft printing.

OCR-A LQ PRINTS AT 42 CHARACTERS PER SECOND TO PROVIDE MACHINE READABLE OUTPUT FOR MANUFACTURING AND RETAIL OPERATIONS.

Greek/Math and APL sets are available and print these characters at 42 cps for special applications:

Greek/Math: πο{)}∫+[₊*′/~Λ⁰¹²³⁴⁵⁶⁷⁸⁹^"Π∓±/∑∇∞Ψ⋄+<Λ¶↑>≡+δ()ι
ΓΘΣ÷Σ∠ΔΩΤ≈√〉≠•˙¨αβΨΦ∈~λη⊑≡κω{νορΥΘστξ×δχυς⊖]⟨α

APL: ")⟨≤=⟩]v≡↑,+./0123456789([;×:\∖∣α⊥η∟∈_∇Δι∘'◻⌈ΤοΗ
?ρΓ~÷∪ω⊃↑c↔⊢↦≷-◊ABCDEFGHIJKLHNOPQRSTUVWXYZ{↴}$

Pitch 17 LQ provides condensed print for compact reports with 17 characters per inch at 70 cps.

Pitch 17 DQ provides 17 characters per inch and 190 cps for volume data processing and draft printing.

In addition to these, Malibu offers foreign character sets, as well as proportional sets for special word processing applications. If what you are looking for isn't here, please ask us about it. We may be working on it already, or we may be able to design a custom set to fit your needs exactly.

Samples of different fonts from a multipass dot-matrix printer. (*Courtesy of Malibu Electronics Corporation.*)

Most multipass printers will also let you choose whether to overprint. Then you can use the high-speed, one-pass mode to produce fast drafts for editing, and the high-quality, overprint mode for the finished copy.

If you're a medium-to-large company (or an eccentric millionaire), you might want to look into **ink-jet** or **laser** printers. But for individual word-processing uses, they're like cracking walnuts with a jack hammer.

I'll be discussing specific printers later on in this chapter. In the meantime, here's a summary of what each major type offers:

Formed-character printers are:
- Relatively slow (10–80 cps).
- Relatively expensive ($1200–$3500, or as little as $700 if you include retrofitted typewriters in this category, where they technically belong).
- Relatively noisy.
- Capable of producing beautiful, crisp, letter-quality copy. Models with microspacing will give you some special effects like boldfacing, proportional spacing, subscripts, and superscripts.

Dot-matrix impact printers are:
- Relatively fast (up to 250 cps, *advertised speed*).
- Relatively cheap (as low as $300).
- Relatively quiet.
- Capable of producing draft-quality copy, with few special effects. Often the copy is barely readable, but if the matrix is dense enough, it can be quite adequate.

Multipass dot-matrix impact printers:
- Operate at various speeds (for example, the Malibu Dual-Mode 200 prints at all the following speeds — 42, 50, 70, 165, 190, and 200 cps; on the other hand, the Centronics 737 only prints at 30 cps).
- Vary widely in price ($700–$4000).
- Are relatively quiet.
- Produce near-letter-quality copy, with many special effects (like elongated and condensed type, different fonts — including foreign alphabets and symbols — you can select without having to change the print element, boldfacing, subscripts and superscripts, and proportional spacing).

Electrosensitive (dot-matrix) printers are:
- Very fast (up to 225 cps).
- Relatively cheap ($700–$1000).
- *Very* quiet.
- Capable of producing copy of varying qualities, up to near-letter-quality on those models with a dense dot matrix, but with few special effects (some won't even let you vary the margins).

I haven't seen enough thermal (dot-matrix) printers suitable for word processing to be able to generalize about them. Normally thermal printers are used when the manufacturer wants the cheapest possible hard copy – to print out narrow adding machine tapes, for example, or for a printer that's integrated into a terminal to reproduce whatever's on the screen.

SPEED

I've given you a slew of cps figures that probably don't mean a lot to you. If you're used to typewriters, printer speeds are a whole new world. For example, although an IBM Selectric's fifteen cps (150 real words per minute, 2½ words a second) may sound pretty fast to you, there are several other factors to consider:

For one thing, you rapidly become spoiled when you don't have to actually sit at a keyboard to produce text. Even a couple of pages a minute begins to feel like a snail's pace.

For another, the standard method for measuring a printer's speed is just to tell it to print a single character over and over again. This is called the **burst speed** and produces the highest possible measurement, because the printer doesn't lose time on carriage returns, waiting for the print element to come around to the right letter, etc. But it's a rare word-processing application that involves filling page after page with the same character.

There are standard tests which put printers through their paces a bit more rigorously. They're called **Shannon tests** — after Claude Shannon, "the father of information theory" who developed them. Shannon tests vary somewhat, but they always consist of a series of real English words which, taken all together, contain each individual letter approximately as often as it occurs in normal text. Thus there are more e's than x's, because e's occur in normal text more frequently than x's do.

Here's a Shannon test used by one printer manufacturer: "The head end in frontal attack on an English writer that the character of this point is therefore another method for the letters that the time of who ever told the problem for an unexpected," repeated over and over again (how's that for found poetry?).

A Shannon test gives a "worst case" score for a printer, typically 80–90 percent of the burst speed. But it's possible to modify a Shannon test so it simulates actual text even more closely, by putting in blank lines, centering lines, and indenting paragraphs. On some printers, that have features which cut down on the time it takes to space vertically or horizontally without printing anything, this will give a score that's actually higher than the official speed (assuming, of course, that you consider every horizontal and vertical space a character).

The first of these features is **bi-directional** printing. Since a computer can't understand what it's printing out, it makes no difference to it whether it starts at the left margin and goes right or starts at the right margin and goes left. In either case it figures out the whole line before it prints any of it. If it can alternate the direction in which it prints lines, it can save itself the time it takes to bring the print element all the way back to the left margin to begin each line.

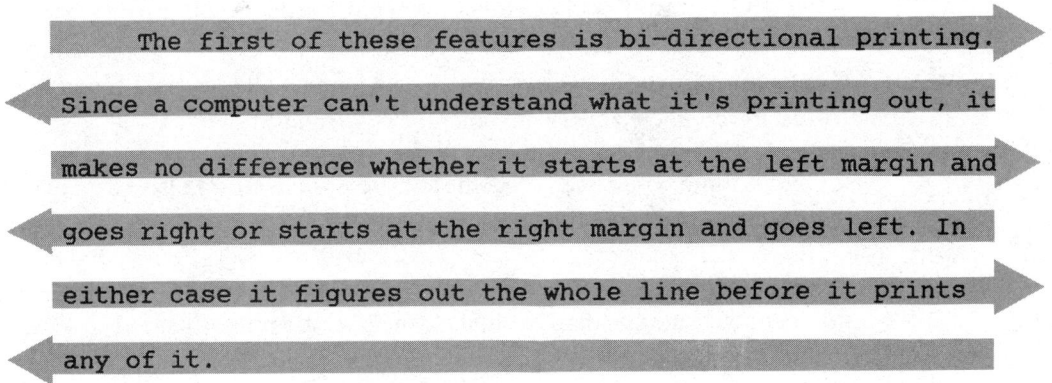

> The first of these features is bi-directional printing.
>
> Since a computer can't understand what it's printing out, it
>
> makes no difference whether it starts at the left margin and
>
> goes right or starts at the right margin and goes left. In
>
> either case it figures out the whole line before it prints
>
> any of it.

Bi-directional printing.

Bi-directional printing doesn't save a whole lot of time in a printout, although it always saves some. But it's great to watch — a constant reminder that what you have here is something way beyond a mere typewriter.

Some printers know enough to go directly to the first place where there's text on a page, instead of spacing down and over to it. This is called **logic seeking.**

Logic-seeking printers usually also have the ability to lump horizontal or vertical spaces together rather than having to do each one individually. Thus an indentation of five spaces will happen in smooth motion, rather than five distinct jumps (and the same for five blank lines). This is called **logically summing** the spaces.

Another feature that helps printers maintain top speed is a **character buffer,** which stores characters transmitted to it by the computer before printing them. So if the computer has to do a complicated calculation at some point, the printer won't have to sit and wait for it; its character buffer will act as a cushion.

One K is probably an average size for a printer buffer, but you can get them up to 48K. With a buffer that size, your computer can transmit a whole 30-page document to the printer (which should only take a minute or two) and then be free for you to use it for

```
    Some printers know enough to go directly to the first

place where there's text on a page, instead on spacing down

and over to it. This is called logic seeking.



    Logic-seeking printers usually also have the

ability to lump horizontal or vertical spaces together

rather than having to do each one individually.
```

Logic-seeking printing.

another job. The only problem with using a printer buffer to achieve multi-tasking is that if there's a mistake on the second page of the printout, there's usually no way to stop it before the buffer empties out — except to actually turn off the printer (which generally isn't a good idea).

(Some manufacturers have figured out a way around that. On their printers you can **flush the buffer** — empty it of all its text — either by a command from the keyboard or by throwing a switch in the printer itself.)

But even if a printer has all the enhancements just described, it may not come close to its advertised speed. That's because —

Advertised speeds are not necessarily true. This is *much* more of a problem with dot-matrix printers than with formed-character printers. In a survey of eight dot-matrix printers done by the weekly microcomputer newspaper, *Infoworld,* real speed turned out to be always slower than the speed claimed — and usually a *lot* slower. One printer that advertised 198 cps actually did less than 50. The mean real speed of all eight printers was only 40 percent of the claimed speeds.

Formed-character printers certainly have a better record. For one thing, I know that my formed-character printer produces about two (double-spaced) pages a minute, which is just what it should do in actual text — given that it's bi-directional, logic seeking, logically summing, and has a Shannon test speed of 48 cps (official speed — 55 cps). I imagine that other formed-character printers will have equally small discrepancies between advertised and actual speeds.

But if it makes a lot of difference to you exactly how fast the printer you buy is, prepare a sample page of text, input it into every system you're considering, and time the printout with a stopwatch. This also tests the effect of other components in the system; for example, the baud rate at which text is sent to the printer is sometimes so slow, and some word-processing programs (like WordStar) do such an inefficient job of transmitting formatted text, that the printer is actually held back from its maximum speed.

PAPER-FEEDING MECHANISMS

It wouldn't make a lot of sense to have all the capabilities of a computer printer only to have to sit next to it and feed it single sheets of paper all day. There are several more efficient ways to handle this task. The easiest and least expensive of them involves fan-fold paper and a tractor feed.

Fan-fold paper is a **continuous form,** like a roll, but with flat sheets folded in a zigzag pattern. Perforations separate each page. It comes neatly folded in a box and will fold into a neat pile again after going through the printer, if you take a little care at the start.

Fan-fold paper comes in many sizes and styles, but for most word processing uses, $9\frac{1}{2} \times 11$ plain white is ideal. In addition to the perforations between each sheet, it has a perforated strip of sprocket holes down each side. When the printout is finished, you just

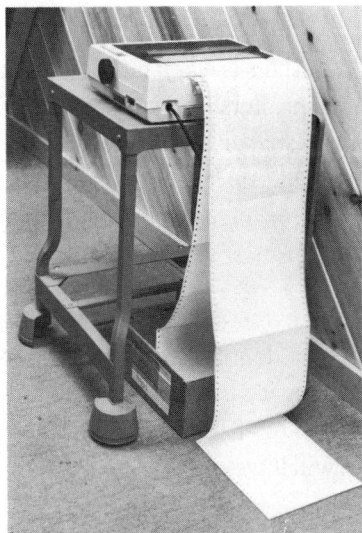

Fan-fold paper in operation.

tear off these strips, separate the pages, and you have single sheets of 8½ × 11 paper. The only clue that it came from a computer is the rough edges (which look a little like the deckle edges on fine, handmade paper).

To pull the fan-fold paper through your printer, you need something that catches the sprocket holes. The least expensive device to do that is a **tractor feed.** Tractor feeds are lightweight and mechanically simple. They attach above the platen in a second or two. When you want to feed single sheets of paper (like letterhead), you just take the tractor feed off and use the **friction feed** (the little rollers that hold the paper against the platen, as on a typewriter).

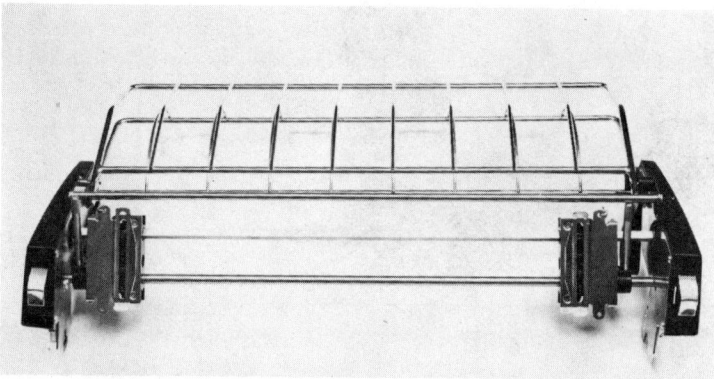

A tractor feed for use on a formed-character printer.

The problem with friction feed is that the registration is not steady. On a printout of any substantial length, the paper wanders out of alignment. Frequently you have to stop the printer, adjust the paper from side to side and top to bottom, and throw out the last few sheets where the adjustment was off.

Some printers come with the teeth to catch the sprockets mounted permanently on each end of the platen. This is called **pin feed** and is not as desirable as a tractor feed, because you can't adjust the distance between the pins; only one width of paper will engage them.

It's also possible to feed single sheets automatically with a machine called a **cut sheet feeder.** Cut sheet feeders are expensive ($1000 +) and complicated pieces of machinery, prone to go out of adjustment and fail with frightening regularity. Unless you really need to do a lot of printing on single sheets (and customized fan fold paper — with your letterhead or other frequently used form printed on it — just won't do), a tractor feed is a better bet.

A cut-sheet feeder.

Some cut sheet feeders have two trays (usually called **bins**), so you can feed envelopes and sheets of paper alternately, and some even have three (so you can feed letterhead, plain paper, and envelopes in whatever pattern you choose). Obviously, your software must be designed to take advantage of these features. You can also get a separate **envelope feeder.**

Another way to handle the problem of letterheads, if you only need to use them occasionally, is to have one printed on a transparent sheet of acetate. You take the printout of your letter, put the transparency in front of it, and make a high-quality photocopy of the two of them sandwiched together.

If you don't need to appear totally professional, there's yet another way to provide yourself with a letterhead. You create a file (called LETTERHEAD, or whatever) and put it on all the disks you use when you write letters. This file contains the instructions on how you want your letters printed out (single-spaced, with a left margin of thirteen, a right margin of 73, etc.), followed by your name, address, and phone number, all centered (and possibly boldfaced).

Here's how such a file might look (in its entirety):

```
.bfon ulon hyon
.sl66 vs8 tm2 hm4 fm4 bm2 hsl2 rm73 lml3 jl
.pnoff
.ce5
Ignatius J. Reilly

512 Constantinople Street
New Orleans LA 70115
(504) 555-3784


                                    MONTH 00, 198_


Name
Address
City State Zip

Dear _____,
```

Whenever you want the first page of a letter to appear on letterhead, you just load this file in first, fill in the blanks, and start writing. The result looks like this:

```
                  Ignatius J. Reilly

               512 Constantinople Street
                New Orleans LA 70115
                   (504) 555-3784


                                    April 4, 1984


Winston Smith
# 702
Victory Mansions
London, England
Oceania

Dear Comrade Smith,
```

TYPESETTING

It's nice to be able to connect a word processor to a **typesetting machine,** but typesetter manufacturers have traditionally made that as difficult as possible — in the hopes, I suppose, of gouging as much money as they can out of every potential user (they haven't had the sense to see that they're also restricting their market). They've been very reluctant to provide the information necessary to make the connection, and they've refused to sell typesetting machines without a lot of (junky) other equipment you don't need at all if you have a computer.

This state of affairs led Jim Warren to rant (justifiably) in his *Silicon Gulch Gazette* about the "dinosaur-like attitudes" and "myopic greed" of these manufacturers: "It's like trying to market a big, overpriced, gas-guzzling Chrysler, complete with chrome sun visors and fox tails on twin radio antennas, to consumers who want a trim, economical, easy-to-handle vehicle. The only difference is that Chrysler management is several years closer to well-earned self-destruction than are the U.S. typesetting manufacturers . . .

"Lest the reader be misled into believing that typesetter makers totally refuse to market a highly desired facility to a major potential market, please understand: Typesetters are available that can be directly computer-driven, for those willing to pay $30,000–100,000 or more. But the economical, $10,000–20,000 models . . . are not available from any major U.S. typesetter manufacturer."*

Fortunately, things have improved considerably since that was written. The codes that let computers interface with typesetters have become more widely available. For example, Marcus Computer Services of New York City markets a product called **Editerm90** which interfaces a TRS-80 with an Alphacomp typesetter. It costs $5000. But you don't need to spend that much. Don McCunn's **Word Worker** word-processing program (which costs about $20 in book form) contains codes for interfacing with several common typesetting machines.

SPECIFIC PRINTERS

When I give a price below, remember that discounts are widely available, and prices tend to drop dramatically over time.

Most of the printers I discuss are read-only (RO) — that is, they have no keyboard. (After all, what do you need a second keyboard for?)

Daisy wheel printers were invented by a company called Diablo. One of their current models, the 630, is a good example of a moderate price, moderate performance formed-character printer.

*Copyright, *Silicon Gulch Gazette.*

A Diablo 630 formed-character printer. (*Courtesy of Diablo Systems, Inc.*)

The **Diablo 630** has a maximum (advertised) speed of 40 cps (bi-directional) and a Shannon test speed of 34 cps with a plastic daisy wheel and 32 cps with a metal one. It does about 45 cps in text with blank lines and indentations. It will take paper up to 15 inches wide, has a 3/4K buffer, and lists for about $2700. An optional tractor feed costs around $300.

There's also a word-processing model for around $3000. It has boldface, proportional spacing, graphics, and an extra 2K of buffer. Diablo is now owned by Xerox, and thus this printer is often known as the Xerox 630.

The 630 has a couple of unusual features. For one thing, it will take either plastic or metal print elements (most printers take one or the other). For another, it has a special "scroll" button which lets you see what's directly in front of the print element. You push it, and the paper moves up several lines. Take your finger off the button, and the paper moves back down to exactly where it was.

Printers are often repackaged when they're sold by different distributors. Sometimes this is because improvements have been made, but other times it's just the same printer with a different name. One good, inexpensive formed-character printer that is frequently repackaged and integrated by OEMs into their word-processing systems is the 25 cps **Itoh Starwriter** (there's also a 45 cps model). You used to be able to recognize the Starwriter by the three vertical buttons on the right side, but the new F-10 model (40 cps) is smaller and lighter than the earlier models and doesn't have the buttons.

Many people, including myself, have been very happy with **NEC** (pronounced "neck") **Spinwriters.** They tend to be extremely reliable, fairly fast, and relatively quiet (about 60 dbs). Rather than daisy wheels, Spinwriters use thimbles, some of which hold 128 characters.

The NEC Series 3500 Spinwriter formed-character printer. (*Courtesy of NEC Information Systems, Inc.*)

There are two Spinwriter model lines — the 7700 and the 3500. The main difference is speed — 33 cps for the 3500 series vs. 55 cps for the 7700 series. The simplest of the 3500 series — a 3510 with no special features — costs about $2300. A 7710 with word-processing assist features costs about $3400.

A variety of paper-feeding options are available for each model — tractor feeds, single- and double-bin cut-sheet feeders, pin feed platens, and friction feed systems.

A company named InterSell modifies Spinwriters to make them smarter. For more than a year I've used a NEC 5500 (a model that's no longer made) with one of their intelligent interface boards in it. Although it has the tackiest product name in the business — **Sellum I** (get it? "sell 'em one"), the machine itself has worked very well.

Intersell was also the first company in this country to sell the **Fujitsu SP830,** which, when it was introduced, was 50 percent faster than any other formed-character printer around (it will do 80 cps; 72 cps on a Shannon test). Their modified version of this printer is called the **Sellum F-86** ("sell 'em F-86" — what does that mean?).

The Sellum F-86 has automatic bi-directional, logic-seeking, logically summing printing; automatic proportional spacing (i.e., the printer does it — you don't have to); RS-232, IEEE-488, and Centronics ports; and a standard 16K buffer (48K optional). It accepts text at rates of from 50 to 19,200 baud, uses 96-character metal or 127-character plastic daisy wheels, and costs around $3500.

One of the cheapest formed-character printers you can get is a **Smith-Corona TP-1** daisy wheel printer. It prints at 12–15 cps, comes in parallel or serial interface versions, and lists at about $900. This printer is designed for use with computers and is not a modification of an electronic typewriter, so it should be fairly reliable.

A Smith-Corona TP-I daisy-wheel printer.

Probably the best machine for the least money is the **Olivetti Praxis**. This is an electronic typewriter that uses a daisy wheel and can be adapted to run directly off a computer. An adapted Praxis, available from the Olive Branch of Hayward, CA, among other places, costs around $700. Another version called the **Bytewriter** is made in Ithaca, NY, and costs about $800. **IBM Selectrics** are also often modified to run with computers.

Oddly enough, the cheapest dot-matrix printer I know of is also called the Bytewriter (**Bytewriter-I,** actually). It costs about $300 and is designed to compete with the 80 cps **Epson MX-80** which, at about $650 list, has been the largest selling printer in the world. The Epson MX-80 uses a 9 $\times$ 9 dot matrix and prints lines a maximum of 80 characters wide (a bigger version, the **Epson MX-100,** prints up to 132 characters on a line). Epson printers have a reputation for great reliability.

The cheapest of the multipass dot-matrix printers is the **Centronics 739,** which some retailers sell for $739 (some sell it for even less). It does automatic proportional spacing, but only in a small type size (16 characters per inch). The advertised speed is 30 cps.

The **Malibu Dual-Mode 200** lists for about $3000. It offers 13 separate font and size combinations, although only two (plus graphics) are included at that price. The Dual-Mode 200 prints near-letter-quality (multipass) copy at speeds ranging from 42 to 70 cps (depending on size and number of characters to the inch) and draft copy at speeds ranging from 165 to 200 cps.

The Malibu Dual-Mode 200 multipass dot-matrix printer. (*Courtesy of Malibu Electronics Corporation.*)

The **Sanders Media 12/7** was the first multipass printer. It lists for around $3500.

Here are some samples of copy produced by each of these three printers. Remember that the smaller a character is, the sharper it's going to look. Always compare type faces of the same size.

The PIE Writer[tm] Word Processing System -- comprising the PIE text editor and FORMAT text formatting program -- is now available from Hayden Book Company. PIE and FORMAT have been rated "...one of the best word processors available..." by Apple Peelings II magazine.

PIE is a free-form, screen-oriented editor for entering and modifying text. FORMAT uses simple codes imbedded in the text to control the formatting of letters, manuals, and other documents. An optional version of the FORMAT program now supports many "specialty printer" features[1], including:

- Multiple FONTS, including ELONGATION

- PROPORTIONAL and INCREMENTAL right justification

- Both SUPERSCRIPTS and SUBSCRIPTS

- UNDERLINING of any font, including subs and supers

Sample printout from Centronics 739.

malibu
Electronics Corporation

Dear Customer:

Thanks very much for your inquiry regarding the Malibu Dual-Mode 200, our "one printer solution to the two printer problem".

Designed for the business system that is used for both data processing *and* word processing, the Dual-Mode 200 can perform high speed DP tasks at an efficient 165 to 200 characters per second, and can produce letters of outstanding quality at speeds of 42 to 70 CPS as well.

Representing the latest developments in technology, the Dual-Mode 200 is a compact, efficient, attractive, and quiet printer, with a broad range of standard features tailored for the computer system of the 80's.

Sample printout from Malibu Dual-Mode 200.

ORIGINAL PRINT SAMPLE
  MEDIA 12/7 PRINTER

Correspondence quality output can be generated by the MEDIA 12/7 in the Messenger typeface. This Messenger 12 is constructed using four passes of the print head per line. Messenger is very applicable to word processing or wherever quality correspondence printing is required. It is available in both 10 and 12 pitch as well as an international set which allows printing in European languages including French, Spanish and German. Messenger International is an additional font set which when added to the Messenger yields a multi-language capability for a small incremental cost.

The standard printer will HAVE UP TO 11 TYPEFACES WHICH CAN BE COMBINED WITHIN THE SAME DOCUMENT AND EVEN WITHIN THE SAME LINE. THE "4 PASS" QUALITY IS PRODUCED BY FOUR HORIZONTAL PASSES OF A 7 PIN PRINT HEAD WITH SLIGHT VERTICAL MOTION OF THE PAPER BETWEEN PASSES. The characters are formed with 12 mil dots placed to 1 mil accuracy *horizontally and 3.5 mils* vertically. Most knowledgeable observers agree our print quality is equal to or slightly better than the IBM ink jet and standard electric typewriters.

High quality text output can be produced using one of the members of the Helvesan family. This paragraph is set in 8 point Helvesan Regular. Helvesan is a proportionally spaced, sans serif typeface which the MEDIA 12/7 prints in four passes of the print head per line. Helvesan is recommended for high quality printing of business documents such as reports and proposals. The "infinite matrix principle" embodied in the MEDIA 12/7 allows this typesetting quality output. Typefaces may be instantaneously switched be the MEDIA 12/7 firmware allowing proportional text for the body of text and fixed pitch text for tables.

Sample printout from Sanders Media 12/7.

The **Comprint 912** is an electrosensitive printer with a fairly dense matrix (9 × 12). Thus it produces quite nice-looking type, and it does that at 225 cps. The main problem with it is that it has to use roll paper that's coated with aluminum. It also offers fewer margin and page options than you're going to want. But it's fast, quiet, and only costs about $700.

The **Silentype** is one of the rare 80-column thermal printers (most have narrower printouts). It interfaces with all Apples, and with the Apple III it lets you specify different type styles. High-resolution graphics are another feature. Printout is at 40 cps, and cost is about $400.

That's a sampling of the many printers that are out there. Use the checklist that follows to evaluate any printer you're interested in.

CHECKLIST FOR PRINTERS

Printer brand and model:

Manufacturer:

Vendor(s) and price(s):

Interfaces provided:
RS-232?
IEEE-488?
Centronics parallel?
Others:

Speed:
advertised _____ cps
Shannon test _____ cps
modified Shannon test, with blank lines,
centered lines, and indentations _____ cps
Bi-directional?
Logic seeking?
Logically sums spaces?
Size of buffer? _____ K
Word-processing features available:
Underlining?
Boldfacing:
if software instructs?
automatically?

Proportional spacing:
    if software instructs?
    automatically?
Justified right margin:
    if software instructs?
    automatically?
Subscripts and superscripts:
    if software instructs?
    automatically?

Minimum **horizontal motion:** 1/_____ inch
Minimum **vertical motion:** 1/_____ inch
Maximum **width of paper** accommodated: _____
Maximum **number of characters** allowed **in line:** _____

Paper feeding mechanisms:
    Friction feed:
        included in price?
        available as an option for $_____
    Tractor feed:
        included in price?
        available as an option for $_____
    Pin feed platen:
        included in price?
        available as an option for $_____
    Cut-sheet feeder:
        included in price?
        available as an option for $_____
    Double-bin cut-sheet feeder:
        included in price?
        available as an option for $_____
    Triple-bin cut sheet feeder:
        included in price?
        available as an option for $_____
    Envelope feeder:
        included in price?
        available as an option for $_____

Range of **transmission rates** accommodated: _____ - _____
Noise level: _____ db
Graphics?
    included in price?
    available as an option for $_____

Other special features:

Reliability:

Service information:

Cost of **ribbons:** $_____ for _____
Additional notes:

FORMED-CHARACTER PRINTERS:

Type of **print element** used:
 Plastic daisy wheel?
 Metal daisy wheel?
 Both?
 Thimble?
 Other?
Maximum **number of characters**
 available on print element: _____
Number of different type styles
 and special **print elements** available:_____
Replacement **cost** of **print element:** $_____

DOT-MATRIX PRINTERS:

Method of putting characters on paper:
 Impact? **Thermal?** **Electrosensitive?**
Density of matrix: _____ × _____
Number of characters it will print: _____
Number of different **fonts** available: _____
Number of different type **sizes** available: _____
 Total number of fonts and sizes: _____
Special paper?
 If so, **cost:** $_____
Multipass?
 Allows **high-speed draft copies** as well?

10

Microcomputers

A lot of what you should look for in a microcomputer system has already been covered in Chapter 8 (screens and keyboards) and Chapter 9 (printers). In this chapter I talk about the computer itself — its capabilities, its memory, the chip it's based on, the operating system it runs, and the kind of storage devices it has (floppy drives or hard disk drives).

If you're primarily interested in a dedicated word processor rather than a microcomputer, you should still read this chapter, because it covers what to look for in terms of computing power and storage. (The discussion near the end of Chapter 3 on the differences between a dedicated word processor and a microcomputer will help you decide which kind of machine you want.) The next chapter covers dedicated word processors in detail.

Oddly enough, picking software, a screen, a keyboard and a printer all involve more crucial decisions than picking the microcomputer itself. In a certain way, it's one of the least important components; basically it just has to support the other elements.

So rather than go on at great length about microcomputers in general, I devote the majority of this chapter to descriptions of specific machines. Even though a lot of that information will quickly go out of date, I want to give you a sense of the incredible number of microcomputers that are available and of how many different companies make them.

IBM, I'm told, plans to capture at least 40 percent of the microcomputer market. *InfoWorld* columnist Jim Edlin sums up my feelings about this when he says that IBM sat ''on the sidelines for 6½ years letting others take the risks and do the spadework, and then [showed] up with a me-too product . . . . If you have participated in or cheered on the entrepreneurial rise of the microcomputer industry, you may find [the idea that IBM will emerge] as the big winner in the microcomputer game . . . infuriating'' (Jim, by the way, has since become a convert to the PC).

This brings me to my first general recommendation:

1) Don't be snowed by a big name.

Sure you want a good, reliable, well-supported product, but IBM, Xerox, Apple, and Radio Shack aren't the only companies that make one. If a company trades on its name, *you* are paying for it. It's like buying Del Monte canned pineapple (or whatever) instead of the generic house brand — you pay more, but you don't necessarily get more.

In the long run, the more small, competitive companies there are around, the better products we'll have and the less money they'll cost. So don't be a sheep. Judge products, and the companies that make them, on their merits, not on their fame.

(Of course, IBM and Xerox got big by providing superb service and are likely to continue providing it. That fact should be part of your considerations. But only part.)

2) Pick the chip, operating system, and/or machine that gives you the software you want.

I've made this point already (in Chapter 4), but it bears repeating. It doesn't do you any good to have the snazziest, most powerful, sexiest computer on your block if the applications programs you need won't run on it. Also remember that —

3) The more popular your machine (or operating system), the more software will be written for it.

Don't think you'll never want any program other than your word processor; you will. And the more programs you have to choose from, the more likely you are to be able to get just the one you need. For example, almost every operating system has a couple of spelling checkers that run under it. But CP/M has at least five, and as a result, one of them — The Word, from Oasis Systems in San Diego — costs only $75 (or $150 for the new, improved version). The other four programs cost between $170 and $300, yet, according to a review in *BYTE* magazine, even the earlier version of The Word ''far surpasses'' them.

Now those other four spelling checkers are no slouches; one of them — SpellGuard — was chosen Software Product of the Year by *InfoWorld*. Only if there are a *lot* of programs do you get one that not only is as good as any of its competitors, but also costs less than half as much money.

In terms of how much software has been written for them, the two most popular operating systems are Apple DOS and CP/M (I'm not sure which has more and, from what I can tell, neither is anybody else). Since an Apple II with a SoftCard can run both of them, it supports more programs than any other computer in the world.

Next comes TRSDOS (I think — all three of these operating systems claim to have the most software). TRS-80s can also be modified to run CP/M (although getting it to run

TRSDOS again after the conversion is more complicated than just popping a card in and out).

In any case, any one of these three operating systems by itself should give you plenty of software to choose from.

4) 8-inch vs. 5¼-inch disks.

Eight-inch disks have two major advantages. The first is obvious — they hold more data (or hold the same amount of data more reliably). The second is that 8-inch disks are often compatible with one another, while each machine's minifloppy format tends to be an island unto itself. (**Format** refers to how data is placed on the disk. It's transparent to you, the user — that is, you never know where the machine is putting the information.) **IBM 3740** is the name of the standard format used on most single-sided, single-density 8-inch disks.

Adapting a piece of software to a new disk format takes a certain amount of time and energy, and software publishers tend never to have enough of either of those. Naturally, the more users a particular format has, the more pieces of software that are going to be adapted to it. Since 3740 is a standard format, it has a lot of users.

Disk format is a consideration above and beyond an operating system. For example, the NorthStar Horizon is based on the Z80 chip and runs CP/M. But its minifloppy drives have their own format; if you want to run a piece of CP/M software, it has to have been adapted for NorthStar-format disks. But almost all CP/M programs are available on standard 8-inch, 3740-format disks.

5) Work in silence.

Many 5¼-inch drives have a feature I wish more 8-inch drive manufacturers would adopt — **automatic shutoff.** This means that if you don't use your drives for some given period of time, they shut off. When you go to use them, they automatically turn on again. This saves wear and tear on the drives — and on you too, because you don't have to listen to them whirring around while you work.

The turning of the disk drives makes up about 90 percent of the noise a microcomputer makes. The fan produces the other 10 percent, but eliminating that courts the risk of heat failure. (Some machines don't even have fans and are always running that risk.)

Some people prefer drives you can turn on and off at will with a switch, but this won't work for programs that are constantly accessing the disk (either because they use overlays or because they swap the workfile on and off disk). In any case, an automatic shutoff is more convenient, and the amount of time the disk spends turning back on is trivial.

6) Remember to get enough memory.

Memory doesn't cost much, and it's really nice to have a lot of it. Get at least 64 K of RAM if you can. For word-processing applications, it's silly to even consider a system with less than 32K of RAM.

How much RAM you have is just an indirect measure, of course. What counts is your workspace. With the operating system and word-processing program loaded into RAM, the remaining workspace should be *at least* 10K; 20K is better, and 30K better still. More than that is gravy (although personally, the idea of a megabyte of workspace makes me drool).

In the case of memory, *more* is more.

7) Leave yourself room to expand.

The easier it is to add new boards and peripherals to your microcomputer, the longer you're going to be able to hold onto it. So, everything else being equal, it's great to have a lot of empty slots and standard interfaces to pop things into.

A standard interface for boards, like the **S-100** bus, is nice because it increases the number of options available to you. (Unfortunately, the S-100 bus isn't as standard as it could be. Not every S-100 board will work in every S-100 machine.)

8) Compare equivalents.

It's easy for one system to be cheaper than another if it doesn't include the same pieces of equipment. Some ads give prices for ''word processors'' that include dot-matrix printers or even no printers at all! (You can process the words, you just can't put them on paper.)

You should get a system that has enough RAM (ideally 64K or more), a keyboard (ideally detachable), a screen (ideally 12″ or more), two disk drives (ideally 8-inch), and a printer (ideally one of the fast formed-character ones); be sure to figure in *all* these components when you compare prices.

9) Connecting with other machines.

There are a couple of ways to do this. The easiest is over phone lines, for which you need a **modem** and an interface (in hardware and/or software) that understands the protocols required by the system you're connecting with — **The Source, Compuserve, Prestel,** or whatever.

(**Protocols** are the rules that govern the exchange of information between two systems — how they know when one should stop talking and listen to the other, say. An everyday example of a communications protocol is the use of the word ''over'' — which means "I'm done transmitting, you transmit now" — on radio channels where only one person can talk at a time. Another such protocol is "over and out," which means, "I'm done transmitting and am going to break the communication." Both of these have exact equivalents in any set of computer communication protocols.)

The problem with modems and phone lines is that 1200 baud is about the fastest data transfer rate they'll handle, and that's pretty slow. If the other machines you want to talk with are physically close to your own, you can hook up with a **local network** to talk to them.

There are several different kinds of local networks and many different brands — Xerox's **Ethernet** (which works with all sorts of machines) is the best known. Local networks have much faster transmission rates than are possible over phone lines.

Some systems (particularly dedicated word processors) come with communications capability included, and others let you add it at additional cost. If you think you're going to want communications capability, make sure the system you buy has a provision for it.

That just about does it for general principles. Following are brief descriptions of several dozen microcomputers, in reverse alphabetical order. (Xerox gave me fifty grand to do it that way. *Just kidding*. I simply think it's only fair to switch around so that the people at the end of the alphabet get equal time.)

Despite its length, this is very much just a *partial* list of what's available. The moral is: shop around until you find a machine (and support) you really like.

The Xerox 820 Information Processor. (*Courtesy of Xerox Corporation.*)

Xerox makes a full line of systems, and I've put all the more expensive ones (including the 8010 Star) in Chapter 11. That leaves the 820, which lists for $3000 with 64K of RAM and two single-sided, single-density minifloppy disk drives that hold 92K each. Eight-inch floppy drives cost $1600 more and hold 250K each. A Diablo 630 formed-character printer costs $2900 more. The keyboard is separate.

The 820 is built around a Z80 chip and runs CP/M. The keyboard has several function keys and a ten-key numeric keypad. The 820 seems to be an intelligently designed machine, but there are dozens of others equivalent (or superior) to it, and some of them cost less money.

Xerox has plans to introduce a less expensive machine than the 820. It will also be built around a Z80 chip, will have 16K of RAM (expandable to 256K), 64K of ROM, and color graphics. It will list for around $1000.

Victor Business Products makes a 16-bit micro called the **9000.** It has 128K of RAM (expandable to 512K) and two minifloppy drives with a capacity of 600K on each disk. The high-resolution screen tilts and swivels and will display either 25 lines of 80 characters or 50 lines of 132 characters. A variety of programs are available for the Victor 9000. It lists for $5000.

The Vector 3005. (*Courtesy of Vector Graphics, Inc.*)

Vector Graphic makes a whole line of micros, including the 2600, which lists for about $6000, and the 3005, which lists for about $8000. The **2600** has 64K of RAM and two minifloppy drives with 600K on each disk. It runs CP/M and is expandable (it's an S-100 bus machine). The 2600 has a special feature: it checks for errors on all disk operations and automatically corrects them (unless there are a whole lot of them). The keyboard is not separate.

The **3005** also checks for errors and automatically corrects them. It has one 630K floppy drive and a 5 MB hard disk as well. It runs CP/M too.

Knowing how to market their products and service their dealers is what made Vector Graphic into a large company. They more or less invented packaging graphics, good documentation, and dealer support in the memory board market, where they started. (Despite their history and reputation, however, Vector Graphic never responded to my letter asking for information on their hardware and software. Maybe they're slipping.)

By the way, Vector Graphic was founded by — and is still run by — two women.

The new Vector 4 dual-processor microcomputer. (*Courtesy of Vector Graphics, Inc.*)

Several **Radio Shack** computers are suitable for word processing. They're called **TRS-80**s, which stands for *T*andy (the parent company's name) *R*adio *S*hack-Z-*80* (although the Color Computer is based on the 6809 chip, not the Z-80).

The first TRS-80 was called the **Model I**; Radio Shack sold more than 200,000 of them before they were discontinued. The Model I is only usable as a word processor in its **Level** II version with an **expansion interface** that lets you add more memory, a printer, and disk drive. Even then, it had a lot of annoying problems, like **key bounce** (which gives you two or more characters when you hit a key once). The Model I was replaced by the **Model III.**

The TRS-80 Model III. (*Courtesy of Tandy Corporation.*)

The Model III comes in a variety of configurations. (In fact, Radio Shack's sales strategy seems to be to charge very little for the basic unit, which is so stripped down you can barely do anything with it, and make its money on everything else you have to buy.)

What Radio Shack calls their Model III Word Processing System costs about $3400 but includes only a dot-matrix printer (their Line Printer VIII). With their formed-character printer (the Daisy Wheel II), the price is about $4600. In either case, the system will include 48K of RAM, two minifloppy drives (306K each), an RS-232 interface, and Radio Shack's own word-processing program, SCRIPSIT. The keyboard is not separate.

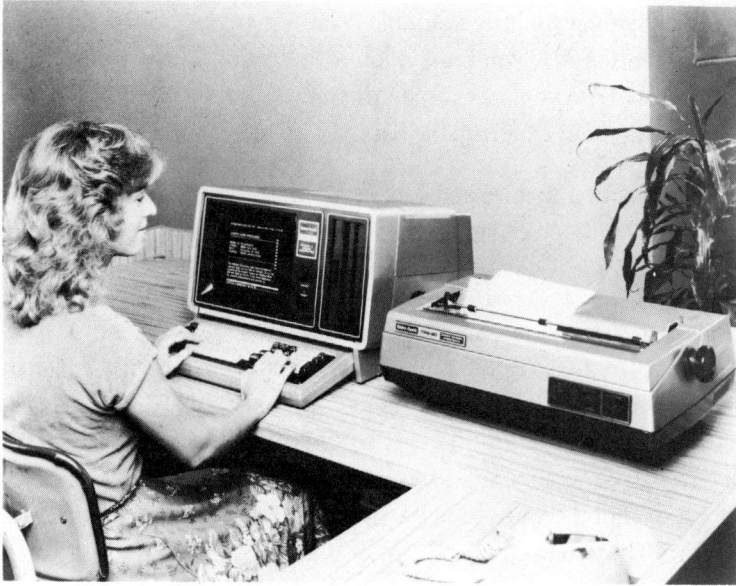

The TRS-80 Model II. (*Courtesy of Tandy Corporation.*)

The TRS-80 **Model II** runs faster (four MHz) than the Model III and has a separate microprocessor in the keyboard which frees up the computer. The keyboard is detachable, with a two-foot cord. The screen shows 24 lines of 80 characters.

A Model II word-processing system with 64K of RAM, a 480K double-density 8-inch floppy drive, Daisy Wheel II printer, printer cable, printer stand, and desk costs about $6400. You can connect up to three additional floppy disk drives (at $780–1150 each, depending on how many you get). An optional 8.4 MB hard disk drive is available for $4500. In fact, you can connect up to three of them, although what you'd need 26 million characters worth of storage for is beyond me.

Like all TRS-80 computers, the Model II runs memory mapped. It and the Model III run under Radio Shack's own operating system, TRSDOS (pronounced "triss doss"). Both can be converted to run CP/M (but Radio Shack themselves won't do it. In fact, Radio Shack refuses to service TRS-80's that have been modified). Two companies that convert TRS-80's to run CP/M are Omikron of Berkeley, California and Field Engineering Consultants of Woburn, Massachusetts; there are many others.

Another operating system for Models I and III is NEWDOS/80, from Apparat, Inc. of Denver. Many users consider NEWDOS a great improvement over TRSDOS.

The TRS-80 **Color Computer** was designed for low-cost game playing, but the people at Softwest have adapted PIE Writer to run on it, and there are likely to be several other word-processing programs available for it. Using the Color Computer for word processing requires the 32K version, which costs around $700. A disk drive is also helpful, and that will run you another $600 for the first drive and $400 for the second. Still, the Color Computer can form the basis for an inexpensive word-processing system.

TRS-80s are quite reliable, and a lot of good, inexpensive software is available for them. Some TRS-80 documentation is quite good, and Radio Shack now has an 800 number you can call with questions (this supplements the support offered by their computer centers).

Texas Instruments is a company whose computer sales have suffered because their machines have been built around their own proprietary chips (the 8-bit **TMS9900** and the 16-bit **TMS99000**), and there isn't much software written to run on those chips. Its **99/4a** is an inexpensive ($525) micro and was the first to offer **LOGO,** which is a great learning language for kids. I don't know of any word processing program that runs on the 99/4a, but there's sure to be one eventually.

TI also makes the **Business System 200,** a 16-bit machine that comes in a number of different configurations and starts at $6200.

Superbrain is the name of a series of micros which begins with a basic system with 64K that costs $3500. You can get 10 and 20 MB hard disks to go with it and connect it with as many as 255 other terminals.

There are a number of machines based on the 6800 and 6809 chips. The major manufacturers are **Southwest Technical Products** of San Antonio; **Smoke Signal Broadcasting** of Westlake Village, California; **Percom** of Garland, Texas; **Midwest Scientific Instruments** of Olathe, Kansas; and **Gimix** of Chicago.

The Otrona Attache portable computer. (*Courtesy of Ortrona Corporation.*)

Otrona Corporation of Boulder, Colorado makes the **Attache,** an 18-pound portable computer that looks — as its name would indicate — like an attache case when carried. It has 64K, two minifloppy drives, and is based on the Z80 chip. Its 5-inch monitor displays lines of either 40 or 80 characters. The Attache costs $4000, and CP/M, WordStar, and an extended BASIC are included in the price.

Six pounds heavier (and $2200 cheaper) than the Otrona is the machine that set the 1981 West Coast Computer Faire on its ear — the **Osborne 1.** The first of the truly portable computers, the Osborne 1 has 64K, two 100K minifloppy drives, a 5-inch screen, a detachable keyboard (with a very short cord), an RS-232, IEEE-4888, and modem interface, and plugs for an external screen and battery pack. Included in the $1800 price are CP/M, WordStar, MailMerge, SuperCalc, and two programming languages — CBASIC and MBASIC.

The Osborne 1 portable computer. (*Courtesy of Osborne Computer Corporation.*)

There are a few problems with the Osborne 1:
- Large numbers of them were reportedly DOA ("dead on arrival") when delivered — but this was apparently just a problem with the first shipments.
- The lines of text on the screen are only 52 characters long (although later models are sure to provide 80-character lines).
- A 5-inch screen is awfully small (but an optional 12″ monitor doesn't cost much extra).
- It's not expandable.
- Not much software has been adapted to run on it yet. One thing that makes adaption difficult is the 52-character line.

But, even with these minor problems, the Osborne 1 offers an incredible amount of value for the money. At the present time there is no other computer that can match it, feature for feature, for less than twice the price. (The Osborne 2, which wasn't out yet when this book was written, may offer even better value.)

NorthStar makes two computer models — the older Horizon and the newer Advantage. The **Advantage** is a 64K Z80 computer with two 360K minifloppy drives. It has a high-resolution screen, graphics capabilities, a numeric keypad, and fifteen user-programmable function keys. Everything comes in one box; the keyboard is not detachable. The Advantage can run either CP/M or NorthStar's own disk operating system, N*DOS. It costs $4000.

For what it's worth, NorthStar wins the prize for being the hardest manufacturer of all the ones I called to get information out of on the telephone. (Magic Wand's publisher, Peachtree, wins the prize for software.) This may or may not translate into bad support from their dealers.

The NEC PC—8001A. (*Courtesy of NEC Informaton Systems, Inc.*)

NEC, which makes great printers, also markets a microcomputer — the **PC-8001A.** It's based on a chip that's compatible with the Z80 and runs an operating system that's compatible with CP/M. It gives you N-BASIC in ROM (24K of it) and 32K of RAM. It offers eight-color graphics and ten special function keys. That much lists for $1300 (and you can get it for $1100 or less).

A one-color (green) 12″ monitor lists for $285. A full-color monitor, to take care of the graphics capabilities, lists for $1100. A double mini disk drive unit (143K each disk) lists for $1300. To do word processing, you need more than 32K of RAM, and the expansion unit, which comes with 32K more RAM and lets you add up to another 96K (for a total of 160K of RAM), lists for $800. It has several additional slots for boards.

So a word-processing system — 64K RAM, one-color screen, two mini drives — lists for about $3700 without a printer. That's not cheap, if you don't need (or want) the color graphics (and if you do, you're talking about $4500 with the color monitor). But it's a nice machine, and once you have the expansion unit, you can add memory to it by just popping in boards.

(NEC stands for Nippon Electric Company — one of my favorite computer names.)

MicroPro International, the publishers of WordStar and other programs, also sell hardware. Their computer manufacturing division, **Performance Business Machines,** distributes the **PBM-1000,** which comes with 80K of RAM, 940K of floppy disk storage, and 5⅔ MB of hard disk storage. It lists for $7000 and comes with the full line of MicroPro software, as well as CP/M.

A third briefcase computer is the **Microdata 8400,** made at the Belvedere Works, Bilton Way, Pump Lane Industrial Estate, Hayes, Middlesex, England (isn't that a wonderful address?). It has a foldaway gas plasma viewing screen and **bubble memory** (an advanced, fast, and expensive technology). 32K of RAM is standard, with an additional 16K optional. The screen measures approximately 5×8 inches and shows 12 lines of 40 characters. It comes in a weatherproof plastic case and weighs about 15 pounds.

Bubble memory and a flat panel screen don't come cheap; the 8400 costs £2750 — about $5500.

The **LNW-80** is a sort of supercharged imitation TRS-80 Model I that outperforms the Model III. Among the features it has that a TRS-80 Model I doesn't are double-density disk drives, high-resolution eight-color graphics, 24 line by 80 character display, extra keys (brackets, control, shift lock), cursor arrows grouped together, a numeric keypad, a metal case, and a fan.

The LNW-80 runs twice as fast as the Model III (four MHz), has an RS-232 interface as standard equipment, and costs less than a comparably equipped Model III ($2250 vs. $2600). All Model I software runs on it. Made by LNW Research of Tustin, California, the LNW-80 also comes in a kit form.

International Systems Marketing of Bethesda, Maryland offers the **Intersystem Model 40,** with 64K of RAM and two minifloppy drives with one MB(!) on each disk. The screen is 12 inches and the keyboard is separate. An RS-232 and a parallel port are standard, as is CP/M. The Model 40 costs about $4200. There are also Models 10, 20, and 30, ranging in price from $2300 to $3600.

The IBM Personal Computer. (*Courtesy of International Business Machines Corporation.*)

Like Radio Shack, **IBM**'s strategy with its **Personal Computer** has been to declare a low price for a basic, stripped-down piece of equipment; at the time of the machine's introduction, $1565 would buy you a "system that, with the addition of one simple device, hooks up to your home TV and uses your own audio cassette." Leaving aside the fact that it's hardly fair to call a keyboard and a computer box with two empty slots for disk drives a "system," the question arises: what will an actual system that can do word processing (for example) cost?

Unfortunately, this isn't easy to figure out because, as *Popular Computing* put it, "IBM's . . . price list is a confusing jumble of options and additions that would make any automobile salesman green with envy."

The Personal Computer comes with 16K of RAM and 40K of ROM standard. The RAM is expandable to 256K by means of circuit boards you can plug in yourself. They cost $90 for 16K, $325 for 32K, and $540 for 64K. So bringing the system up to 48K will bring the price up to about $1900; at 64K, the price becomes about $2000.

The 160K, 5¼-inch minifloppy drives are $570 each, and the disk adapter to run them costs $220. The 11½-inch green phosphor monitor that IBM sells with the system costs $345. So a good word-processing configuration (64K, two mini drives, etc.) will run about $3700 — in other words, just about what you'd expect to pay from most manufacturers. The question is, will you get more value for your money from IBM? And the answer is . . .

Yes and no. In certain ways, the IBM Personal Computer is a well thought-out machine, with unusual and advanced features. In other ways, it's perfectly ordinary, no better and no worse than dozens of competitors.

The 40K of ROM that comes standard is a nice feature, and an unusual one; it contains an extended version of the MBASIC programming language. It's also nice to be able to increase your memory all the way up to 256K just by plugging in boards.

The PC is also a fast machine for a personal computer, in part because it runs at 4.77 MHz, and in part because of the chip it's based on. The Intel **8088** processes data internally 16 bits at a time, but takes data in and sends it out eight bits at a time (in technical jargon, it's a 16-bit chip with an 8-bit **data bus**). Since characters are each one byte anyway, it makes sense to transmit text eight bits at a time; but the 16-bit internal operations speed things up. So this is a nice combination.

The problem with the 8088 chip is that there isn't much software written for it (or wasn't much before IBM used it in the Personal Computer; since then, everybody and her brother are busy converting programs to it). The Personal Computer will run CP/M, but it's CP/M-86, not the original 8080/Z80 CP/M that has all the software on it.

When the Personal Computer came out, there was almost no CP/M-86 software, and IBM took a long time supporting CPM-86, doubtless in the hope that eager programmers would come out with software to run on IBM's own operating system in the meantime. IBM is wisely encouraging independent programmers by offering to publish their software for them. They are also providing information that makes it easy for "the existing cottage industry" to design boards and peripherals for the PC.

If you're going to get a PC, it makes a lot of sense to get plug-compatible boards (and other components) made by other manufacturers. They generally are more technologically advanced and offer better value than IBM's own hardware. The same goes for software. The word-processing program IBM itself originally offered — EasyWriter — is reviewed in this book. Since they obviously considered a number of programs, it's hard to see how they ended up with this one, which is both weak and hard to use.

The PC is an attractive machine and benefits from IBM's usual dedication to human engineering. For example, the keyboard is separate, with a six-foot coiled cord, and you can adjust the angle at which the keys tilt toward you. There are cursor arrows, a numeric keypad, auto-repeat on all keys, and ten function keys. RS-232 and Centronics parallel interfaces are standard.

When you turn the Personal Computer on, it automatically tests itself to make sure things are working OK. You can play music on its speaker. With a color monitor you can get either high-resolution graphics or 16 foreground and eight background colors.

IBM offers service contracts on the Personal Computer and its components for 10–15 percent of the purchase price per year. That may seem like a lot, but it buys you IBM's own unique brand of S*E*R*V*I*C*E — for example, they'll send you a replacement keyboard, printer, or computer box, by courier, within 48 hours of your call. [Stop Press: I've just heard a report of IBM's giving at least one company absolutely wretched service on their PC's.] You can also bring components into an IBM Product Center, Sears business machine store, or Computerland, regardless of where you bought them. For support, of course, you should depend on your vendor; ask what their policy is on calling up with questions.

So that's the IBM Personal Computer — a good, solid, well-designed machine, but not the Second Coming.

The Hewlett-Packard HP 125 Personal Office Computer. (*Courtesy of Hewlett-Packard Company.*)

Hewlett-Packard is a company famous for building solid products, giving them great support, and understating what they can do. They charge top dollar for all of this (although recently they've been bringing their prices down). So if you want a fully supported, high-quality micro and can afford to pay for it, you should look at the **HP-125.**

It's built around two Z80A chips and has a separate microprocessor to control the terminal. There's 64K of RAM (plus some additional memory for the screen), a 12-inch CRT with characters in a 9×15 matrix (very well defined, in other words), and a detachable keyboard with numeric keypad and eight soft keys whose current functions are labelled by the software on the screen. The machine tests itself when it turns on.

CP/M is standard, and comes with a rewritten, and indexed, manual (thank God!) instead of Digital Research's unreadable seven manuals that all have to be looked at together to be understood (and can't be understood even then). HP sells a customized version of Spellbinder, called Word/125. Spellbinder is evaluated in Chapter 5.

You can get the HP-125 with twin mini drives (256K each) for around $5000. They sell a 40 cps Diablo daisy-wheel printer to go with it for about $4000. You can also get twin 8-inch disks (1.2 MB each), but the drive unit costs around $6800 all by itself. There's also a 4.6 MB Winchester hard disk, with an integrated 270K floppy for backup; this unit costs $5500 and is therefore a much better deal than the 8-inch floppies.

Godbout Electronics of Oakland, California has a reputation for making top-of-the-line microcomputer hardware, which it sells under the inelegant name of **CompuPro; G & G Engineering** of San Leandro, California is one OEM that assembles components from CompuPro (and other manufacturers) into finished systems. For about $5000 they'll give you 64 K of **static RAM** (which uses less power and is accessed faster than the normal **dynamic RAM**), two 8-inch floppy drives (1.2 MB per disk), CP/M, WordStar, and MBASIC. The system runs at 6 MHz.

A state-of-the-art micro is the **Fortune 32/16,** from Fortune Systems of San Carlos, California. It's based on the 16-bit 68000 chip and offers 128K of RAM (expandable to four MB), two minifloppies (750K each), a high-resolution monitor that tilts and swivels, a detachable keyboard, and the UNIX operating system. It costs about $5000.

The **Exidy Sorcerer** is a Z80-based micro with 4K of ROM and up to 32K of RAM. It runs CP/M and can also be adapted to connect with other terminals.

Epic Computer of San Diego makes the **Episode,** a compact computer containing a Z80 CPU, 64K of RAM, and two minifloppy drives in a box measuring $7\frac{1}{2} \times 9\frac{1}{2} \times 14\frac{1}{2}$ inches. It runs CP/M and the special CP/M menu, Supervyz.

Durango Systems of San Jose, California makes the **Colt,** which is configured in an unusual way. The keyboard is part of the dot-matrix printer (which therefore looks like a typewriter); there's also a separate screen.

Digital Equipment Corporation is known to everybody in the computer field as **DEC** (pronounced ''deck''). For some reason, they don't seem to like that, and lately they've been signing their ads **Digital.** Whatever you call them, they're one of the major minicomputer manufacturers and, as of this writing, are just about to move into the micro field as well. Whatever they come up with, it will have a lot of muscle behind it.

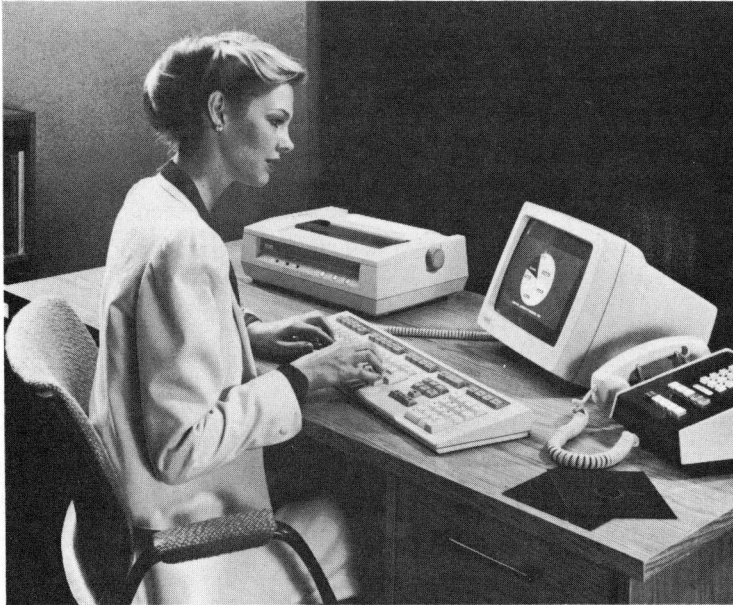

The Professional 350, the top of Digital Equipment Corporation's new personal computer line, priced at $4995. (*Courtesy of Digital Equipment Corporation.*)

Data General is another mini manufacturer which has moved into the micro market with its **Enterprise 1000.** Based on the proprietary 16-bit microNOVA chip, the Enterprise 1000 has 64K of RAM, two minifloppies (358K each), and Data General's Business BASIC. With a 150 cps dot-matrix printer, it costs around $7200.

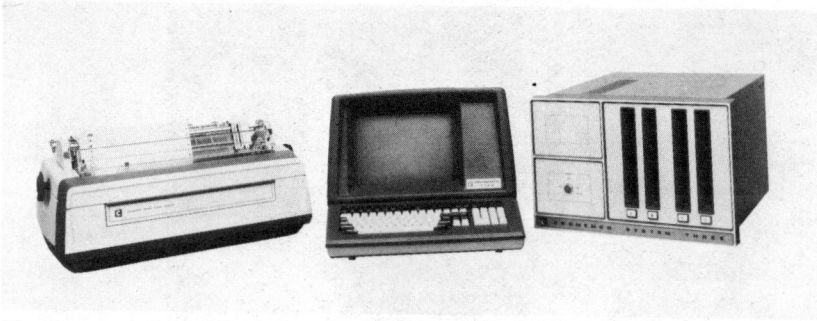

The Cromemco System 3. (*Courtesy of Cromemco, Inc.*)

Cromemco of Mountain View, California is one of the oldest microcomputer manufacturers; they go all the way back to the *mid-70's!* Cromemco makes a full line of micros with a bewildering multiplicity of possible configurations. I'll discuss a good system for word processing, the System 3, Model CS-3. It's based on a Z80A chip running at four MHz and an S-100 bus. The motherboard will hold up to 21 boards and slides out through a hinged front panel to make it easy to put new ones in.

The Model CS-3 has 64K of RAM (expandable to 512K) and 4K of ROM. There are slots for four 8-inch drives, and two come standard. Each disk holds 1.2 MB. The CRT displays 24 lines of 80 characters; the keyboard is not detachable. Cromemco supplies either a 180 cps dot-matrix printer or a 55 cps formed-character printer. With the latter printer, the system lists for $11,500, but you can find one for under $10,000 if you look around.

Cromemco has its own word-processing program, Writemaster. Since their micros run CP/M, you have a large number of other ones to choose from if you don't like Writemaster.

Cromemco's new C-10 personal computer for $1785, which includes more than $1000 worth of free software. The printer is extra, bringing the system price to $2785. (*Courtesy of Cromemco, Inc.*)

The **Commodore Pet 4016** has a 12-inch green screen, a numeric keypad, and a standard IEEE interface. With 16K, it costs $1000. Minifloppy drives are also available; each disk holds 500K.

AVL of Campbell, California also makes a computer called the Eagle — The **Eagle II** in this case. It has 64K of RAM and two disks that hold 250K each. It's built around the Z80 chip, runs CP/M, and costs about $5000. AVL has extensively modified the VTS-80 word-processing program for the Eagle II.

The **Archives III** (made by Archives, Inc. of Davenport, Iowa) is built around a 5¼-inch hard disk which holds 5½ MB. The computer runs CP/M and has a detachable keyboard. It sells for $8500.

Which brings us to **Apple.** Although they didn't invent the personal computer (as they have claimed), they were among the first companies to market and support it in an intelligent way.

The **Apple I** was a kit, and not many were sold. The **Apple II** is the machine that made Apple famous. It comes with 16K of RAM, expandable to 48K, and 8K of ROM, which holds the BASIC programming language and is expandable to 12K.

A TV set can be used for a monitor and displays 24 lines of 40 characters. (You can, and probably should, use a computer monitor instead.) There are eight expansion slots to put new boards in, a fifteen-color graphics capability, and a loudspeaker. And — most important — there's tons of software.

The Apple II + personal computer. (*Courtesy of Apple Computer, Inc.*)

The **Apple II +** has a better BASIC, with high-resolution graphics commands and automatic startup. At the time I'm writing this, you can get an Apple II + with 48K for about $1250. Mini disk drives will run about $500 for the first and $400 for the second.

Lots of hardware enhancements are available for the Apple II. One of the most basic is a **lowercase adaptor,** without which you're stuck with the Apple's standard capital letters. For word-processing purposes you'll also need an **80-column card,** which doubles the length of the lines displayed on the screen. Videx, M & R Associates, Apple themselves, and several other manufacturers all make 80-column cards. Videx's includes a lowercase adaptor and costs about $300.

It often makes more sense to get a separate terminal for the Apple rather than investing in an 80-column card and a monitor. A 12-inch green screen capable of 80 columns will cost you about $150. So, with the lowercase adaptor and 80-column card, you're talking about $450, which is more than the cost of many terminals. (Of course if you're going to use your TV for a monitor, switching between the mindless pap of the airwaves and the beautiful elegance of computer programs, the 80-column board route will be cheaper.)

Another useful addition is a **type-ahead buffer** (this prevents you from losing keystrokes when you type too fast for the Apple to keep up with you). Good software will have a type-ahead buffer built into it, but it's good to have one in hardware too. Vista Computer (of Santa Ana, California) makes type-ahead buffers in hardware, as does Lazer Micro-Systems.

The Apple II is based on the 6502 chip, and there's lots of software written to run it directly under its own Apple DOS. But there are also special boards that let you run software designed for other chips and operating systems. **Microsoft's SoftCard** is the most famous of these. You just pop it into slot seven and you have a Z80-based computer running CP/M and CP/M applications programs.

There's a board that turns the Apple into a 6809 computer, and the **MetaCard** from **Metamorphic Microsystems** of Boulder, Colorado does the same for the 8088. This is the same chip the IBM Personal Computer is based on, and thus the MetaCard lets an Apple run software developed for the PC (if it runs under CP/M-86). The MetaCard also provides 4K of RAM (expandable to 128K); it costs about $1000.

Some people say that Apples are good only for games, but this is manifestly untrue. They've been used in many, many serious commercial applications, and there's hardly any sort of business program you can get on any microcomputer that you can't get on an Apple. (Some — like **VisiCalc,** the first of the "electronic spreadsheet" programs — began on the Apple and were subsequently adapted to every other sort of machine.)

The **Apple III** is also based on the 6502 chip, but it runs at twice the speed of the Apple II. Its RAM is expandable to 128K, its minifloppy disks hold 140 K each, and there's room in the computer case for one drive. An 80-column display is standard, as are self-diagnostics and the ability to produce either sixteen-color graphics or high-resolution black-and-white graphics. The basic system (with one disk and a black-and-white monitor) costs about $4000.

There's an optional hard disk for the Apple III — the **Profile** from **Seagate** of Scotts Valley, California. It holds five MB and costs $3500.

The Apple III uses an operating system called SOS (for "sophisticated operating system"). Because this is different from the Apple II's operating system (Apple DOS), the Apple III has relatively little software available for it. But there is an emulator that lets you run Apple II software on the Apple III, albeit less efficiently. MicroSoft makes a SoftCard for the III so it can run CP/M software.

Neither the Apple II nor Apple III have a fan, and both are therefore vulnerable to failures caused by heat buildup. Documentation for both machines is good.

Apple is bound to keep expanding its product line. At the time I'm writing this, at least three new products are planned. The first (known by the internal code name **Lisa**) is a 68000-based, 16-bit machine. It will have 128K of RAM, expandable to a megabyte, and is designed to compete with the Xerox Star (described in the next chapter) at a lower price.

A second project (code named **MacIntosh**) is a portable computer also based on the 68000 chip. A third project (code name **Diana**) involves putting the whole Apple II onto a chip, which will make for a much smaller, much less expensive machine that nevertheless will run all current Apple II software.

Altos of San Jose, California makes microcomputers that have done very well in the *DataPro* reports (which are described in the next chapter and in Appendix A). Every single one of the Altos users who responded to the survey said they would recommend the system to someone thinking of buying one for the same applications, and their overall satisfaction rating was an incredible 3.8 (three = good, four = excellent).

The **ACS8000** is a series of Z80A-based machines running at four MHz. The smallest is the ACS8000-2 — with 64K of RAM and two single-sided 8-inch floppies that hold 500K each. It costs $3,650. The series continues on up through the $5,000 ACS8000-15 (with 208K of RAM) into hard disk and multi-user systems costing up to $15,000. They all run either CP/M or Oasis.

Altos also makes 16-bit micros — the **ACS8600** series. They're based on the 8086 chip and run CP/M-86, Oasis-86, or a version of UNIX called XENIX.

I don't know if they actually ship their computers in them, but at every trade show, Altos' display is stacked high with fruit crates, each bearing the colorful Altos label. (You may not know it, but fruit crate labels are a real art form.) This makes for a good looking display, and also hearkens back to Silicon Valley's agricultural origins.

Alpha Micro is a Southern California manufacturer of a full line of 16-bit, multi-user business systems. The **AM-1010** and **AM-1011** use floppy disks that hold 1.2 MB each; the **AM-1050** and **AM-1051** use a *90 MB* hard disk (that's a *lot* of data), 15 MB of which is in the form of a removable cartridge. 128K of RAM is standard on all the machines.

Alpha has its own operating system (**AMOS**) and word-processing package, composed of an editor called **AlphaVUE** and a text formatter called **TXTFMT** (say "TXT-fmt").

As I said when I began, this list is definitely incomplete; I doubt that I've discussed a third of the microcomputers available today. But I have included all the major ones and, hopefully, by piling up the examples, you have a pretty good idea of what to look for and what you can expect to get.

RECOMMENDATIONS

By the time you read this, what I'm about to say will probably be out-of-date. On the other hand, some machines stay bargains for quite a while. I suggest you check out the machines I recommend first and then see if you can find any new ones that are better deals.

If I didn't already have a microcomputer and were buying one to use as a word processor myself, I think I would go for an Osborne (with the optional larger screen). It's hard for me to imagine more value for the price. It does just about everything that systems costing twice as much can do.

One disadvantage of the Osborne 1 is the fact that, although it runs CP/M, there isn't a lot of software that's been converted to its particular idiosyncracies yet. This is sure to change, however, as it becomes both more popular and less idiosyncractic (with an 80-column screen, for instance).

I could live with WordStar as my word-processing program; although it isn't my favorite, it has a lot of features, it's thoroughly debugged, and MicroPro is constantly improving it. And anyway, many other CP/M word processors will be available on the Osborne 1, and especially on later model Osbornes with 80-column displays.

As I mentioned above, many of the first Osborne 1s were DOA, but I imagine this was just the inevitable shaking out that happens with any new product. I can't believe Adam Osborne, knowing what he does about the power of the press, would be stupid enough to put out a product that doesn't work right.

I love the Osborne's portability but regret that its disks, like all 5¼-inch disks, are not compatible with those of other machines. With a slow but inexpensive formed-character printer, the whole system (with larger screen) would come to about $3500 (and this includes more software than just word processing). A dot-matrix printer would shave about $500 off the price, as would an Olivetti Praxis adapted to run off a computer.

If you need graphics, a color display, or games to relax with, it's also worth considering an Apple II or Apple II + running PIE Writer. Although more expensive than an Osborne and not as portable, the Apple II (as I've said) can run more software than any other computer (of any size) in the world. This is partially because of all the programs that have been written directly for it, and also because it can take the SoftCard, which gives it access to CP/M software. And, as I've said, there are also cards which convert the Apple II to 6809 and 8086/8088 operation.

Software for the Apple tends to be cheaper than CP/M software, and, unlike the Osborne 1, it's expandable, with seven card slots.

I would modify the Apple to provide upper- and lowercase and an 80-column screen. I'd make sure that the shift key works as it does on a typewriter, and that the reset button requires more than one keystroke. It often makes more sense to buy a separate terminal to run with the Apple than to use an 80-column card with a monitor. Naturally, I'd get two disk drives; unfortunately, they'll have to be minifloppies.

With an inexpensive formed-character printer, an Apple II+ based system should run around $4000 ($2700 without the printer). Here again, using the Olivetti Praxis or a dot-matrix printer will save you money. It might also make sense to wait until Apple puts this whole machine on a chip (if they already haven't by the time you read this).

Both the Osborne and the Apple II are among the cheapest microcomputers you can buy. Of course you can pay more money for a microcomputer and get more power, but you could also buy two or three of these machines instead. It's like one of my favorite old Volkswagen ads. The first half of the headline reads: ''For the price of this station wagon, with all its optional extras . . .,'' and the picture above it shows a standard Detroit station wagon; the second half of the headline reads: ''. . . you can get our station wagon, with this optional extra,'' and the picture above it shows a Volkswagen bus with a Volkswagen bug sitting next to it.

It's too bad that neither the Osborne or the Apple have 8-inch drives. But you can't have everything.

I don't make any recommendations for higher budgets because there are dozens of different uses that require more expensive systems, and dozens of different systems that accommodate them. The next chapter discusses some top-end systems for word-processing applications — the dedicated word processors.

CHECKLIST FOR MICROCOMPUTERS

Machine name:

Manufacturer:

Vendor(s) and price(s):

Included in the price:

Chip the machine is based on:
    Running at _____ MHz
Operating system(s) it runs:

Memory: _____ K RAM   _____ K ROM
    RAM expandable to: _____ K

Runs in terminal mode/memory-mapped/both
Upper- and lowercase letters/caps only

Storage:
Cassette recorder?
Floppy disk drives?   How many? _____
   3½-inch?   5¼-inch?   8-inch?
   Single-sided?   Double-sided?
   Single-density?   Double-density?   Quad-density?
   Drive manufacturer: _____ Model: _____
   Format: standard IBM 3740 / _____
Hard disk drive?
   Size: _____"   Capacity: _____MB
   Manufacturer: _____ Model: _____
   Media removable?
   Backup system: _____

Chapter

11

Dedicated Word Processors

A dedicated word processor is basically a microcomputer — with a keyboard, screen, and printer — that's running a word-processing program. Thus everything I've said in Chapters 5, 8, 9, and 10 applies to dedicated word processors, and you can use the checklists at the end of those four chapters when evaluating them.

Seven dedicated word processors are evaluated from a software standpoint in Chapter 5 (and described in Chapter 6). In this chapter, I'll discuss several systems from a hardware standpoint. And I'll also tell you how to get more information on dedicated word processors. (If you need to figure out whether you want a dedicated word processor or a microcomputer, see the discussion at the end of Chapter 3.)

As you've no doubt noticed, this book has more to say about microcomputers and word-processing programs that run on them than about dedicated word processors. There are a couple of reasons for this:

1) A microcomputer with a word-processing program is likely to be less expensive and more powerful dollar for dollar than a dedicated word processor; thus it's the first option you should consider. Move on to a dedicated word processor only if you need its more advanced features and can afford to pay for them.

2) There's much more information already available on dedicated word processors than there is on microcomputer programs. There are literally dozens of specialized report services that do nothing but review dedicated word processors, and several magazines are entirely devoted to that subject. But there isn't a single microcomputer publication that even emphasizes word processing. (*InfoWorld* and *Popular Computing* come closest.)

Probably the most useful of the report services is **Datapro.** Their full word-processing report service — two volumes updated monthly — is priced for business users who will be buying more than one system; it costs about $500 a year. But there's also a 30-page summary report you can get for around $20. This tabulates the responses of thousands of users to lengthy questionnaires about their word processors. More than 70 models are covered.

The questionnaires cover many different topics and end with user ratings for reliability, documentation, ease of use, repairs, support, and overall satisfaction. Each area is rated poor, fair, good, or excellent by the users, and Datapro figures the composite score like a grade-point average: excellent = four, good = three, fair = two, and poor = one. (The averages for overall satisfaction seldom go above 3.6 or below 2.6.)

I was very impressed with the usefulness of this report (the one I saw was *Word Processing Systems User Ratings,* October, 1981). Here's a (slightly rearranged and abridged) table from it, so you can see what I mean:

Stand-alone word processors	Overall satisfaction	Lowest rating in any area	Number of responses
Compucorp Omega	3.6	3.1	20
Phillips Micom 2000/2001	3.6	2.7	91
Lexitron 1202/1303	3.5	3.0	102
NBI 3000	3.5	2.9	120
Lanier LTE-3 No Problem	3.4	3.0	179
CPT 8000/8100	3.4	3.0	171
Dictaphone Dual Display	3.3	3.0	32
Xerox 860	3.2	2.9	121
IBM Displaywriter	3.2	2.9	75
Xerox 350	3.2	2.7	118
DEC WS78	3.2	2.7	41
Multi-terminal systems			
NBI OASys 8	3.6	3.2	33
A.B. Dick Magna SL	3.5	3.2	65
Wang OIS 130A	3.2	2.7	53

You can also set up comparisons of your own, based on data in the user ratings. For example, here's another table I was able to put together from information in that same report:

Stand-alone word processors	Percent of users who say they'd recommend system	Number of responses
Compucorp Omega	100	20
AM Jacquard	100	11
Radio Shack TRS-80	100	7
Phillips Micom 2000/2001	99	91
NBI 3000	97	120
CPT 8000/8100	95	171
Lanier LTE-3 No Problem	93	179
Dictaphone Dual Display	93	32
Xerox 860 IPS	91	121
Multi-terminal systems		
Wang OIS 125A	100	14
Comptek Barrister	100	10
Wang OIS 140	98	174
Wang WPS 25	97	123
NBI OASys 8	97	33
IBM 5520	95	74
A.B. Dick Magna SL	94	65
Wang OIS 130A	94	53
Wang WPS 20	93	31

Datapro also publishes reports on small computers, and on microcomputer software.

Another good resource for information on dedicated word processors is the **Seybold Report** (the Seybold Report on Office Systems, that is; there's another, older Seybold Report that's about typesetting equipment). Twelve monthly issues plus occasional special bulletins cost around $100.

While Datapro reports tend to be factual and non-committal, Seybold reports are more subjective and often more critical. They also discuss industry trends, new technologies, and other issues larger than a single, specific machine. And they are *thorough*.

A good approach might be to use DataPro's comparison charts and user ratings to narrow your search down to a few systems you want to consider, and then read the Seybold Report on each of them to get an in-depth picture of what they do.

The Seybold Report organization also gives seminars, mostly in Boston, Atlanta, and San Francisco. Details about everything they, DataPro, and other information resources offer, as well as where to order them from, are in Appendix A.

Now I'll give you brief descriptions of several specific dedicated word processors.

Thomas Edison invented the mimeograph machine in collaboration with Albert Blake Dick. The two went into business together, and that business today is **A.B. Dick** (the Edison family sold their shares in the '30s).

The A.B. Dick Magna SL dedicated word processor. (*Courtesy of A.B. Dick.*)

A.B. Dick makes all kinds of office equipment; the word processor they promote most is the **Magna SL.** SL stands for **shared logic,** and this system does indeed have as its center a large computer box that stands on the floor and supports up to four workstations, three printers, and seven disk drives.

The central processing unit (CPU) itself comes with 28K of RAM and one 8-inch, 300K disk drive (expandable to four). Each workstation has a drive of its own and an additional 12K of RAM. The screens are tiltable, with brightness controls and detachable keyboards. Characters are displayed at three levels of intensity (i.e., bright, regular, dim). Workstations can be up to 200 feet away from the main CPU, much farther than shared resource systems allow.

The basic system costs about $14,500 (the price includes all software and updates). But it's silly to have that huge CPU sitting out on the floor to service just one user (additional workstations cost around $7000 each).

The Magna SL will interface with typesetting machines and with its own OCR reader, which costs $11,500. (An **OCR reader** can read documents typed in the special OCR typeface, thus allowing workers to input text into the system using nothing more than a typewriter.)

A.B. Dick also makes a single-user stand-alone word processor, the **Magna III,** as well as a thin-line display and an intelligent typewriter. Their overall satisfaction score for all models was 3.3 on the DataPro survey; they did best in ease of operation (3.6) and worst in documentation (3.1).

The CPT 8000. (*Courtesy of CPT Corporation*).

The **CPT** Corporation of Minneapolis makes a line of word processors that users have been very satisfied with. The 6000 series machines show a half page of text (23 lines) on a 10-inch screen and have a single 8-inch disk drive; the 8000 series machines show a full page of text (54 lines) on a 15-inch screen and have double 8-inch disk drives. The disks hold 315K. The keyboards are separate.

In order to make the changeover to a word processor as painless as possible for typists, CPT has tried to make the screen display look like a piece of paper in a typewriter. The display is black on white and there's a black ''ruler'' line across it that resembles the paper bail. (Text is entered directly above this line, and margins and tabs are shown on it.)

You can change where the ruler line falls on the screen, and you can display a separate file below it. I found the CPT's split screen capabilities *very* impressive. It takes just a few keystrokes to bring up another file, and even fewer to add a paragraph from it to the file you're working on.

CPT has an unusual method of moving around in the text, which I describe when I discuss CPT software in Chapter 6. I haven't used it extensively, but my brief impression was that it works pretty well. It can do all sorts of things other than word processing, including play Bach. You can even compose your own music on it.

CPT got a DataPro rating of 3.4 for overall satisfaction with all models. They were weakest in troubleshooting and training (3.0) and best in ease of operation (3.6).

The half-screen CPT **6000** has 48K of RAM and sells for around $5500; the **6100** has 64K of RAM and sells for around $6500. The full-screen **8000** has 64K of RAM and sells for around $11,000. The **8100** has 96K of RAM and sells for around $12,000. All prices include software.

The **Dictaphone Dual Display** is made by **Artec,** which Dictaphone owns. (Dictaphone, in turn, is owned by Pitney Bowes.) It's an impressive machine. There are two displays — a single-line, red gas plasma display that runs across the top of the keyboard, and a 15-inch CRT that shows a full page of text (66 lines of 102 characters) in virtual representation — boldfacing, double underlines, proportional spacing, etc. (although it won't display double spacing, you usually don't want to display it anyway, because it halves the amount of text on the screen).

The basic system costs $13,500 and comes with 96K of RAM scattered all over the place — 32K in the keyboard, 16K in the CRT, 16K in the printer, and 32K in the disk drive. There's one 8-inch floppy drive (500K), and you can add up to three more. The printer is a 40 cps Diablo. The keyboard is separate and has a number of function keys, many with small red lights on them so you can tell whether they're turned on or off.

The screen is tiltable and has a couple of nice features:
● The cursor is a non-blinking underline which boldfaces the character it's under.

- If no text or commands are entered for 20 minutes, the display blanks out. (You can get it back by pushing one key.) This prevents damage to the screen that could be caused by burning one particular pattern into the phosphor.
- Since a 66 × 102 screen displays six and a half times as many characters as a 16 × 64 and three and a half times as many as a 24 × 80, it's nice to be able to make the characters bigger when you want. The ZOOM feature doubles the size of each character (and shows you a half page of text surrounding the cursor).

The main advantage of the thin-window display is to cut the cost of expanding the system. If you're willing to have someone work without a screen, you can add a workstation for just $2200. (With a CRT it's about $3900.)

Dictaphone got a DataPro overall satisfaction score of 3.4 for all its models. It did best in maintenance and ease of operation (3.4) and worst in documentation (2.8).

The Lanier TypeMaster. (*Courtesy of Lanier.*)

Lanier is one of the most highly rated makers of dedicated word processors. They have several model lines, starting with the **No Problem** systems. These are integrated units, with the disks drives, screen, and (non-detachable) keyboard all packaged together. There are eighteen different configurations, with disk storage from 70K to almost 1.2 MB. As of this writing, the No Problem runs CP/M, but it's only available in certain test markets.

The **TypeMaster** looks a lot like the No Problem, but it's even more integrated — a 30 cps daisy-wheel printer sits on top of the screen, in the same box. Thus the whole unit takes up no more desk space than a typewriter. It has an instant print feature so it can be used like a typewriter too.

Lanier's idea of specs seems to be things like the maximum altitude at which you can operate their equipment (10,000 feet — a heartbreaker for those of you who live in Cuzco), so I can't tell you non-essential information like how many K of RAM any of these machines have. However, I was able to dig out the following facts about the TypeMaster:

Its screen measures 12 inches diagonally and displays 16 lines of 80 characters (fourteen of which you can use for text — the other two are for control messages). One (70K) minifloppy drive is standard, and there's room in the case for another one. The machine costs $8000.

An even less expensive Lanier is the $6000 **EZ-1.** This comes with a separate keyboard and a screen that displays 27 80-character lines (they don't say how large the screen is, but don't try to store it at less than 40° below zero). There are twelve different models. The disk storage on the basic system is a 147K minifloppy drive; this is expandable to 600K. The basic printer is a 43 cps daisy-wheel, and two others are available.

The EZ-1 has some unusual features, like the ability to handle footnotes and compile a table of contents automatically. It also lets you print one file while editing another and has a merge-print program.

Lanier got a DataPro overall satisfaction score of 3.4 for all its models combined. It did best in ease of operation (3.5), and it did worst in training (2.9).

Philips Information Systems makes a series of impressive word processors called **Micoms.** The Micom **2001** has 128K of RAM (expandable to 256K) and a 15-inch screen that displays 31 eighty-character lines (28 of text). The characters are very well defined (11 × 15 dot matrix). There are one or two 8-inch disk drives that hold 300K each. The keyboard is not separable.

Micom has a lot of powerful software features that are described in Chapter 6. The basic 2001 costs around $12,000 and the **2002,** which is able to cluster with other units, around $14,000. These prices include software and all updates of it.

There's also the Micom **1001** — a supplementary input station with a one-line screen. Up to 20 pages of text can be edited and reviewed in the 40-character LCD display, and it gets recorded on a microcassette. It can then be transferred to the diskette on a main unit for final editing and printout. The 1001 costs about $1400, which cuts down the cost of adding work stations to a system.

In the DataPro user ratings, Philips got an overall satisfaction score of 3.6 for all Micom models together; no dedicated word processor manufacturer scored higher. (Compucorp, Lexor, and Royal also got 3.6's, but none of them had more than 20 users responding.) Philips did best in reliability (3.7) and worst in documentation (2.9).

Sony has come up with an interesting machine: it's called the **Typecorder** and consists of an integrated keyboard, microcassette recorder, and one-line LCD display. It's small enough to fit in a briefcase and light enough to take anywhere. You can edit text on the Typecorder, store it on tape, and even transmit it to other machines. The Typecorder lists for $1400.

The Wangwriter II. (*Courtesy of Wang Laboratories, Inc.*)

The Wangwriter II is a Z80 machine with 96K of RAM (expandable to 128K) that can run CP/M. It displays 24 lines of 80 characters and comes with one or two minifloppy drives which hold 320K each.

Wang got an overall score of 3.3 for all its stand-alone models in the DataPro users ratings. It did best in ease of operation (3.7) and worst in training (2.5).

Leading Edge, of Canton, Massachusetts, has come out with a new word processor called **Wordsworth.** It consists of integrated screen, computer and (non-detachable) keyboard with 48K of RAM (expandable to 64K), and a built-in 100K minifloppy drive (upgradable to 2.8 MB, the brochure says, but it doesn't say how; a hard disk, I guess). The 12-inch green-phosphor CRT shows 24 lines of 80 characters. The keyboard has twelve function keys and a numeric keypad. The printer is an Itoh Starwriter.

Wordsworth runs CP/M and comes with its own word-processing program. I've seen some of the preliminary documentation for it and it's adequate, but not great. The whole system costs $5000.

In the DataPro user ratings, Wordsworth got an overall score of 3.0. It did best in ease of operation (3.6) and worst in troubleshooting (2.3).

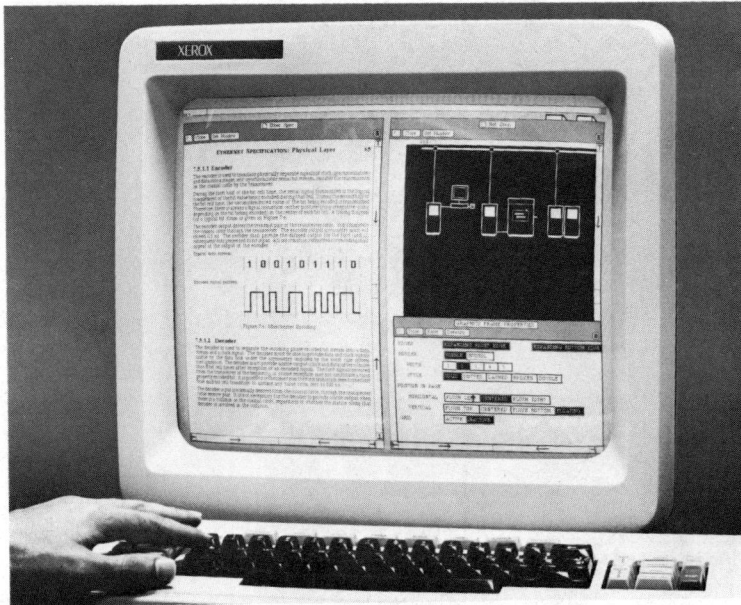

The Xerox Star displaying two full pages of text mixed with graphics. (*Courtesy of Xerox Corporation.*)

Xerox makes a number of dedicated word processors; the most interesting of them is their top-of-the-line **Star.** The Star is aimed at business professionals and is designed to make them more independent and efficient. It costs about $16,600 for a single work station with standard software and 10 MB of disk storage (one floppy and a hard disk); this doesn't include a printer. But the Star has some unique features that justify its high cost.

For one thing, its 11 × 14-inch screen is capable of displaying two full pages of text. It also has the ultimate in split screen capabilities — it can display portions of *six* different documents at the same time. You can mix graphics with text and choose different type fonts, ranging from eight to 24 point and including boldface, italics, bold italics, subscripts, and superscripts. (This is virtual representation with a vengeance.)

There's a library of pre-drawn graphic symbols (arrows, boxes, and the like). They can be moved around the screen, enlarged, or reduced. The Star can make a hard copy of what's on the screen by sending it to a laser printer, thus letting you set type without a typesetting machine and/or do graphics without a plotter. Santa Claus, if you're reading this — I want a Star with a laser printer for Christmas.

Because the Star is aimed at people higher up the corporate ladder than secretaries, they've had to make it very easy to use. There's a mouse to move the cursor around (explained in Chapter 8), and you can choose a function by placing the cursor next to a symbol that represents it and pressing a button on the mouse's back.

The Xerox 860. (*Courtesy of Xerox Corporation.*)

Next down from the Star is the **860.** It only displays one page of text (66 lines of 102 characters) and has a CAT in the keyboard, rather than a mouse. (A CAT is a rotary control knob for moving the cursor.) The screen is tiltable, and you can choose between a dark-on-light or light-on-dark display. The keyboard is separate.

You have a choice of two different 35 cps printers — one with a standard 15-inch carriage, the other a super-wide 28-inch carriage. Both print bi-directionally, use metal daisy wheels, and do proportional spacing. The printer can be shared between work stations.

The standard system costs about $15,300 and includes 128K of RAM, two floppy drives (300K each), and the smaller printer. You can expand the floppy disk capacity to 1.2 MB each and attach a 5 or 10 MB hard disk. The **860** also comes with **partial page display** (24 lines of 102 characters). It sells for about $11,600 with a Xerox 630 printer.

The 860 will run CP/M, which can save you a lot of money on software. For example, the spelling checker program for the Star costs $1500, while there's a CP/M spelling checker for just $75.

All of these machines can connect with each other over Xerox' local network, called **Ethernet.** Xerox got an overall score of 3.1 for all models in the DataPro user ratings. They did best in reliability and maintenance (3.2) and worst in training, troubleshooting, and documentation (2.8).

RECOMMENDATIONS

It's hard to recommend a dedicated word processor, both because there are lots of systems I haven't seen and also because most of the ones I have seen are almost all very capable and powerful. I was particularly impressed with the Dictaphone's virtual representation, and I think the Micom has a nice balance of features, particularly in the areas of indexing, sorting, and statistical typing.

If I had to choose a dedicated word processor for my own use from the ones I've seen, I'd probably go with the CPT. I love its split screen and file-merging capabilities and the fact that it runs CP/M. But I'd also love to have a Xerox Star, if I could afford it (and its software).

I'm not sure it would ever be worth it to me personally to spend as much money on a word processor as any of these machines cost. But if you're rich and/or if you really need the features these machines offer, you can certainly get a system that will make you happy.

And I think that should be my basic advice: Shop around till you find a dedicated word processor that does *exactly* what you want it to. Given the quality of what's out there, and what it costs, there's no sense in settling for anything less than your heart's desire.

APPENDICES

Appendix

A

Resources

MICROCOMPUTER MAGAZINES AND NEWSPAPERS

Probably the best publication to start off with is **Popular Computing** (formerly **onComputing**). It carries articles on very basic subjects (''Printers: Why You Need One, How to Choose One,'' for example), and they're written for readers who know virtually nothing about computers. Each issue has a glossary of essential terms, called ''In Other Words.''

Having read this book — no fair reading the appendices until you've read the book — you may find *Popular Computing* too elementary for you. But it's worth looking at a copy to see. You can order it directly from Box 307, Martinsville, NJ 08836 (subscription WATS line — 800-258-5485). It comes out monthly and costs $15 per year; individual copies are $2.50.

When you've outgrown *Popular Computing,* move on to **InfoWorld.** It comes out weekly and carries up-to-the-minute news on new products and industry trends; software, hardware, and book reviews; classified ads; and debates on issues like the morality of censoring pornographic programs or of carrying ads for programs that let you copy software that manufacturers have tried to make uncopyable.

For me, *InfoWorld* consistently manages to find a middle ground between technical gobbledygook I can't understand and basic information I already know. A number of my friends feel the same way (although some of them feel that it's been going downhill). Unfortunately, *InfoWorld's* product reviews are neither systematic nor critical enough to be terribly useful.

InfoWorld costs $1.25 a pop, or you can subscribe for $25 per year by writing 375 Cochitutate Road, Framingham, MA 01701 (it's edited in Palo Alto, California, though). The toll free subscription line is 800-343-6474 (outside of Massachusetts).

If you do word processing on your system and not much else, **BYTE** magazine will probably be too technical for you. But you should look at one issue at least, for a couple of reasons:

1) *Everything* is advertised in *BYTE*, and there's an alphabetical list of the pages on which each advertiser's ads appear. This is essential, since the average issue of *BYTE* looks more like a phone book than a magazine. Even if you don't want to read it, it's useful as a catalog.

2) In addition to articles telling you how to build your own bar-code scanner or how to link a Pascal microengine to a Cyber 170, there's some very helpful stuff for users of word processors. For example, in the same issue that those two articles appeared, there was a *very* thorough and informative review of five CP/M spelling checkers. There are also Sol Libes' monthly feature, "BYTELINES," which is an excellent compilation of the most useful and interesting industry news, and "What's New," a descriptive list of new microcomputer products.

BYTE costs $3 an issue — certainly one of the greatest pounds per dollar bargains in all of publishing. Subscriptions are $19 a year (it's a monthly), from Box 590, Martinsville, NJ 08836. The subscription WATS line is 800-258-5485.

Creative Computing's main focus is games, and their main market is computer hobbyists. But they do run a fair number of articles about word-processing programs and microcomputers capable of being used as word processors. **Creative Computing** is a monthly and costs $2.50 per issue. Subscriptions are $20 a year, from 39 East Hanover Avenue, Morris Plains, NJ 07950. The toll free subscription number is 800-631-8112 (except in New Jersey).

You don't have to decide whether to subscribe to these magazines based merely on what I've told you about them; most computer stores carry the current issues, and usually several back issues, of all of them. Browse through them there and take home a sample copy of the ones that seem interesting.

One magazine that may be hard to find in the stores, but which can be very helpful, is **DataCast.** This was started by Jim Warren, who also originated *InfoWorld,* the West Coast Computer Faire, and the *Silicon Gulch Gazette* (all discussed in this appendix). Like all of Jim Warren's activities, *DataCast* was designed to fill a need.

It calls itself "the reference publication for major microcomputer systems' software" (particularly CP/M) and provides users with readable documentation, application-oriented tutorials, and feature articles on consumer issues. The first two issues contained a series of much-needed tutorials on various aspects of CP/M, a similar tutorial for WordStar, and a number of other interesting articles.

DataCast comes out every other month and costs $18 a year from 333 Swett Road, Woodside, CA 94062. Individual issues are $4.

Also available from the same address is the **Silicon Gulch Gazette.** This comes out irregularly — four times a year — and consists mostly of information on the West Coast

Computer Faire and other conferences run by the same organization and reprinted press releases about new products. If you live in Northern California, you should definitely get it, and you may find it interesting even if you live elsewhere and never make it to the Faire.

The official subscription price is $6 a year, but I doubt that many people pay it. Just request a sample copy and you'll find yourself on their mailing list.

Buying used computer equipment requires a fair amount of technical expertise, but I'll give you the names of a couple of papers that carry ads for it anyway:

Computer Shopper, monthly, $1.50 per copy, $10 a year, from Box F, Titusville, FL 32780.

Horsetrader, $5 to be on mailing list forever. Box 11712, Santa Ana, CA 92711.

REPORT SERVICES

I mentioned **Datapro** in Chapter 11. You can write them at 1805 Underwood Boulevard, Delran, NJ 08075 for a list of all the reports they offer; you can also call them, from outside of New Jersey, at 800-257-9406. Here are a few of the reports you're most likely to be interested in (with approximate lengths and prices, and a few comments):

Word Processing Systems User Ratings (30 pp, $19) Some examples of the information available in this report are given near the beginning of Chapter 11.

All About 112 Word Processing Software Packages (57 pp, $15) Not, of course, *all* about them, but just some basic factual information on each one — who sells it, what machines it runs on, etc.

All About 150 Word Processors (110 pp, $19) A comprehensive list of the physical features of dedicated word processors from over 50 vendors.

Glossary of 263 Word Processing Terms (12 pp, $15)

All About Personal Computers (70 pp, $30) Reports on eighteen popular personal computers.

All About 278 Small Business Computers (67 pp, $15) A comprehensive list of the physical features; more than 67 vendors are represented.

All About 190 Microcomputers (45 pp, $15) Also a list of physical features; models from 61 vendors.

There's also the full two-volume word-processing report, which contains detailed reviews of specific dedicated word processors and word-processing software, as well as several of the smaller reports listed above and additional information. It's updated monthly and costs about $500 a year. There are similar reports on small computers (which cost around $325), microcomputer software (around $350), and other subjects.

The **Seybold Report on Office Systems** is also mentioned in Chapter 11. It comes out monthly and is usually 16 to 18 pages. A yearly subscription costs about $100 and includes special bulletins covering late-breaking news (an average of two or three a year). The address for subscriptions is Box 644, Media, PA 19063. (Be sure to specify the report on office systems; they also publish one on typesetting equipment.)

The Seybold Report organization also holds seminars at least once or twice a year in Boston, Atlanta, and San Francisco, and occasionally in other cities. They usually last three days and cost around $500.

In addition to reporting on one specific machine, the Seybold Report sometimes reviews a whole range of products for a particular marketplace or application or devotes an issue to describing a major show and all the equipment introduced there. It also carries broad survey pieces on industry trends and new technologies.

At their seminars, the Seybold Report staff sometimes distributes 26 pages of worksheets you can use when evaluating a word processor on your own. Patty Seybold says she will send you a free copy of these if you request them by writing her at Suite 801, 44 Broomfield Street, Boston, MA 02108.

The **Information and Word Processing Report** consists of six to eight pages and comes out twice a month. It's aimed at "the professional community involved with automated business communications and related office systems" and costs $106 a year, so it probably isn't worth your money unless you fit into that category. It's published by Geyer-McAllister, 51 Madison Avenue, New York, NY 10010. Single copies cost $3.75 to $7.75.

There are many other report services. They often publish selections from their reports in magazines, and that's one of the best ways to find out about them.

MAGAZINES ABOUT DEDICATED WORD PROCESSORS

I'll just list two; there are a number of others:

Word Processing and Information Systems (formerly Word Processing Systems) comes out monthly. It costs $2.50 a copy and $16 a year, from Geyer-McAllister (address above).

Words is the journal of the International Word Processing Association, headquartered in Willow Grove, Pennsylvania. It's issued every two months and seems to be primarily aimed at managers of word-processing departments and other people professionally involved in the field. A subscription is included with membership in the association, which costs $50 a year.

OTHER RESOURCES

There are various lists of software that include word-processing programs. The **Small Systems Group** puts out one for **CP/M Software.** The second edition costs $6 and includes 740 programs (just their names, the category they fall in, and the address of the publisher). You can order it from Box 5429, Santa Monica, CA 90405.

There's a similar list of programs that run under **UNIX** and/or that are written in the **C** programming language. It costs $18 from **InfoPro Systems,** Box 33, East Hanover, NJ 07936.

Commodore, Apple, and Radio Shack all have catalogs of programs that run on their machines.

Conventions and fairs are great places to learn about various products. The **West Coast Computer Faire** is particularly wonderful, because of its informal, down-home atmosphere.

Be sure that the convention you go to features *micro*computers (or microcomputer-based word processors). The machines you'll find at some computer conventions are about as close to what you need as one of those ten-story-tall earth-moving machines is to a moped.

If you want to get some custom programming done inexpensively, try a computer club or put a notice on the bulletin board in the computer science department of a nearby university. Both methods will put you in touch with people who will be making $50 an hour in about five years, but will probably work for $10 an hour or less now.

Since they spend most of their time absorbing knowledge rather than making use of it, they love to impress you with how much they know; the money is almost secondary. Here — as with picking a doctor or a mechanic for your car — it helps to be a good judge of people, whether or not you know anything about the particular field they're experts in.

Appendix

B

Conversions

K TO WORDS TO PAGES

Let me begin by recapping what I said in Chapter 2:

> It's a convention to define a ''word'' as five characters (including spaces). Whenever you see the speed of a printer advertised in words per minute (**wpm**), it's these five-character words they mean. But in reality, it's a rare piece of text whose words average only four letters (plus a space).

> Because my word processor gives me the number of K and the number of words in a file, I've been able to do a little research into how long the average word actually is. In my writing, at least, it's about six characters (including the space) — not five. Since, as you can see, I'm not fond of fancy, sesquipedalian words (except for that one), it's not likely that my words are longer — on the average — than most people's. If anything, they're shorter.

> So, I think six-character words should become the standard. To do my little bit in that direction, I call six-character words ''real'' words, and speak of ''real words per minute'' (**rwpm**). I call the five-character words ''official'' words, and refer to ''official words per minute'' (**owpm**). (When I refer to ''words'' in this book, without qualifying the term, I usually mean real words.)

> To find out how many real words per minute a printer will do, multiply the wpm figure in the ad or brochure by .83, or multiply by 5 and divide by 6. Wpm figures in ads will overstate the actual number of words per minute by 20 percent. (This assumes, of course, that the figure in the ad is accurate in the first place. See Chapter 9 for some reasons to doubt that.)

> There is no such thing as a standard ''page,'' so I've defined it to mean 250 words, which is about how many there'll actually be on an 8½ by 11 page with double-spaced pica type, one-inch margins, and long paragraphs (27 lines of 65 characters, minus 15 percent for short lines and indentations). Short paragraphs can bring the count down to as low as 200 words.

If you use elite type (twelve characters to the inch, instead of ten for pica), a "standard" page will average around 300 words. Single-spaced text with blank lines between each paragraph will average about 400 words per page with pica type and 500 words with elite type.

If the pages you type differ from the standard page, multiply the number of pages indicated in the chart below by these conversion factors:

For text with long paragraphs:
  Double-spaced elite: .8
  Single-spaced pica: .6
  Single-spaced elite: .5

For text with short paragraphs:
  Double-spaced pica: 1.2
  Double-spaced elite: 1
  Single-spaced pica: .7
  Single-spaced elite: .6

K to words to pages
(all values are approximate)

K	(real) words	("standard") pages
1*	170	2/3
1.5	250	1
3	500	2
6	1000	4
10	1700	7
15	2500	10
20	3400	13
25	4200	17
30	5000	20
40	6800	27
50	8500	33
60	10,000	40
75	12,500	50
100	17,000	67

*1K = 1024 characters

Cps to wpm to pph

Typical printer	cps*	owpm**	rwpm***	pph****
Teletype terminal	10	120	100	24
IBM Selectric	15	180	150	36
(driven at top speed by a computer)				
Itoh Starwriter I	25	300	250	60
Diablo 630	40	480	400	96
(with plastic wheel)				
NEC Spinwriter 7710	55	660	550	132
Sellum F-86	80	960	800	192
Malibu Dual-Mode 200	165	1980	1650	396
(at draft speed)				
Comprint 912	225	2700	2250	540

*characters per second (advertised speed)
**(official) words per minute (word = 5 characters)
***(real) words per minute (word = 6 characters)
****(standard) pages per hour (page = 250 real words)

Here are formulas for the relationships:

$$rwpm = \frac{5\ owpm}{6} \qquad cps = \frac{owpm}{12} \qquad cps = \frac{rwpm}{10}$$

$$owpm = 12\ cps \qquad rwpm = 10\ cps \qquad pph = 2.4\ cps$$

There's also **lpm** (lines per minute) — a totally bogus unit of measurement, in my opinion, since the number of characters in a line varies. In any case, here's how you get from cps to lpm (and back again):

$$lpm = \frac{60\ cps}{\#\ of\ characters\ in\ line} \qquad cps = \frac{lpm\ \times\ \#\ of\ characters\ in\ line}{60}$$

Appendix

C

Full Disclosure

As I said in the Introduction, I don't see how any human being can hope to be objective. I do, however, want to be fair. So this appendix tells you the name of every piece of word-processing software or hardware I've ever used, my opinion of it, and all the programmers and engineers who I'm more than casually acquainted with. You can use this information to figure out what my prejudices are, although I've tried to make them obvious (when I'm aware of them). For example, you don't need to be Sherlock Holmes to know that I despise flashing cursors.

This appendix will probably bore you to tears, if you're foolish enough to continue reading it. What's important is that the information is here.

I think I first heard about word processors from my friend Ron Lichty, who had an SWTP micro put together by his friend Tom Crosley. I was impressed by what I saw, even though this was a primitive system with no lowercase letters and a cursor that only moved right and down.

I couldn't afford to get a machine of my own, but I was able to wangle an account on the University of California's UNIX system on the Berkeley campus. I used this for about a year, and found a lot of things hard to take — too many users slowing down the system, bleak computer rooms, unreadable documentation, training classes with teachers who weren't used to dealing with people (''But they ask questions I didn't *program* them to ask! It's almost as if they have a will of their own!''), and a bureaucracy that makes Kafka seem like a Pollyanna.

(To be fair, some of the documentation was terrific, particularly when written by Bill Joy or Ricki Blau. And although the word-processing program I was using — first ex and then vi — was clumsy, it was powerful.)

Meanwhile, I was trying frantically to get a computer of my own. My first attempt was with Basic Business Computers of Palo Alto. My roommate and I were going to sell their systems and get one wholesale to use as a demonstrator. The system was composed of an Altos ACS8000 series micro, a TEC terminal, and WordStar.

I took the WordStar manual home, ploughed through it, and hated it (I should have sat at the machine while I was doing it, but the machine was 45 minutes away from home). But that didn't matter in the long run, because my roommate and I couldn't get the loan we needed to finance buying the system.

Then I read an article by Jerry Pournelle in *onComputing*. He talked about Electric Pencil, Magic Wand, and WordStar, and said that while each program had its virtues, his friend Tony Pietsch, the computer genius, was going to put together one that did "everything."

Figuring I had nothing to lose, I guessed what city Tony must live in, got his number from information, and called him up out of the blue. We had a long conversation in which I told him how desperate I was for a word processor and asked him questions about his program (subsequently named WRITE).

A few days later I sent Tony a package containing a booklet I'd written on advertising for small businesses and an offer to trade my writing for a machine. He liked what he read and agreed to put together a system for me at a big discount, in return for my writing a training manual for him. I paid the wholesale cost of the printer ($2300) and traded writing for the remaining $3300.

The system, which I'm still using, is a 64K, Z80-based, S-100 micro that runs CP/M, put together out of OEM components. If you needed a name for it, I suppose you'd call it a Pietsch. It runs memory-mapped on a 10½-inch Hitachi monitor, and the keyboard is a used Imsai. I've had a lot of problems with the system, much to Tony's mystification (all the other systems he's installed have run perfectly). But he's been really good about fixing things up. (The printer — an adapted NEC Spinwriter called a Sellum I — has been rock-solid.).

I began with WRITE version 1.1 and beta-tested that and versions 1.2, 1.3, and 1.4 over the next year and a half. Some of the features of the current version of WRITE were originally my idea, since I put a lot of energy into suggesting improvements in the program. I spent a lot of time on the phone with Tony and came to consider him a friend. He read an early version of Chapter 5 and suggested some changes.

When I travelled to Tony's to pick up the system, we transferred my files off the UNIX system over phone lines. I finished my first book (*Every Goy's Guide to Common Jewish Expressions*) on the machine and then wrote the WRITE training manual on it. Since I was ecstatic about word processing by then, and since there were no good books on the subject, I decided to write one.

I first approached Sybex (in Berkeley) with the idea, but they already had a book planned on that subject and hired me to write *Introduction to WordStar* instead. I wrote it on my machine, using WRITE, and checked it out on an Apple II (with a Zenith Z-19 terminal and SoftCard) running WordStar. Then I began this book.

In the meantime, Ron Lichty decided to become a programmer instead of an author and went to work for Tom Crosley, author of PIE Writer. Both Ron and Tom read parts of this book and made many, many suggestions and corrections. They have particularly concentrated on trying to shake me free from my CP/M provincialism. They also talked up the Apple II's flexibility, all the good, inexpensive software available for it, and the power and efficiency of the 6809 chip.

In the spring of 1981, I did a couple of months of freelance work for an advertising agency in San Francisco, writing ads for a variety of Hewlett-Packard computer products. In 1982, I did freelance brochures for some TeleVideo and Apple products.

In picking products to cover in this book, I wanted to make sure I didn't overlook any simply because I hadn't heard of them. So I sent letters out to a hundred manufacturers and publishers, requesting information on their products. Each letter was modified slightly, but the basic form was as follows:

Sales Manager [for _____]
Company
Address
City State Zip

Dear Sales Manager,

I am currently writing a book for BYTE Books entitled **Word Processing Buyer's Guide.** I would like to review your product(s), _____ , in the book. In order for me to do that, I will need to receive from you, within three weeks at the latest, the following materials:

— all user documentation for _____
— copies of any magazine reviews of _____
— any brochures or sales materials you have for _____
— the price(s) of _____ (to end users, in quantities of one)
— any other material you have that you think would help me understand the capabilities of _____
— the address and phone number (ideally an 800 number) of a person I can contact with further questions

At some future date, I may send you an evaluation questionnaire or ask for a demonstration of _____ . For the time being, however, the material requested above will suffice.

If you have a question, or if there's a problem getting these materials to me on time, please feel free to call me at the above number. You can call any time; if I'm not in, please leave a message on my answering machine.

Thanks for your help.

This letter went out to 53 publishers of word-processing programs. They're all listed in Chapter 6, and I've noted, for each, whether or not they responded. (Chapter 6 also lists many publishers I heard of too late to send the letter to.)

The letter also was sent to fourteen dedicated word processor manufacturers — Burroughs (Redactron), A.B. Dick, CPT, Dictaphone, IBM (Displaywriter), Lanier, Leading Edge (Wordsworth), Lexitron, Lexor (Alphasprint), NBI, Philips (Micom), Royal, Vydec, and Wang — and thirteen printer manufacturers — Comprint, DEC, Diablo, Intersell (Sellum), Itoh, Malibu, NEC, Pertec, Qume, Radio Shack, Sanders, Teletype, and a small company that adapts Selectrics.

Finally, I wrote to 20 microcomputer manufacturers: Alpha, Altos, Apple, Atari, Canon, Casio, Commodore, Cromemco, HP, IBM (for the Personal Computer), Microdata, NEC, North Star, Ohio Scientific, Osborne, Radio Shack, Sharp, Vector Graphic, Xerox, and Zenith/Heath.

Every company that sent the information I asked for is discussed in this book. Since few responded, many others — who sent inadequate information or nothing all — are also covered.

Like a lot of people, I was knocked out by the Osborne 1 when it was introduced at the Sixth West Coast Computer Faire in April, 1981. I have no connection of any kind with Osborne Computer or Adam Osborne himself, except that Osborne/McGraw-Hill was one of the places I went to with the idea for this book before I sold it to BYTE.

That's about it — except, of course, for the beach house in Malibu that was given to me by . . .

Appendix

D

Glossary

---

acoustic coupler: A device you put a telephone receiver in so information can be transmitted to and from a *modem*.

addressable cursor: A *cursor* you can move all over the screen.

alpha testing: Trying a new product out on the employees of your own company.

alphanumeric: Composed of letters and numbers (as opposed to just numbers or numbers and symbols). For example, text is alphanumeric.

applications programs (or *software*): Programs that do tasks like word processing or accounting. Distinguished from *operating systems, programming languages,* and *utility programs*, but not in any clear-cut way. Basically, applications programs do jobs that are specific, complicated, and immediately practical.

archive: A synonym for *save*, used mostly with dedicated word processors.

ASCII: (ASK-ee) The code most commonly used for transmitting text between computers or between a computer and its peripherals. The name stands for ''American Standard Code for Information Interchange.''

assembly language: Programming languages that talk fairly directly to the computer, as opposed to *high-level languages*, which are farther away from *machine language* and close to human speech.

auto-repeat: A feature of some keyboards that automatically repeats rapidly any key you hold down. A delay (usually about half a second) is built in to minimize accidental repeats.

auxiliary memory (or auxiliary storage): Other names for *storage*.

backup:　An extra copy of a file or disk, kept in case the original is harmed or destroyed.

BASIC:　A *high-level programming language,* very popular on microcomputers. The name is an acronym for ''Beginners' All-purpose Symbolic Instruction Code.''

baud rate:　(bawd) Bits per second. Baud rates are most commonly used as a measurement of transmission speeds, as on a *modem.* Named after Baudot, who devised a pre-ASCII communications code.

beta testing:　Having people who don't work for your company (friends, business associates, customers, etc.) try a new product out. If a company is large, testing a product in another division or group from the one that developed it is sometimes also called beta testing.

bi-directional:　Refers to printers that print one line from the left to right, the next from the right to left, and so on. This eliminates carriage returns and speeds up the printout.

bin:　On a *cut-sheet feeder,* a tray that holds blank paper or envelopes.

binary numbers:　The numbers computers themselves understand. Composed entirely of zeros and ones, they express all values in powers of two.

bit:　The smallest possible unit of information. All a bit can say is yes or no, on or off, or — as it's expressed in binary numbers — 0 or 1. Short for ''**b**inary dig**it**''.

block move:　The electronic equivalent of ''cut and paste,'' this feature allows you to mark a block of text and move it anywhere you want in a file. It is also possible to *block copy* (the block stays in its original position as well as appearing in the new place) and *block delete.*

board:　A piece of fiberglass or pressboard on which *chips* are mounted. The connections between the chips can be wires, or metallic ink printed on the board.

boilerplate:　Pieces of text that get used over and over again, word for word, in different documents.

boot:　To start up a computer by loading the *operating system* into it. If you're just turning the system on, it's a *cold boot.* If you've been working on it, it's called a *warm boot,* or *rebooting.*

box: A name sometimes used to refer to the computer itself, or the case it comes in (which also contains the *motherboard, bus,* and *power supply*).

bps: Bits per second.

bubble memory: An advanced, and expensive, sort of storage device featuring extremely fast access.

buffer: A portion of *memory* set aside for the temporary storage of data. In word processing, the *workspace* is a buffer.

bug: A mistake in a piece of *software* (or, less frequently, *hardware*).

bulk storage: Another word for *storage*.

bundled: Said of a system sold together as one package, rather than each component separately.

burn-in period: The first 168 or 200 hours of a component's life, during which time it's much more likely to fail than later on; the computer equivalent to infant mortality. To burn something in, you just turn it on and leave it on for the burn-in period (although you can also cycle the ambient temperature up and down). Some manufacturers do this for you (if they don't, you do it yourself . . . inevitably). Once something has been burned in, you can usually depend on it for a while.

burst speed: The top speed of a printer, usually the speed at which it can repeatedly print one letter.

bus: Circuits that connect *boards* and other devices in a computer. A common microcomputer bus is the *S-100*.

byte: A character (or, more precisely, the amount of information required to define one character). A byte consists of eight *bits*.

card: Another name for a *board*.

CAT: (1) Acronym for "computer-aided training." (2) A device on some Xerox keyboards that's used to move the cursor around (I don't know what the letters stand for).

catalog: A list of all the files on a disk (also called a *directory*).

character: The generic name for a letter, number, or symbol.

character buffer: On a printer, a buffer that lets you pump text over to it to free the computer up for other jobs. On a terminal, the buffer where data is sent before being displayed on the screen.

chip: A piece of (mostly) silicon about the size of a baby's fingernail incorporating any one of several different kinds of miniaturized computer circuitry. More loosely, the package in which the chip is contained (properly called a *DIP*). A chip is about the most impressive thing you can do with sand.

Whole computers (as powerful as an IBM 370) have been reduced to a chip. Hewlett-Packard talks about a chip of theirs being ''faster than a speeding bullet.'' A quarter inch on a side, it can perform 500 operations in the time it takes a bullet to travel across it.

Chips are distinguished by how much circuitry is on them:

SSI's (small-scale integration) are the smallest. they contain (the equivalent of) relatively few transistors per chip and cost about half a cent to produce (for just the chip itself, without leads — not the DIP).

Next in size are *MSI's* (medium-scale integration), followed by *LSI's* (large-scale), which cost about 50¢, *VLSI's* (very-large-scale), and *SLSI's* (super-large-scale), which can contain up to *half a million* transistors. Compare that to a transistor radio, which typically contains about half a dozen.

Chips are usually mounted onto *boards*.

chip family: A group of related chips, all made by the same manufacturer, which evolved from one another.

clock: *Not* what it normally means (although the meaning is related); a computer's clock sends out electronic pulses that are used to synchronize the various things a computer does.

clustering: Linking several word processors to one printer (or other expensive peripheral that isn't constantly used). Also called *sharing resources*.

code: The actual instructions in a program. (''Have you seen his code? Kluge city!'')

code key: What the *control key* is called on some systems.

column: A horizontal space. An 80-column screen displays 80 characters on each line.

compatible: Able to work together.

computer: A machine for processing information.

computer box: See *box*.

computer letters: *Personalized form letters* produced by a *merge-print program*.

conditional carriage return, hyphen, or **page:** See *soft carriage return, hyphen* or *page*.

continuous form paper: Paper that comes in a roll or a series of sheets connected by perforations. *Fan-fold* is the kind most commonly used in word processing.

control character: The result of holding down the control key while holding down another key (or keys). Control characters usually *do* things rather than appearing in the text themselves.

control key: A special key on computer keyboards that, like the shift key, changes the meaning of every other key, if it's held down when they're struck. Unlike the shift key, the control key usually generates commands rather than new characters.

controllable cursor: A cursor you can move all over the screen.

copy: This term means just what it usually means, except that in word processing, the copy is in the form of electromagnetic impulses rather than marks on paper.

CP/M: One of the most common *operating systems* for microcomputers.

CP/M-86: A version of CP/M that runs on machines built around the *8086* CPU chip.

CPU: The ''central processing unit'' — the central part of the computer. It contains the *CPU chip* or *microprocessor*. In a microcomputer, the CPU is usually all on one board (called the *CPU board,* of course), or even on part of one board.

cps: Characters per second. Used to describe the speed of printers. To convert from cps to words per minute, multiply by ten if you want actual words, and by twelve if you want official, five-character, typing words. (Also see *word*.)

crash: Noun and verb which mean your computer (or a program you're running on it) has stopped working — or, worse, is working wrong.

CRT: A "cathode ray tube" — a screen like the one on a television set.

cursor: A marker which tells where you are in the text.

cursor arrows: Keys with arrows printed on them that move the cursor in the direction indicated.

cursor diamond: Keys (*cursor arrows* or otherwise) arranged in a diamond, so that the top key moves the cursor up, the right-hand key moves it right, and so on.

customized form letters: *Personalized form letters* produced by a *merge-print program.*

cut-sheet feeder: A machine that fits on top of a printer and feeds separate sheets of paper into it.

CVT: A "constant voltage transformer" — a device used to correct high, low, or fluctuating line voltages which can wreak havoc on a computer.

daisy wheel: A flat, circular device made of plastic or metal with characters mounted on it. Certain *formed-character printers* use it as their *print element.*

dangerous key: A *reset button* or other key that can result in the loss of text if hit and is in a position where it can be hit fairly easily.

data file: A file composed of data; as opposed to a *program,* which is a file composed of instructions.

debugging: The process of getting the *bugs* out of a piece of software or hardware.

decimal tab: A tab stop that automatically aligns numbers on their decimal points.

dedicated key: A *function key* with only one function (*cursor arrows* are an example). The command it executes is written on it and doesn't change.

dedicated word processor: A computer designed specifically to do word processing, usually with limited ability to be used as a general-purpose computer.

default: What happens if you don't specify something else. Often used in the phrase *default value.* ("Singlespacing is the default.")

descenders:　The little tales on g's, y's, j's, p's, and q's that descend below the line. On some primitive printers and CRT's, they don't actually extend below the line (we say they lack *true descenders*).

dictionary:　In a spelling checker, the list of words the program checks text against.

DIP:　(pronounced as one word, not as three letters) A "dual in-line package" — what most chips are packaged in. The DIP protects the chip and connects it to the board with its prongs.

DIP switch:　Some DIPS have little switches on them. For example, the video board in my computer has a DIP switch that gives me reverse video (dark-on-light) if I push it one way, regular video (light-on-dark) if I push it the other.

directory:　A list of all the files on a disk (also called a *catalog*).

dirty power:　Electricity coming into a computer that has any one of several things wrong with it — noise, spikes, consistently low voltage, etc.

disk:　When I use this word, I'm usually talking about a *floppy disk*. There are also *hard disks*.

disk drive:　A device that *writes* information onto, and *reads* information off of, a floppy disk or a hard disk. As the drive spins the disk at high speed, an arm (something like the tone arm on a record turntable) moves back and forth to various tracks on the disk and either absorbs or deposits information by means of the *read/write head* that's mounted on it.

diskette:　The bland official name for a *floppy disk*.

distribution disk:　The actual disk you get from a software publisher or store, with the program you bought on it. Also called a *master disk*. Copy it and put it away.

DMA:　"Direct memory access" — a common form of *memory-mapping*.

DOA:　"Dead on arrival." Used to describe something that doesn't work when you take it out of the box.

document:　The generic name for whatever it is you're writing.

documentation:　Written information about computer hardware and software — instructions, training manuals, and reference materials of all sorts.

DOS: "Disk operating system." See *operating system*.

dot matrix: A system for forming letters and other characters out of small dots. All CRTS and many *printers* use dot matrixes.

The more dots in the matrix, the higher the quality of the character formed in it (i.e., the higher the *resolution*). Typical low-resolution dot matrixes are 5 by 7 dots (a total of 35 dots) or 7 by 9 (63 dots); high-resolution dot matrixes range up to 11 by 13 (143 dots) and beyond.

double-density: A system for putting information onto a floppy disk that crams twice as much into the same space.

double-sided: Refers to floppy disks which store information on both sides, rather than just one.

down: Not working (as opposed to *up*).

draft mode: On multipass printers, draft mode prints out fast, without overstriking. The text produced doesn't look great, but it's good enough to use for editing a draft.

drive: A *storage* device that *writes* information onto a *disk* and *reads* it off.

drop-ins: Characters not typed by you that appear in your text because the system is malfunctioning.

dropouts: Characters that are deleted from your text because the system is malfunctioning.

dumb: Having little or no computational ability of its own. Said of terminals, keyboards, printers, etc.

Dvorak keyboard: An arrangement of keys that strives to make typing easy — unlike *QWERTY*, which was designed to make it hard.

editor: The part of a *word-processing program* that edits the text (as opposed to the *formatter*). Sometimes a stand-alone program (in which case it's usually called a *text editor*).

eight-bit chip: A *microprocessor* that handles data eight bits at a time. The *8080*, *Z80*, *6502*, and *6800* are some examples.

8080: An eight-bit *microprocessor*, the first to be widely used in personal computers.

end users: People who use the computer products they buy themselves. As opposed to *OEMS,* who resell them.

EPROM: An ''erasable programmable read-only memory'' chip — a kind of PROM that is particularly easy to reprogram.

error message: Text that appears on the screen to tell you something is wrong.

ESC or **ESCAPE:**   A special key found on most microcomputer keyboards. Its function depends on the software you're running.

expandable: Said of a computer that can be improved and made capable of performing new functions, usually by putting extra boards into it.

expansion interface: Some computers which aren't expandable nevertheless do support an expansion interface, which allows you to add disk drives, more memory, and other enhancements.

extension: In CP/M, another word for *type.*

fan-fold paper: Continuous form paper made up of single sheets with perforations between them. It folds into the box like a fan.

fatal bug: A bug that crashes a program, forcing you to reboot and lose all your work since the last time you saved.

fatal error: A mistake you make that crashes the program. If you think it's the program's fault, you call it a fatal bug.

field-upgradable: Capable of being transformed into a more powerful model ''in the field'' (at the store where you bought it) rather than having to be sent back to the factory.

file: A bunch of text, or a program. What makes it a file is that you call it by one name.

fixed disk: A *hard disk* that can't be removed from its drive.

flag: To mark. Or, a marker.

flat panel: Any one of several technologies that substitute for *CRTs* and require much less depth.

Flex: An operating system for 6800/6809 machines.

flexible disk:　　Another bland, corporate name for a *floppy disk*.

flexible diskette:　　Ditto.

floppy disk or **floppy:**　　A device for the permanent storage of computer data. The information is stored magnetically on material similar to recording tape. It's called a floppy to distinguish it from rigid, *hard disks*.

　　Floppies are round, but come in square protective envelopes made of cardboard about 1/16 inch thick. There are two basic sizes — 8-inch and 5¼-inch *minifloppies*. (Smaller 3½-inch floppies have also been introduced.)

　　Floppies come *hard-sectored* and *soft-sectored, single-sided* and *double-sided, single-density* and *double-density*. A typical single-density, single-sided, soft-sectored 8-inch floppy holds about 240K.

font:　　A typeface. Fonts vary in terms of their size (e.g., pica or elite), design (e.g., serif or sanserif), boldness (e.g., regular or bold), and style (e.g., italic or Roman).

footer:　　A piece of text repeated at the bottom of each page.

form feed:　　A page break — the "form" (paper) "feeds" (moves up) to the start of the next page.

form-letter program:　　Same as a *merge-print program*.

format:　　To prepare text for printout. Formatting involves setting the page length, margins, line spacing, character spacing, page numbering, headers, footers, line justification, etc.

　　To *format a disk* is to prepare it to accept information.

formatter:　　The part of a *word-processing program* that formats the text (as opposed to the *editor*). Sometimes a stand-alone program.

formed-character printers:　　The most common kind of *letter-quality printers,* they produce images the same way typewriters do — by pushing the shape of a character against an inked ribbon and then against the paper. They're relatively slow and relatively expensive.

　　Most formed-character printers use a flat, circular device called a *daisy wheel* on which the characters are mounted. NEC Spinwriters use a *thimble*. The daisy wheel or thimble spins very fast, and a high-speed hammer hits it when the desired character is in front of it.

Forth: A high-level programming language whose many fans remind you that the word is short for ''fanatic.''

friction feed: Moving paper through a printer by means of rollers pressing against the platen, the way a typewriter does.

friendly: Said of a piece of software or hardware, it means you don't need a Ph.D in Computer Science to understand how to use it. Also called *user-friendly*.

full-screen editing: Being able to move the cursor all over the screen to alter text.

function key: A special key that doesn't produce a character on the screen but rather executes a command or series of commands. There are two basic kinds: fixed-function, *dedicated keys,* and programmable function keys or *soft keys,* whose function varies with the software you're using.

gas plasma: A kind of *phosphorescent flat-panel* display.

getting (a file):   Another name for *loading* (a file).

GIGO   (GUY-go) ''Garbage in, garbage out.'' In other words, you can't expect a computer to outsmart your stupid mistakes.

glare: Reflections from a CRT screen.

glitch: A sudden voltage surge or burst of electromagnetic noise that causes a piece of hardware to malfunction.

global editor: That part of the *editor* that makes changes everywhere in a document, not just where the cursor is.

global find and replace: The ability to find a *string* anywhere it appears in a document and to substitute another string for it.

Hall-effect key switches: When you depress the key, a plunger passes through a magnetic field that sends the signal from the keyboard to the computer. Since the key and the switch never touch, these are also known as contactless key switches.

hanging indent: Another name for an *outdent*.

hard copy: An actual piece of paper with text on it, as opposed to what you see on your screen (or copy onto a disk).

hard disk: The next step up from a *floppy disk*. Hard disks hold more data, get to it more quickly, and cost more money.

hard-wired: Built right into the hardware. Hard-wiring is more convenient than having to load a program, but much more difficult to change.

hardware: The actual physical components of a computer system, the machinery (as opposed to *software*).

hash: Visual static on the screen.

head: The actual device that magnetically stores information on a disk or reads it from one.

header: A piece of text repeated at the top of each page.

hertz: The number of cycles of an electrical current per second. Abbreviated Hz.

high-level languages: Programming languages fairly close to natural languages like English, with commands that each translate into several instructions to the computer. As opposed to *assembly languages*, which talk fairly directly to the computer. *BASIC*, *Pascal*, and *Forth* are three examples.

highlight: To make parts of the text brighter than the rest of the text on a screen, or to show them in *reverse video*, in order to distinguish them from the rest of the text.

hologram: A three-dimensional image produced in thin air by lasers interacting with each other.

home: The upper left corner of the screen.

home computer: A microcomputer used at home.

home row: The row of keys on the keyboard where touch typists rest their fingers between keystrokes.

horizontal scrolling: Moving text on the screen to the left, so the right end of lines too long to fit on the screen can be seen.

human engineering: Designing a product as if human beings were going to use it.

Hz: Abbreviation for *hertz*.

IC: Abbreviation for *integrated circuit*.

IEEE-488:   (''eye triple ee'') An industry-standard *parallel interface*. IEEE stands for the Institute of Electrical and Electronic Engineers.

impact printer: Any printer that forms characters by hitting the paper.

implement: To make something work. (''We hope to have PIE Writer implemented on the IBM PC by the end of next month.'')

incremental spacing: A synonym for *microspacing*.

indexer: A program that generates an index for a document.

insert mode: When a word-processing program is in this mode, it inserts text at the cursor, pushing all text after the cursor right and down.

instant print: A feature that lets you use a word processor as a typewriter. Each time you hit a key, the character is immediately transmitted to the printer.

instruction set: All the basic instructions a CPU chip understands. Each chip's instruction set is different.

integrated circuit: A complicated electronic circuit that has been shrunk down and put on a *chip*. An *integrated circuit board* is a *board* which contains integrated circuits.

intelligent: Even smarter than *smart*.

interface: The hardware and software needed to connect one component with another, or one computer with another.

I/O: ''Input-output'' (of information).

justification: Making lines of text straight at the margin. *Left justification* (a straight left margin) is the most common format for typed text, and *justification to both margins* is the most common format for typeset text. *Right justification* (straight right margin, ragged left) is also possible, but it looks very strange.
  The phrase ''justified text'' all by itself implies justification to both margins.

K or **KB:**   Abbreviations for *kilobyte*. Although K always refers to a kilobyte in this book, it's also sometimes used to refer to a kilo*bit* — 1024 *bits*. For example, a 16K memory chip handles 16,384 bits, not bytes. It takes eight of them to give you 16 kilo*bytes* of memory. (KB, however, always refers to kilobytes.)

keyboard: Oh, you know what this is. The important thing to mention is that it can be bought separately, or as part of a *terminal*. Keyboards vary in terms of how they feel to type on, how *smart* they are, number of keys, layout of keys, etc. (The standard layout is *QWERTY*.)

key switch: When you push down on a key, you close a switch. When the key switch is closed, the character on the key you pushed is transmitted to the computer.

key tops: The part of the keys your fingers hit. Also, little labels supplied with software designed to be stuck on the top of the keys to remind you of what various commands are.

kHz: Abbreviation for *kilohertz*.

kill: To delete (a file, for example).

kilobit: 1024 bits. Abbreviated K.

kilobyte: 1024 *bytes*. Equal to about 170 (actual) *words,* or about ⅔ of a standard *page*. Abbreviated *KB* or just *K*.

kilohertz: A thousand cycles of an electrical current per second. Abbreviated KHz.

kluge: To solve a problem by patching rather than finding the root cause and correcting that. Also, the result of such patching.

KSR: "Keyboard send/receive." Refers to printers that have keyboards and thus can give instructions to a computer, as well as follow a computer's instructions. Also see *R/O*.

LCD: "Liquid crystal display" — a common sort of *nonemitter flat-panel* technology.

LED: "Light-emitting diode" — a type of *phosphorescent flat-panel* display.

letter-quality printer: A printer that produces printouts you wouldn't be ashamed to send out as business letters. *Formed-character printers* are the main kind, but *multipass printers* are also capable of producing letter-quality text.

line break: A command to move the printout onto the next line, whether or not the present line is full.

line conditioner/stabilizer: A device which combines a *surge suppressor,* a *line filter,* and a *CVT*.

line editor: An *editor* that requires you to specify the line (and word) you want to make your changes on, rather than letting you just move the cursor there. As opposed to a screen editor.

line feed: Another name for a *line break*.

line filter (or *isolater*): A device to correct electromagnetic interference (more commonly known as *noise*).

line printer: This is not a very precise term. Strictly it means a printer that prints a whole line at a time, but it's commonly used to describe any dot-matrix printer. In fact, Radio Shack's Line Printer VII only prints 30 cps — hardly a line at a time.

load: To copy a *file* from *disk* to *RAM*.

logged disk: The disk that is currently in the *logged drive*.

logged drive: The disk drive the computer will use by default if another drive is not specified.

logic seeking: The ability of some printers to go immediately to the first point on the page where a character will appear, instead of having to space over to it.

logically summing: The ability of some printers to lump several horizontal or vertical spaces together and to move across them in one fell swoop.

lpm: Lines per minute — the least meaningful way to talk about printer speeds.

machine: Another name for a computer.

machine language: The actual *binary code* a computer understands. All programming language commands — whether high-level or assembly — must ultimately be translated into machine language before the computer can obey them.

magnetic media: A generic name for floppy disks, hard disks, tapes, and any other object or substance that stores data in the form of magnetic impulses.

mainframe: The largest kind of computer, bigger than a minicomputer. Mainframe is also another name for a *computer box*.

mass storage: Another name for *storage*.

master disk: Another name for a *distribution disk*.

MB: Abbreviation for *megabyte*.

media: A shorthand way of referring to *magnetic media*.

megabyte: 1024 *kilobytes;* 1,048,576 *bytes*. Abbreviated *MB*.

megahertz: A million cycles of an electrical current per second. Abbreviated *MHz*.

memory: Just what it normally means, except that the term does include information held in external media like disks or tapes. There are three basic kinds of computer memory — *RAM, ROM,* and *PROM*.

memory mapping: A system for transmitting information to a screen in which it's read directly from the *memory* or the *bus* of the computer, as opposed to *terminal mode*.

menu: A list on the screen of commands you can choose from.

menu-driven: Said of a program which uses *menus* extensively.

merge-print program: A program that lets you produce *personalized form letters* and the like by combining information from various sources during the actual printing of each document.

message: Text that appears on the screen when the computer wants to tell you something.

MHz: Abbreviation for *megahertz*.

microcomputer (or **micro**):   A computer built around a *microprocessor*. The next size down from a minicomputer, the computer box itself can be carried in your arms. A complete word-processing system built around a microcomputer costs between $3,000 and $20,000.

microjustification: The ability of some word-processing programs, when working with printers with *microspacing,* to justify lines by adding little slivers of blank space between letters of words as well as between words.

microprocessor: The actual computing part of a computer, squeezed onto a tiny *chip*. Also called a *CPU chip*.

microspacing: A feature of some printers which allows them to move distances as small as 1/120 inch horizontally or 1/60 inch vertically.

mini-diskette: Another name for a *minifloppy*.

minicomputer (or **mini**):   A middle-sized computer, larger than a *microcomputer* and smaller than a *mainframe*.

minifloppy: A *floppy disk* 5¼ inches in diameter.

mnemonics: Giving a command (or anything else) a name that's easy to remember, usually because it derives from a word that describes what the command does. So, for example, the command ^P to go to the print menu is mnemonic; the command ^J to go to the help menu is not.

modem: (MOE-dum) A device that lets computers or terminals talk to one another over phone lines. Short for *mo*dulator-*dem*odulator.

modem board: A *board* that plugs into a computer's *motherboard* and functions as a modem (usually it has a phone company modular plug attached to it on a cord, which you snake out through a hole in the back of the computer).

monitor: Usually this word is used to refer to a *CRT* — the television screen on which you see your work.

But monitor also has a technical meaning — a program (or collection of programs) that controls certain basic aspects of a computer's operation.

motherboard: A slotted board in the computer box that other boards are mounted into.

mouse: A device attached to some Xerox keyboards that lets you move the cursor by rolling it around on the table.

MPU: The ''microprocessor unit'' — another name for *CPU*.

MTBF: ''Mean (i.e., average) time between failures'' — a measure of the reliability of a piece of hardware.

MTTR: ''Mean (i.e., average) time to repair'' — a measure of how easy a piece of hardware is to fix.

multi-tasking: Doing more than one job at a time; for example, editing one file while printing out another.

multi-user: Allowing more than one person to use a computer at the same time.

multipass printer: A kind of dot-matrix printer that can go back and overstrike text to produce more fully formed, readable characters.

no-break space: A space which will not be broken over the end of a line; the words on either side of a no-break space always appear on the same line.

no-screen word processor: A word processor without a screen (oddly enough); printout and display are the same process.

noise: Electromagnetic interference caused by electrical engines, fluorescent lights, television sets, etc.

nonemitter: A display technology that doesn't shine with its own light. *LCD* is one example.

nonimpact printers: Dot-matrix printers that produce images chemically, thermally, or electrostatically, rather than by impact through an ink ribbon.

numeric key pad: Ten number keys arranged in a square, the way they are on a calculator.

OCR reader: A device that can literally read text printed in certain typefaces and transmit it to a computer. The name stands for "optical character recognition."

OEM: An "original equipment manufacturer"; actually, a company that assembles computer systems using components many (or all) of which were manufactured by other companies. A better name for this is *system integrator*. Distinguished from *end users*, who don't resell what they buy.

official word: In this book, a five-letter word (four letters and a space). So called because this definition of word is used to calculate typing speeds in advertising, although actually the average word is longer. Also see *real word*.

on-line: On the computer. For example, on-line documentation appears on your screen rather than in a manual.

on-screen formatting: Showing on the screen how a piece of text will look on paper. (I reserve the term *virtual representation* for showing *exactly* how the printed text will look and use on-screen formatting to indicate rough approximations of that).

operating system: The basic program that tells your computer what to do. Operating systems are usually specific to the particular chip on which a computer is based. Operating system is often abbreviated *OS* or *DOS* (for disk operating system). Thus the TRS-80 operating system is called TRSDOS.

orphan: The first line of a paragraph sitting alone at the bottom of a page.

OS: Abbreviation for "operating system."

OS-9:   An operating system that runs on machines built around the 6809 chip.

outdent: A line of text (usually the first) which extends farther to the left than other lines in the same paragraph.

overlay: A portion of a program that sits on the disk until the main part of the program calls it (or a part of it) into action.

overstrike: To have two or more characters print on the same space.

owpm: *Official words* per minute. Equal to the number of characters per minute divided by five.

page: Although this word has a technical, computer meaning, I always use it to mean a standard page of double-spaced pica text, with one-inch margins all around — which contains about 250 *words* (or about 1½ K).

page break: A command to move the printout onto the next page, whether or not the present page is full.

parallel interface: An *interface* on which several bits of data travel over separate wires simultaneously, next to each other.

parameter: A variable. So, for example, a formatting parameter is any aspect of the printout that can be varied (the margins, for example).

Pascal: A *high-level programming language,* said to be one of the most logical and least klugy.

PC: "Printed circuit." "*The* PC" is a nickname for the IBM Personal Computer.

peripheral: Any device connected to a computer — e.g., a monitor, keyboard, printer, terminal, etc.

permanent storage: A synonym for *storage*.

personal computer: A microcomputer that belongs to, and is mostly used by, one person.

personalized form letters: Generated by a *merge-print program,* each of these is more or less identical to every other, but personalizing data (like the name of the addressee, where he or she lives, how much he or she owes, etc.) is inserted into each one. The program gets this personal information from a mailing list, data file, or directly from the computer operator while the letter is being printed out.

phosphor: The stuff on the inside of CRT's that glows when the electron beam hits it. It continues to glow for a moment, giving the picture a bit of permanence.

phosphorescent: When speaking of *flat-panel* displays, those that glow with their own light.

pin feed: Pins, set at the either end of the platen, engage sprocket holes on the edge of the paper and pull it through the printer.

PIP: A CP/M utility program for copying files from one disk to another.

plotter: A computer *peripheral* that draws things.

plug compatible: Although made by manufacturer X, all you have to do is plug it into manufacturer Y's equipment and it will work.

port: A sweet wine that . . . no, uh, *here* it means a place to connect other devices to a computer. Also called an *I/O* (input/output) port. I/O ports can be *serial* or *parallel*.

power supply: The device that converts the 110-volt electricity in your wall socket to DC electricity of the proper voltages for use by the computer, printer, etc.

pph: Pages per hour.

print element: The piece of a printer that actually puts the characters on the paper. Usually it's removable.

printed circuit board: A *board* on which the chips are connected by circuits printed with metallic ink rather than by wires.

printer: A computer peripheral that produces hard copies of text on paper.

printer terminal: A keyboard and printer combination capable of being connected to a computer. Distinguished from a *VDT*.

printout: A *hard copy* of your file(s), prepared on a printer.

program: A set of instructions that tells a computer what to do. Also called *software*.

programmable function key: A key whose function varies with the software you're using.

programmer: Someone who uses a programming language to write programs, as opposed to a *user*.

programming language: A tool for writing programs. Programming languages occupy a middle ground between *machine language* and human speech.

PROM: (prahm) ''Programmable read-only memory.'' It tells the computer what to do, and you can only change it with a piece of hardware called a PROM programmer. It usually comes as a DIP, and is referred to as *a* PROM.

proofing program: Another name for a *spelling checker*.

proportional spacing, (true):   Proportional spacing is the main thing that makes something that's typeset easier to read than something that's typed.
  In typing, all letters get the same space, regardless of how wide or narrow they are. For example, look at the word ''`commission`.'' Because the m's are wider than the average letter, they looked squeezed together. Because the i's are narrower than most letters, they look like they're floating alone. The ''co,'' ''ss,'' and ''on'' look OK, because c's, s's, o's, and n's are of average width. Capitalization makes the situation even more extreme. A capital M or W is *much* wider than a small i or l.
  Proportional spacing takes the varying widths of letters into account and gives each character exactly the width it needs — no more, no less. Compare the word ''commission'' when it's typeset. The m's get more room, and the i's get less.
  Because proportional spacing involves a lot of computation, the software that does it takes a lot of memory; for this reason, it's sometimes put into a separate program from the word-processing program or into an *overlay*.
  I refer to ''true'' proportional spacing because some word-processing programs claim to have proportional spacing when all they really have is *microjustification*.

proprietary: Belonging to just one company and not widely used outside of that company (e.g., a proprietary chip).

QWERTY: The standard layout for keyboards, where the first six letter keys on the second line are q, w, e, r, t, and y, and where you can spell "typewriter" with the keys on that line, as opposed to newer, more efficient keyboards where a letter's location depends on how much it's used.

ragged left: An unusual format in which the right margin is straight but the left is uneven.

ragged right: The normal format for typewritten text. The left margin is straight but the lines are of different lengths.

RAM: (pronounced as in "battering ram") "random-access memory." Actually, most sorts of memory are randomly-accessed, but the term RAM has come to mean what is more correctly called *read/write memory* — that is, memory you can both input data into and read data out of (as opposed to *ROM*).

The amount of RAM a word processor has is an important measure of its usefulness, because RAM is where you do all your writing. Whatever is in RAM normally disappears when you turn the computer off.

read: To absorb information from.

read/write: Capable of both absorbing and depositing information, or of having information absorbed from it and deposited in it; e.g., *read/write memory* (see *RAM*), *read/write head* (see *head*). As opposed to read-only.

real time clock: An actual clock (in the usual sense of the word) that keeps track of how long things take when you're working on a computer (and thus can tell you how long you've been working on a given file, for example).

real word: In this book, a six-letter word (five letters and a space). Distinguished from an *official word* (four letters and a space).

reboot: To dump whatever you're working on and boot the operating system again.

reference card: A small card designed to be propped up near the keyboard which lists the commands a given program makes available.

reference manual: A manual designed to be referred to after a program is more or less learned.

refresh rate: How often the image on a CRT is renewed.

release version: The first version of a program that's sold to the public.

repetitive document generator: A synonym for a *merge-print program*.

reset button: A key or button on a computer that flushes memory, throwing out whatever programs, text, etc. had been loaded into it.

resolution: The number of little dots in a character or on a screen. The more there are, the more fine detail there will be (high resolution); the fewer there are, the grosser and clumsier the image will be (low resolution).

By the way, don't confuse the size of a screen with its resolution. On a big screen with low resolution, the dots *(pixels)* are just bigger.

RETURN: A key found on all computer keyboards. Its function varies with the software. Usually (but not always) it does what the equivalent key on a typewriter keyboard does — i.e., moves you to the beginning of the next line.

reverse video: Dark on light, the opposite of the usual light-on-dark CRT image.

rewrite flicker: On systems that operate in *terminal mode* with relatively slow *baud rates,* the resultant flickering of the screen when the image changes.

rigid disk: Another name for a *hard disk*.

R/O (also **RO**): ''Receive only.'' Usually refers to a printer without a keyboard which can only do what the computer tells it to do and can't send information back to the computer. Also see *KSR*. Also, ''read only'' (that is, able only to be read from, not written to).

ROM: (rahm) ''Read-only memory.'' It tells the computer what to do, but you can't change what it says (as opposed to RAM). ROM usually comes in the form of a DIP, which is referred to as a ROM.

rotary control knob: A device mounted in some HP keyboards that moves the cursor when you press down on its perimeter.

Route 128: Silicon Valley East (Route 128 encircles the greater Boston area).

RS-232: An industry-standard *serial interface*. RS stands for ''recommended standard.''

(X) runs on (Y): X (program) will function on Y (machine).

(X) runs under (Y):   In order for X (program) to function, Y (program) must have first been loaded into the machine.

R/W: Abbreviation for *read/write*.

rwpm: *Real words* per minute. Equal to the number of characters per minute divided by six.

S-100 bus: A common microcomputer *bus*.

san serif: Without *serifs*.

save: To copy a *file* from *RAM* to *disk*.

screen: A *CRT*.

screen editor: An *editor* that lets you move the cursor all around the screen (as opposed to a *line editor*).

screen update: Changing of the screen to reflect new information (despite the use of the word date, it happens very quickly).

screenful: The amount of text it takes to fill the screen.

scrolling: Moving through the text (usually vertically, unless *horizontal scrolling* is specified). Scrolling is often used in this book to indicate automatic scrolling — i.e., moving through the text without having to hold a key down.

secondary memory: A (misleading) synonym for *storage*.

serial interface: An *interface* on which all the data moves over the same wire, one bit after the other.

serif: A little hook or line on the end of a letter. Also used as an adjective: ''Palatino is an elegant serif typeface.''

service contract: You pay a certain amount per year (or per month), and if anything goes wrong with the hardware, they fix it for free.

shadow printing: Printing a character, moving right a tiny bit, and printing it again (and so on). Only printers with *microspacing* can do this.

Shannon test: A piece of text designed to approximate the speed of a printer in actual use, as opposed to its *burst speed*.

shared-logic: More than one terminal connected to one computer.

shared-resource: More than one computer connected to one printer, disk drive, or other expensive peripheral.

Silicon Valley: The Santa Clara Valley, south of San Francisco, where about two-thirds of all American computer products are designed and built.

single-density: The original system for putting information on a floppy disk. It only gives you half as much capacity as *double-density*, but it's more reliable.

single-sided: Refers to floppy disks that store information on only one side.

sixteen-bit chip: A *microprocessor* that handles data 16 bits at a time. The *68000*, *8086*, and *Z8000* are some examples.

16 × 64:   A common screen format — sixteen lines of 64 characters.

6502:   An eight-bit *microprocessor* used in the Apple II and Apple III, among other computers.

6800:   An eight-bit *microprocessor*.

6809:   A *microprocessor* that handles data in 16-bit chunks internally, but takes it in and sends it out in eight-bit chunks.

68000:   A 16-bit *microprocessor*.

slave: To make one computer (or computer component) do what another computer (or component) tells it to do.

slots: The openings in the *motherboard* the other *boards* plug into.

smart: Having some computational ability of its own. Said of terminals, keyboards, printers, etc.

smooth scrolling: The ability to scroll text without having it jerk from line to line.

soft carriage return: A symbol, usually invisible, that generates a line break when it falls at the end of a line and a space otherwise.

soft hyphen: A symbol, usually visual, that prints as a hyphen when it falls at the end of a line and disappears otherwise.

soft key: A *programmable function key;* what it does depends on the software you're using.

SoftCard: A board that plugs into the Apple II and allows it to run CP/M by slaving the Apple's own 6502 microprocessor to the Z80 on the SoftCard.

software: The instructions that tell a computer what to do (as opposed to the actual *hardware*). Also called *programs*.

SPACEBAR: The long, narrow key at the bottom of all alphanumeric keyboards that generates spaces.

spelling checker: A program that goes through a file and checks for spelling errors.

spike: Another name for a *surge*.

split screen: A feature that allows you to see more than one piece of text on the screen at the same time.

spooling: *Swapping* the file you're working on from memory into disk, and vice versa. Spool stands for "simultaneous peripheral operations on-line."

stand-alone: Not hooked up to other hardware; capable of operating on its own.

storage: A permanent place to put files you want to use later. Floppy disks, hard disks, cassette tapes, and streaming tapes are common forms of storage.

string: A sequence of characters.

support: 1) Verbal advice and help with hardware or software problems, e.g., "We support what we sell."

2) Said of a piece of hardware or software itself, supports means works with, e.g., "Magic Wand supports the TEC terminal."

The connection between the two meanings is this: computers are so complex that you're crazy to try to make two things work together if someone doesn't promise to help you with any problems that come up — unless, of course, you think you can solve every problem yourself (but everybody needs *some* level of support).

support contract: You pay money just so you can ask the people who sold you a product questions about it. The time you can spend talking to them is usually measured in hours.

surge: A very sudden, and very sharp, increase in voltage.

surge suppressor: A device that evens out surges.

swap: To take what's in memory and put it on disk, automatically replacing it with more of the same file from disk.

system: A computer plus its *peripherals* — terminal, printer, keyboard, monitor, disk drives, etc. Sometimes system also includes software.

system disk: A disk that has the operating system (and often other programs) on it. If a disk isn't a system disk, you can't *boot* it.

system integrator: A company that assembles computer systems using components most (or all) of which were manufactured by other companies. Usually called an *OEM*.

terminal: A device used to give instructions to a computer and to get information back from it. It consists of a keyboard and a CRT (a *video terminal* or *VDT*) or a keyboard and a printer (a *printer terminal*).

Terminals vary in terms of how *smart* or *dumb* they are — that is, how much computational ability they have.

terminal mode: A system for transmitting information to a screen in which it's first sent to the terminal's character buffer and then formatted for display on the screen, as opposed to *memory-mapping*.

text editor: Another name for an *editor*.

text file: A file that contains text (rather than, say, a program).

thermal printer: A printer that uses heat to form characters on special paper.

thimble: The *print element* used on NEC Spinwriter *formed-character printers*.

thin-window display: A non-CRT display that shows just one line or part of a line. Typically, it runs across the top of the keyboard.

time sharing: Using phone lines to share a large computer with many other users. You're usually billed by the hour.

toggle: Any command that switches back and forth between two possible alternatives (insert mode and writeover mode, for example).

tractor feed: Gasoline. But when talking about computers, it means a lightweight, mechanically-simple paper-feeding device that attaches to the top of a printer and engages sprocket holes in the paper with pins. The distance between the pins can be altered to accommodate papers of different widths.

training manual: A manual designed to be used while a program is being learned. Also called a *tutorial*.

tutorial: Another name for a *training manual*. (Be aware that, in the world of computers, this usually means a book, not a class.)

324 × 80: A common screen format — 24 lines of 80 characters.

type: In CP/M, the three-letter addition to the file name which comes after the period and is used to indicate what type of file it is (e.g.,.TXT,. LET,. BAC).

type-ahead buffer: A *buffer* that remembers which keys were struck when the computer, for some reason or another, can't pay attention to them right at that moment.

UNIX: (YOU-nix) An operating system for 16-bit machines.

up: Working (as opposed to *down*).

user: Someone who uses programs written by other people, rather than writing her (or his) own. As opposed to a *programmer*.

user memory: Another name for *RAM*.

user-friendly: Another name for *friendly*.

utility program: A relatively simple program that usually sits on every disk you use. Typical utility-program tasks are copying files or disks or doing simple sorts.

VDT: A "video display terminal" — i.e., a keyboard and a CRT combination capable of communicating with a computer. As distinguished from a *printer terminal*.

VDU: A "video display unit" — the British name for a *VDT*.

vendor: The company (or person) who sells you something. Usually as distinguished from the manufacturer or publisher who actually makes the product.

verification (of a save):   A process whereby, after a file has been saved, the program goes back and makes a character-by-character comparison of what's on disk with what's in memory.

versions (of programs):   Progressive refinements and enhancements, numbered in ascending order.

video board: In memory-mapped mode, the *board* which controls the display on a monitor; together with the CRT, it substitutes for a terminal.

video terminal: A *VDT*.

virtual representation: Showing on the screen exactly what a piece of text will look like on paper. It goes beyond *on-screen formatting* by displaying a whole page of text, right justification, proportional spacing, boldfacing, underlining, and double underlining as such.

visual editor: A *screen editor*.

warm boot: Another name for *rebooting*.

widow: The last line of a paragraph sitting alone at the top of a page.

wildcard: A symbol which stands for any character (or any letter, any number, etc.)

Winchester: A kind of *fixed hard disk* that features very light read/write heads positioned very close to the disk.

word: Word has a technical, computer meaning (which you can ignore), and also a traditional meaning in typing — five characters, including spaces (*official words*). But I most often use it to refer to actual English words which — in my writing at least — average about six characters (*real words*).

Thus 1K contains 205 official typing words but only about 170 actual words. Likewise, a 55 *cps* printer actually prints out about 550 words per minute, not the 660 you may find in brochures and the like.

word processing: Using a computer to edit and format text.

word-processing program: A *program* that tells a computer how to accept, edit, and format text.

word processor: A computer set up to accept, edit, and print out text. It can be a *dedicated word processor* or a general purpose computer running a word-processing program. Sometimes a *word-processing program* is referred to as a word processor.

word wrap: A feature that automatically moves a word, all in one piece, to the beginning of the next line if there isn't room for it at the end of the line it started out on.

work disk: A disk you alter, as opposed to a *master disk*. Also, on systems with small disk capacities, the work disk has your text files on it, as opposed to the *system disk,* which has programs (like the operating system and word-processing program) on it.

workfile: The text file currently being edited.

work space: The portion of *RAM* set aside for you to put your text in.

work station: A chair, desk, terminal, etc. — the place where one person works. This is mostly a business term, you wouldn't refer to the place where you use a home computer as a work station.

wpm: ''Words per minute.'' See *owpm* and *rwpm*.

write: To deposit information on.

write-protect slot: On some floppy disks, this prevents the disk from being written to unless it's covered over with a small sticker.

writeover mode: When a word-processing program is in this mode, it substitutes characters you type for ones that are already on the screen.

Z80:   The most common eight-bit *microprocessor*. (Later versions are called the *Z80A* and the *Z80B*.)

Z8000:   A 16-bit *microprocessor*.

zoom video: A feature that lets you magnify a portion of the text on the screen (usually found on full-page screens where the normal text is rather small).

Index